ROMANTICISM
& GENDER

ROMANTICISM & GENDER

ANNE K. MELLOR

ROUTLEDGE · NEW YORK & LONDON

Published in 1993 by

Routledge
An imprint of Routledge, Chapman and Hall, Inc.
29 West 35th Street
New York, NY 10001

Published in Great Britain by

Routledge
11 New Fetter Lane
London EC4P 4EE

Library of Congress Cataloging-in-Publication Data

Mellor, Anne Kostelanetz.
    Romanticism and gender / by Anne K. Mellor.
        p.   cm.
    Includes bibliographical references and index.
    ISBN 0-415-90111-1 (HB) ISBN 0-415-90664-4 (PB)
        1. English literature—Women authors—History and criticism—Theory, etc.   2.
English literature—19th century—History and criticism—Theory, etc.   3. English
literature—18th century—History and criticism—Theory, etc.   4. Feminism and
literature—Great Britain—History.   5. Women and literature—Great Britain—
History.   6. Authorship—Sex differences.   7. Romanticism—Great Britain.   8.
Sex role in literature.   I. Title.
PR468.F46M45   1992
820.9'9287'09034—dc20   92-22902
                                                                                         CIP

ISBN 0-415-90111-1 (HB)
ISBN 0-415-90664-4 (PB)

FOR LYNNE TIDABACK HANLEY
in sisterhood

Contents

Acknowledgments

I am grateful to the Humanities Research Centre of the Australian National University for providing both the time and the support necessary to complete this project. Many friends and colleagues were generous with their suggestions and criticisms: I especially wish to thank Susan Wolfson, Peter Manning and Ruth Bernard Yeazell, to whom this book owes an enormous debt, as well as Paul John Aikin, R. A. Foakes, Paul Sheats, Alexander Welsh and John Bender. I learned a great deal from the participants in the Seminars which I gave in Australia on aspects of this material, from the members of the UCLA Romantic Study Group, from the members of the Ad Hoc Faculty Feminist Theory group at UCLA and from the students in my graduate seminars on Romanticism and Gender, to all of whom I am deeply grateful. Portions of chapter four appear in *Rebel Daughters: Women and the French Revolution*, ed. Sara Melzer and Leslie Rabine (New York: Oxford University Press, 1992).

For their continuing support and affection, I thank Ron and Blake Mellor. I dedicate this book, with love and admiration, to my sister.

Introduction
Romanticism, Gender and Genre

What difference does gender make to our understanding of British literary Romanticism? Does Romanticism have a gender? In this speculative book, I will argue that our current cultural and scholarly descriptions of that historical phenomenon we call Romanticism are unwittingly gender-biased. Whether we interpret British literary Romanticism as a commitment to imagination, vision and transcendence, as did Meyer Abrams, Harold Bloom and John Beer, or as a questioning, even systematic demystification, of the very possibility of a linguistically unmediated vision, as have Geoffrey Hartman, Paul de Man and a host of others, or as an ideology located in specific political and social events, as urged by Carl Woodring, Jerome McGann and the school of new historical Romanticists inspired by their work, or as a complex configuration derived from all of these recent critical approaches, we nonetheless have based our constructions of British Romanticism almost exclusively upon the writings and thought of six male poets (Wordsworth, Coleridge, Blake, Byron, Shelley and Keats).

What happens to our interpretations of Romanticism if we focus our attention on the numerous women writers who produced at least half of the literature published in England between 1780 and 1830? It will be the argument of this book that a paradigm shift in our conceptual understanding of British literary Romanticism occurs when we give equal weight to the thought and writing of the women of the period. The establishment of the lending library, which spread rapidly through England in this era, meant that books were widely accessible to a new and ever-growing readership, a readership composed in large part of upper- and middle-class women who preferred to read literature, and especially novels, written by women. When we look at this female-authored literature, we find a focus on very different issues from those which concerned the canonical male Romantic poets. For the purposes of this book, I will take as representative of this enormous body of female literary production (there were over 200 publishing women poets and at least as many novelists, as well as several playwrights, essayists, memoirists and journalists) only twenty or so women writers acknowledged at the time or later to be the most influential, gifted, or widely read: Jane Austen, Joanna Baillie, Anna Laetitia Barbauld, Mary Brunton, Frances Burney, Maria Edgeworth, Susan Ferrier, Mary Hays, Felicia Hemans, Letitia Landon, Hannah More, Amelia Opie, Sydney Owenson (Lady Morgan), Ann Radcliffe, Mary Robinson, Mary Shelley, Charlotte Smith, Jane Taylor, Helen Maria Williams, Mary Wollstonecraft and Dorothy Wordsworth. Some of these writers have already received extensive critical attention to which my discussions will be much indebted (e.g. Jane Austen, Frances Burney, Ann Radcliffe, Mary Shelley, Mary Wollstonecraft, Dorothy Wordsworth); but most of them are relatively or entirely unknown to current scholarship. I realize that my selection is both limited and arbitrary: no description of this female literary corpus can be reliably accurate until we know the work of most of the women writing during this period.

This book can attempt only an initial, exploratory mapping of this new literary terrain, the uncharted expanse of women's literary Romanticism. It will require decades of research and hundreds of books before we fully grasp the complex intellectual and formal configurations of this terra incognita. But even a cursory, introductory survey reveals significant differences between the thematic concerns, formal practices, and ideological positionings of male and female Romantic writers. To mention only the most immediately obvious, the women writers of the Romantic period for the most part foreswore the concern of their male peers with the capacities of the creative imagination, with the limitations of language, with the possibility of transcendence or "unity of being," with the development of an autonomous self, with political (as opposed to social) revolution, with the role of the creative writer as political leader or religious savior. Instead, women Romantic writers tended to celebrate, not the achievements of the imagination nor the overflow of powerful feelings, but rather the workings of the rational mind, a mind relocated—in a gesture of revolutionary gender implications—in the female as well as the male body. They thus insisted upon the fundamental equality of women and men. They typically endorsed a commitment to a construction of subjectivity based on alterity, and based their moral systems on what Carol Gilligan has recently taught us to call an ethic of care which insists on the primacy of the family or the community and their attendant practical responsibilities. They grounded their notion of community on a cooperative rather than possessive interaction with a Nature troped as a female friend or sister, and promoted a politics of gradual rather than violent social change, a social change that extends the values of domesticity into the public realm. These introductory and necessarily crude generalizations will in the future need to be refined by taking into account the many subtle distinctions that exist, not only between the men and women writers of the Romantic period, but also—and more importantly—between one woman writer and another.

In writing this book, I have used a structural model which is in itself deeply problematic and whose limitations I wish to acknowledge at the outset. In order to recover the erased and neglected voices of Romantic women writers, I have grouped their writings together under the heading of what I have called "feminine" Romanticism. I have tried to identify the concerns and ideological positions which they held in common with the other women writers of their day, and I have contrasted this material to what we have traditionally defined as "Romanticism," which I have rechristened "masculine" Romanticism. This binary structure has the initial, and it seems to me necessary, advantage of allowing us to *see* what has hitherto been hidden, the difference that gender makes in the construction of British Romantic literature.

But the use of a model grounded on polarity is both theoretically dubious and critically confining. As the obsession of the male Romantic poets with the principle of polarity might indicate—think of Blake's Contraries, Coleridge's enduring concern with the relation of the subject to the object, Shelley's opposition of analytical reason to synthetic imagination—a binary model is already deeply implicated in "masculine" Romanticism (it receives its ultimate philosophical statement in Hegel's dialectic). The principle of polarity, of Fichte's ego versus non-ego, of thesis versus antithesis, requires the construction of an Other which is seen as a threat to the originating subject. At both the theoretical and the psychological level, the women writers of the Romantic period resisted this model of oppositional polarity (as the foundation of both the natural and the human worlds) for one based on sympathy and likeness.

In order fully to understand their ways of knowing the world, we need to learn how to think *beyond* a dialectic based on polarities.

Moreover, the construction of British literary Romanticism as a rigid binary opposition based on gender does not do justice to the critical complexity of many of the literary texts produced in England between 1780 and 1830. As I will show in detail in my last two chapters, where I discuss the Wordsworths and Keats and Emily Brontë, and as I will illustrate more briefly in a moment here, the relationship between "masculine" and "feminine" Romanticism is finally not one of structural opposition but rather of intersection along a fluid continuum. Any writer, male or female, could occupy the "masculine" or the "feminine" ideological or subject position, even within the same work. In an attempt to show that gender-biased Romantic ideologies are grounded not on biological sex but rather on socially constructed and therefore fluid systems of discourse, I will argue in Part III that the writings of John Keats can be in part embraced within what I call "feminine" Romanticism while Emily Brontë's *Wuthering Heights* can be seen as an example of "masculine" Romanticism. After we have identified the poles of a gender continuum, we can and must explore sensitively all the ways in which gender and sex intersect and complicate each other in particular Romantic texts.

To clarify this broad argument, let me briefly explore here the relation of gender to genre in the Romantic period. Poetry has dominated the discussion of genre in academic literary studies of British Romanticism; at least five of the six canonical writers of Romanticism are known primarily as poets (Wordsworth, Blake, Byron, Shelley and Keats) and Coleridge's poems, although a very small part of his overall literary oeuvre, are more famous than his prose writings. The Romantic novel, whether by Scott, Godwin, Hogg, Austen, Edgeworth or the writers of Gothic fiction, and despite valiant efforts by such critics as Alexander Welsh, Robert Kiely and Susan Morgan to redress this imbalance, has been relegated to the margins of "Romanticism," while drama (by Joanna Baillie, Byron, Coleridge and Godwin among others) and the literary essay (by Lamb, Hazlitt, De Quincey, Clara Reeve, Anna Barbauld and many others) have until very recently received even less attention.[1] What are the gender implications inherent in this academic definition of poetry as *the* canonical Romantic genre? This is a large topic, and one that needs a book to itself, building on Stuart Curran's study of how six poetic genres function in the writings of the canonical poets in *Poetic Form and British Romanticism*

(1986). Although Curran acknowledges that in the early nineteenth century, there were "women poets everywhere—writing sonnets, writing epics" (17), and rightly identifies Charlotte Smith as the herald both of the rebirth of the sonnet and of a literary Romanticism grounded on the expression of intense feeling (30–31), he does not consider the role played by gender either in the choice or the performance of a given poetic genre. The central issues concerning the interrelationship of genre and gender in the Romantic period, which I can sketch out only briefly here, are yet to be explored.

As students of the history of the novel are now coming to accept, the English novel probably originated in those modes of writing we associate primarily with upper- and middle-class women—letters, journals, diaries—and with an oral tradition sustained by lower-class women—ballads, folk-tales, fairy tales, "old wives' tales," and gossip.[2] Both the epistemological assumptions and the ideological content of the genre of the English novel, which Michael McKeon has argued was conceptually stabilized by Richardson and Fielding in the 1740s,[3] are present in the texts of late seventeenth- and early eighteenth-century women writers. The debate between skepticism and the idealist epistemology of romance, between an aristocratic conservative and a more progressive political ideology, together with the rhetorical strategies of free indirect discourse and a dialogic form characterized by techniques of indirection and the lack of a central narrative authority—which for McKeon are the defining characteristics of the English novel—all occur in the early eighteenth century in the novels and conduct-books of Eliza Haywood.[4] Moreover, the ideological issue foregrounded in the novel—the proper relation of the public sphere to an increasingly powerful private sphere, the dialogue between questions of truth and questions of virtue described by McKeon[5]—was from the start the central concern of women writers anxious to define the correct relationship between knowledge, romance, sexuality, familial obedience, and the constraints of both property and propriety on the lives of women. The development of a literature of sensibility, together with the emphasis on the situation of women in the major novels of Fielding and Richardson, produced by 1780 what Terry Eagleton has called "the feminization of discourse" in the novel,[6] referring to the cultural construction of the novel as an ideological arena in which the social contract is translated into a sexual exchange[7] and the desirable characteristics of the good woman are both defined and appropriated by the hegemonic masculine culture.

This "feminization of discourse" in the novel could be construed as locating the genre of the novel, in some meaningful sense, within the private or domestic sphere assigned to the feminine gender. In contrast, as Irene Tayler and Gina Luria have suggested, the derivation of poetic and dramatic forms from classical models might locate the genres of poetry and drama within the public sphere of the masculine gender. This is the case, they argue, because the use of such classical models presupposed a knowledge of both Greek and Latin, an education from which women in the eighteenth century were excluded.[8] The writing of poetry thus became in theory a masculine occupation, and one associated especially with the aristocratic or leisured classes. Byron consciously adopted the persona of the "poet-statesman" inherited from Sir Philip Sidney and other Renaissance courtiers, Percy Shelley laid claim to it ("Poets are the unacknowledged legislators of the world"), and Keats desired to become a "Man of Achievement" in letters. The other tradition of poetic performance appropriated by the male Romantic poets was that of the poet-priest, the inheritor and transmitter of a Judaeo-Christian prophetic tradition originating in the Bible and passed on by England's greatest bard, Milton.

Both these representations of the vocation of poetry elevated certain genres within poetry: the epic, with its implicit assumption that the male hero embodies the character and aspirations of the nation and thus is a "representative" of mankind; the tragic verse drama, inherited from the ancient Greeks and Shakespeare, with its depiction of the hero as a scapegoat who bears the burdens or consciousness of civilization itself; the prophetic ode; the elegy; and the satire as the public voice of moral denunciation and correction. The canonical Romantic poets all worked within these "higher" genres of poetry, writing epics (*Jerusalem, The Prelude, Don Juan, Hyperion*), heroic verse tragedies (*Prometheus Unbound, Manfred*), elegies (*Adonais*), and developing new forms both of the satire (*Don Juan*) and especially of the prophetic ode, namely, the Pindarick (*Immortality Ode*) and that form which more than any other, Meyer Abrams claimed, characterised Romanticism, the "Romantic odal hymn" (*Ode to the West Wind, Ode on a Grecian Urn, Dejection: An Ode, Tintern Abbey*). Significantly, the Romantic odal hymn presupposes what I will argue in chapter six is a "masculine" or oppositional construction of subjectivity, the concept of an autonomous and self-conscious "I" that exists independently of the Other, in this case of a divine creative power which the poet seeks to possess.

Such a description of genre in the Romantic period would erect a firm gender barrier between literary forms: the novel would be assigned to the realm of "feminine" discourse, the higher forms of poetry and drama to the realm of "masculine" discourse. Before we become comfortable with this construction of gender difference in romantic genre, however, we must recognize that the ideological "feminization" of the novel proved historically problematic for women authors. As male writers appropriated the discourse of the feminine for the novel, they effectively trivialized the voices of actual women writers. Gaye Tuchman has shown that by the end of the nineteenth century, male authors and reviewers had created a theoretical distinction between the "high-brow" novel of philosophical enquiry (authored by and for men) and the "low-brow" novel of feminine romance (authored by and for women), thus relegating women writers to the realm of the sentimental, fanciful and forgettable.[9]

Similarly, before assigning poetry to the discourse of the masculine, we need to account for the fact that between 1780 and 1830, women dominated not only the production of the novel—of the dozen most popular novelists in the period, ten were women, and as Mitzi Myers has commented, the period's "most prolific fictionalist was surely 'A Lady' "[10]—but also the production of poetry and drama.[11] Stuart Curran has identified 339 women poets publishing in England between 1760 and 1830 in addition to 82 anonymous female poets.[12] The leading playwright of the day was a woman, Joanna Baillie. We need to know a great deal more about these women writers who flourished in the Romantic period, several of whom managed to earn a living from their writing. The popularity and widespread growth of the circulating library during this period made books easily accessible not only to upper-class male and female subscribers, but also to women and men of the middle classes; since women of these classes had more leisure time at their disposal than men, and since reading (especially novels) was thought to be a particularly genteel occupation for such women, the majority of the reading public, for all genres, was female.[13] Thus a "feminine" discourse was present in all the literary genres in the Romantic period. Any attempt to preserve a firm gender barrier between genres in the Romantic period breaks down in the face of the statistical evidence.

Let me speculate further about the implications of this large body of female-authored literature for our understanding of Romantic genre and gender. Although several of these women writers invoked a modesty *topos* in introducing their work to the public, the sheer bulk of their publications would suggest that they did not succumb to the debilitating "anxiety of authorship" assigned to them by Mary Poovey, Margaret Homans, Sandra Gilbert and Susan Gubar.[14] Many were capable of the authorial self-confidence, even arrogance, of Harriet Lee, who, in introducing the Standard Novels edition of her *Canterbury Tales* in 1832, claimed:

> I think I may be permitted to observe, that when these volumes first appeared [in 1797], a work bearing distinctly the title of "Tales," professedly adopted to different countries, and either abruptly commencing with, or breaking suddenly into, a sort of dramatic dialogue, was a novelty in the fictions of the day. Innumerable "Tales" of the same stamp, and adapted in the same manner to all classes and all countries, have since appeared; with many of which I presume not to compete in merit, though I think I may fairly claim priority of design and style.

The rapidly growing number of salons and associations for women writers, critics and readers attests to their increased literary self-confidence, presence, and power. Keats, Byron and Thomas Moore were openly hostile to these "bluestockings"[15]—Byron repeatedly denounced the "vile jargon" of literary ladies in *The Blues* (1821), *Beppo* and *Don Juan*, while Moore parodied women's pretensions to scientific knowledge in his comic opera, *M. P. or The Blue-Stocking*, where he portrays Lady Bab Blue as a woman whose head was "stuffed. . .with all that was legible and *illegible*" and whose literary employment is the writing of "a *chemical* Poem" upon "the *Loves* of *Ammonia*." But these poets' hostility (produced by the success of their female literary rivals?) must be balanced against the admiration for literary and intellectual women expressed by Leigh Hunt in his *Blue-Stocking Revels or, The Feast of the Lilacs* (1837) and by William P. Scargill in *Blue-Stocking Hall* (1827). The broad public awareness of these women of letters (who often appeared in broadsides and cartoons), and the ways in which they figure both negatively and positively in so many literary texts of the Romantic period by both men and women, are a significant index to the increasing impact of women's literary performances and opinions upon the general reading public.

Despite the tendency of modern academic critics of the history of the novel to think so,[16] Romantic women novelists did not resign the construction of "feminine discourse" to men, obediently reproducing in their novels the hegemonic ideology of bourgeois capitalism, now relocated in an idealised middle-class patriarchal family. In the Romantic period, women novelists frequently employed the novel as a site of ideological contestation and subversion, exploiting its generic capacity for heteroglossia and dialogism, for disruptive laughter and a sustained interrogation of existing social codes, to invoke Bakhtin's terms. As I shall discuss in chapter three, the debates between Emily Lindore and Mary Douglas in Susan Ferrier's *Marriage* open up a radically new concept of an egalitarian marriage in which the wife has as much power as the husband, and thus propose a revolutionary model for state government based on individual as well as gender equality.

Charlotte Smith, for example, in *The Old Manor House*, offered a wide-ranging critique of masculinity in all its cultural forms. She first condemns the new man of feeling by parodying Wordsworth: the overflow of powerful feeling in a man, expressed in her protagonist Orlando's *Ode to Poverty*, functions in her novel as a sign of self-indulgence and social irresponsibility, of Orlando's momentary failure to provide his wife with a home and income. She then calls into question the masculine code of chivalric honor from which Orlando's name is derived, not in the name of the rights of the common man, as did William Godwin that same year in *Caleb Williams* (1794), but rather in the name of gender transformation. In this novel, Orlando finally gives up both these social constructions of masculinity in order to take up the subject position of a woman. He is finally portrayed as *feminine*, as the vulnerable dependent of a wealthy aristocratic woman, as delicately featured, refined, loving, loyal and passive, in short as a modest heroine.[17] When he goes to America to fight in the war against the colonies, he is immediately captured and cared for by a noble Indian chief. Orlando's femininity embodies a critique not just of the ideology of feudal aristocracy but also of the ideology of patrilineal bourgeois capitalism; his revulsion at the brutality of modern war, at primogeniture and the indulgence of the eldest son, and at the greed of modern commerce are all endorsed by the novel.

Rather than reinscribing the appropriation by a manly public sphere of the private domestic affections, rather than celebrating the triumph of the benevolent man of feeling, many female-authored Romantic novels implicitly contested the domination of this benign patriarch. Some reversed the political dynamic of the literature of sensibility. Rather than allowing the public realm to usurp the prerogatives and virtues of the private realm, they recolonized the public sphere under the governance of women and feminine virtue, celebrating the social and political domination of a domestic sphere located either in an idealised version of the feudal past or in an utopian future, as did Charlotte Smith and Ann Radcliffe. Others denied the moral and thus the legal legitimacy of the public sphere altogether, as did Mary Wollstonecraft in *Maria, or The Wrongs of Woman* or Mary Hays in *A Victim of Prejudice.*

Romantic women writers challenged the masculine "feminization of discourse" from another direction, by unmasking the oppression of women encoded within the eighteenth-century bourgeois construction of femininity. Following Frances Sheridan's *Memoirs of Sydney Biddulph* (1761), Mary Wollstonecraft, Mary Hays, Ann Radcliffe, Susan Ferrier, and Mary Shelley all explored the physical and psychic price paid by women who too fully subscribed to the ideology of maternity and domesticity.[18] In the Romantic period, then, in ways we have only begun to perceive, the "femininized" novel was in fact the site of a powerful struggle over the very construction of gender.

Women poets also engaged in ideological contestation, one that affected their choice of both subject and poetic form. One of the most popular poets of the Romantic era, sharing that accolade with Byron and Thomson, was a woman, Felicia Hemans. As I discuss in detail in chapter six, the thematic content of Hemans' poetry pits a masculine public code of heroic chivalry against a feminine private code of domesticity, only to reveal the inadequacy of each. Hemans' most famous poem, *Casabianca* ("The boy stood on the burning deck. . . ."), suggests that the attempt to preserve the doctrine of the separate spheres, to stabilize the relation between the private domestic affections and the public demand for loyalty to the state, is not only futile, but counterproductive: the boy would have lived had he disobeyed his (now dead) father's command to remain at his post.

Hemans comfortably worked within the "highest" poetic genre—heroic verse tragedy—but she devoted most of her poetic output to shorter verse narratives, Spenserian romances, songs and sonnets. Other leading women poets (Charlotte Smith, Mary Tighe, Mary Robinson, Helen Maria Williams, Anna Laetitia Barbauld, Joanna Baillie, Letitia Elizabeth Landon, Jane Taylor) also preferred to write odes, romances, ballads, shorter verse narratives, sonnets, "occasional verse," and nursery rhymes. Before describing this as an inability to master the "higher" genres of poetry, we might ask what they achieved through their choice of poetic genre. Memorability, most obviously—probably no poem in English has been so often memorized as Jane Taylor's *Twinkle, twinkle, little star;* and Hemans' *Casabianca, The Homes of England* and *The Graves of a Household* were set pieces in popular poetry recitals until the Second World War.[19] These women engaged in their poetry in the production of a studied simplicity that was later devalued by Modernist and New Critical demands for poetic irony, complexity, and ambiguity. Short lyrics which combined the details of the quotidian with the expression of a single feeling implicitly assume the overriding value of ordinary, daily interactions with other people, of a self experienced in relation to other selves, of social interactions that are not available to the self-absorbed, often abstracted meditations of either the epic poet or the odal hymnist. Occasional verse, as the name of the genre indicates, records a shared event, either a moment of communal ritual—a birthday, wedding, anniversary, funeral—or a personal communication, the exchange of gifts (as when Helen Maria Williams insists that flowers are valuable, not because they inspire "Thoughts that do often lie too deep for tears," but because they are brought to her *by a friend,* James Forbes; or when Dorothy Wordsworth records the buying of gingerbread she does not need in order to succor her neighbors).

The poetic genres chosen by Romantic women poets thus function to create and sustain community. Frequently published in pocketbook albums and such annual gift books as *Forget Me Not* and *The Keepsake,* advertised as "tokens of remembrance, friendship, or affection,"[20] they are designed to employ memory in the service of human experiences shared by both men and women over time. Women poets' choice of genre thus exists in contestation both with the eighteenth-century ordering of the arts and the masculinist poetics this hierarchy reflects; they implicitly rejected the egotistical sublime that sustains, however precariously, the Romantic epic and the odal hymn. We need to learn once again how to read these alternative poetic genres in a way that acknowledges their cultural power, their creation of a *popular* culture that perhaps more than other literary productions defined British literary Romanticism to itself.

With the all-important caveat that "masculine" and "feminine" Romanticism in this book are finally not binary opposites but rather the endpoints on a continuum that ranges not only through the entire range of literary Romanticism but also through the corpus of individual writers, let me turn now to a more extended analysis of the manifestations of gender difference in British literature between 1780 and 1830.

PART I

MASCULINE ROMANTICISM

There is no need to remap the contours of masculine English Romanticism here; numerous insightful critics and scholars over the last thirty years have put forth increasingly complex and sophisticated descriptions of the thematic, formal and theoretical pursuits of the canonical Romantic poets. For the purposes of the dialogue which I wish to initiate, it will be sufficient to recall only a few major signposts. We might begin at Meyer Abrams' magisterial summation, in *Natural Supernaturalism* (1971), of the way Romanticism had been constructed in the previous decade: as a "spirit of the age" (to evoke Hazlitt's term) which responded directly to the major political events of the late eighteenth century, the American and French Revolutions. Identifying Romanticism with the Enlightenment beliefs in democracy and the rights of the common man, Abrams argued that the greatest Romantic poems traced what he called a "circuitous journey" from innocence to experience or a higher innocence, a quest that begins with the child's unconscious conviction of a primal oneness between himself and Mother Nature and his fall away from that communion into an experience of alienated self-consciousness and isolation.[1] But this fall, like Milton's, proves finally fortunate, for it enables the poet to learn the powers inherent in consciousness itself. He can thereby spiral upward to a higher state of consciousness, even a sublime transcendence, in which he comes to understand the ultimate harmony between the workings of nature and his own mind and to consummate a marriage with nature through his "spousal verse." For

Abrams, Romantic poetry finally constitutes a humanistic secular-ization of the Judaeo-Christian myth of a paradise lost and re-gained, a rewriting as epic autobiography of the myth that has dominated Western culture for over two thousand years.

Abrams' paradigm of English Romanticism was challenged by numerous scholars and critics during the 1970s and early 1980s, primarily on the grounds that it omitted Byron and the self-ironizing practices within Romanticism which Byron's *Don Juan* so notably represented. Many critics have demonstrated that a rec-ognition of the prison house of language was fundamental to the poetry not only of Byron but also of Wordsworth and the other ma-jor Romantic poets.[2] A deconstructive concern with romantic irony, questioning habits of mind, and the instabilities of poetic forms and figures replaced the apocalyptic certainties of *Natural Supernaturalism*. The publication in 1983 of Jerome McGann's *The Romantic Ideology* posed a challenge both to Abrams' paradigm and to deconstructive reading methods, this time from a historical rather than a rhetorical position. Arguing that the critics of En-glish Romantic poems have themselves imbibed the values and ideological commitments of the Romantic poets, McGann insisted that we must recognize the historical and social specificity of En-glish Romanticism, the ways in which these texts promote the cul-tural and economic interests of a particular class of people in a particular society at a particular time. Only by detaching our-selves from the class interests inherent in Romantic poems can we begin to understand their "false consciousness" or "bad faith." Many new historical and cultural critics have offered increasingly sophisticated interrogations of the role of ideology and histori-cal discourse in Romantic texts—I think especially of Alan Liu's *Wordsworth—The Sense of History* (1989).

Whether we have focused on the social and historical, or the psy-chological, or the rhetorical maneuverings of the English Roman-tic poets, we have concurred in grounding English Romanticism on a reading of a highly selective group of texts, almost all poetry, al-most all written by men. David Perkins has recently tracked the way in which English Romanticism came to be conceptualized as a coherent literary movement only in the early twentieth century, and has further emphasized the historical instability of the aca-demic construction of that very coherence, which shifted between Victorian political identifications of Romanticism and later aes-thetic definitions.[3] We need to learn still more about how Roman-ticism came to be defined (by whom, when, and most important, with the privileging of what texts and for what cultural purposes), and the shifting role of gender within that process of historical literary canonization. Preliminary investigations by Gaye Tuchman and Paula Feldman suggest that women novelists dominated the publishing field in England until the middle of the nineteenth century, while female Romantic poets retained their great popularity until the beginning of the twentieth century.[4] What forces in the period of literary Modernism in England, from 1900 onwards, contributed to the exclusion of women writers from the canon of Romanticism, forces so powerful that the once-canonical woman writer of the Romantic period, Jane Austen, came to be defined as "non-Romantic"?[5] Such an inquiry would require a thorough examination of both the publishing practices in England in the nineteenth and twentieth centuries, as well as the establishment of the academic curriculum of "English Studies" at Oxford and Cambridge Universities during this period, and is beyond the scope of this book.

Here I will explore the role played by gender in the construction, not of the canon of Romanticism, but of Romantic literary texts themselves. The canonized male-authored texts of what we have been taught to call English literary Romanticism share certain attitudes and ideological investments which differ markedly from those displayed by the female-authored texts of the period. In emphasizing these large differences, I am fully aware that many individual exceptions exist, in the writings of both men and women, exceptions which I shall try to acknowledge. Nonetheless, there *are* important differences between the body of canonical masculine Romantic literature and the body of writing by women now excluded from this canon, and it is these differences (rather than similarities and local exceptions) which we must first recognize if we are to comprehend the full range and complexity of English Romanticism.

1

Gender in Masculine Romanticism

How does gender function in the canonical texts of masculine Romanticism? What shared definitions of the nature and function of the female do we find in the poetry of Wordsworth, Coleridge, Blake, Byron, Shelley, and Keats, in their treatments of the nature of the imagination, of the creative process, of erotic love, of the development of the self, of the value and rights of the common man, of the epistemological relation of the "philosophic mind" to the natural world?

In attempting a brief and necessarily preliminary answer to this large question, I wish to maintain the linguistic distinction between sex and gender. I will confine the term sex to the difference between male and female reproductive organs, and use gender to refer to the socially constructed roles and functions allotted to an individual on the basis of perceived sexual difference. I am aware that binary sexuality (or biology) is itself a social construction, as has been shown by Foucault and recent studies both in the history of sexuality and in the cultural variations of sex differences (some cultures recognize only one sex, others construct a third sex or "berdache").[1] For the purposes of clarity, however, in this book I will reserve the terms male and female for the binary sex differences established by Western culture and use the terms man/

woman, boy/girl, masculine/feminine to refer to the products of the social definition and organization of gender.

When Wordsworth, in the climactic passage of *The Prelude*, triumphantly climbs, "in opposition set/ Against an enemy" and "foremost of the Band," to the top of Mount Snowdon, where "lo!/ The Moon stood naked in the Heavens" and a fractured sea of mist is spread beneath his feet, he explicitly represents himself—as Marlon Ross has argued[2]—as the weary but nonetheless heroic conqueror of a Nature whose Soul, "the Imagination of the whole," is not his own. Defining the landscape as "the perfect image of a mighty Mind," Wordsworth acknowledges the power of Nature to exert a "domination. . .upon the outward face of things," to so mould, endure, abstract, combine or "by abrupt and unhabitual influence" to "make one object so impress itself/ Upon all others," that even the "grossest" human minds "must see and hear/And cannot chuse but feel" this power. As Wordsworth celebrates the power of Nature, he genders Nature as feminine—"that domination which *she* oftentimes/Exerts" (my emphasis). It is a woman's power to arouse, create and control that he has encountered, a power that first appeared as explicitly sexual ("the Moon stood naked"). Meyer Abrams has described this encounter as an "apocalyptic marriage" of mind and nature consummated in Wordsworth's "spousal verse." But a more subtle gender politics is at work here. While Wordsworth acknowledges the power which a female Nature "thus/ Thrusts forth upon the senses," both physical and mental, he also immediately appropriates that power, insisting that it is a "genuine Counterpart" of the "glorious faculty" which the "higher minds" of poets "bear with them as their own." Not only does Wordsworth insist that the poetic imagination "can send abroad/ Like transformations" and "create/A like existence"—equalling the creative power of Nature—but he also insists that this power is "truly from the Deity" and that the poets who possess it are endowed with sovereignty, emotions entirely trustworthy, cheerfulness, moral truth, and unfailing delight. Most readers who have noted the gender roles implicit in this passage have argued that Wordsworth has equated the capacities of his masculine imagination with those of feminine Nature, his mighty mind working in harmony with her mighty mind.[3] However, a closer reading of this passage suggests that Wordsworth has actually usurped Nature's power, leaving her silenced, even absent. For the "domination" or power which a female Nature exerted at line 81 becomes by line 89 the "Brother" of the poet's imagination, "a genuine Counterpart/

And Brother of the glorious faculty/ Which higher minds bear with them as their own." Since a female faculty can only be a "sister," Wordsworth has here subtly regendered nature's power as masculine and thus attempted to eliminate her otherness, her difference, her separate being.

Wordsworth's rhetorical strategy, the precariousness of which I shall explore in chapter seven, illustrates a common tendency in masculine Romanticism. These six poets' descriptions of the growth of the individual mind frequently posit a split between the subject and the object. So long as the object—nature—is gendered female, that split cannot be resolved into the unity in multeity of which Coleridge dreamed. Therefore these poets often subtly regender both the subject and the object as male and in the process erase the female from discourse: she does not speak; she therefore has no existence. As Margaret Homans has persuasively argued, by identifying Nature as female and the female as Nature (or not-human), Wordsworth effectively denied to women the ability to enter what Lacan called the symbolic order.[4] Rarely allowed to speak for themselves, the female figures in Wordsworth's early poems exist only as embodiments of an undifferentiated life cycle that moves inexorably from birth to death. They do not exist as independent, self-conscious human beings with minds as capable as the poet's. In this sense, almost all of Wordsworth's women are dead, either literally (as in the cases of Lucy, Margaret and Martha Ray) or figuratively (they are mad, or allowed to live only vicariously through the words and experiences of male narrators). Dorothy remains a silenced auditor in *Tintern Abbey*, a less conscious being whose function is to mirror and thus to guarantee the truth of the poet's development and perceptions, even as the poem itself acknowledges the existence of an unbridgeable gap between the poet's forever-lost past subjectivity and his present self, a gap also troped in the division between his sister's "wild eyes" and his own "eye made quiet by the power /Of harmony."

Even more troubling, the masculine mind can receive pleasure from the silencing of the female. Margaret's inability to survive without her husband and her gradual mental and physical decay, represented in the decay of both her home and her garden, becomes in *The Ruined Cottage* a source of "comfort" and "happiness" for both the Old Man who tells her tale of unrelieved suffering and the Pedlar who hears it.[5] Wordsworth's desire, as Marlon Ross has stressed, is rhetorically to conquer and absorb the female,[6] and the philosophic mind he so precariously achieves is thus masculinist in its usurpation and exploitation of the (female) objective world. Recasting Geoffrey Hartman's argument[7] in terms of gender, we might say that Wordsworth finally replaces (feminine) nature with the productions of the (masculine) imagination, inevitably substituting for his felt experiences of the physical world a linguistically mediated memory of them, mediations which confine his consciousness to a solipsistic subjectivity, one that is specifically troped as male.

The Prelude is not the only canonical Romantic poem that attempts to reassign the all-creating powers of a nature gendered as female to the masculine poetic imagination. In Coleridge's *Kubla Khan*, the sacred river Alph, the source of life itself, is procreated from a natural chasm which is initially imaged in terms that suggest the female birth canal: "That deep romantic chasm which slanted/ Down the green hill athwart a cedarn cover." The earth mother, "with ceaseless turmoil seething,/ . . .in fast thick pants . . .breathing," both in orgasm and in the labor of childbirth, forces out the mighty fountain. But this bursting fountain, "Amid whose swift half-intermitted burst/ Huge fragments vaulted like rebounding hail,/ Or chaffy grain beneath the thresher's flail," also suggests male orgasm and ejaculation. Together, female and male produce Kubla's kingdom and the sun and ice of his "miracle of rare device." But in the final stanza, this procreative power has been potentially usurped by the male poet: inspired by a damsel with a dulcimer (whose song we never hear, who can sing only of a fallen or lesser paradise, of Mount Abora), the male poet "with music loud and long,/. . .would build that dome in air/ That sunny dome! those caves of ice!/ And all who heard should see them there." Admittedly, this male poet is portrayed as a pariah about to be exorcised from the human community ("Weave a circle round him thrice"). Moreover, his control over the female voice is precarious at best—"*Could I revive within me/ Her symphony and song*" (my italics)—does he possess her or she him? Nonetheless, the poet's desire remains one for total absorption of the female: "*within me.*"

The male poet's attempt to usurp female procreative power is troped again in Coleridge's *Eolian Harp*, where the window harp is imaged first as phallic, "Placed length-ways in the clasping casement" (the long, rectangular, Aeolian box harp fashioned by Robert Bloomfield in 1808 measured 31 ½ inches long by 4 ⅝ inches wide by four inches high[8]), and then, remarkably, as female, "by the desultory breeze caress'd,/ Like some coy maid half yielding to her lover." The male poet is then figured as the harp: "as on the midway slope/ Of yonder hill I stretch my limbs at noon,/ . . .And many idle flitting phantasies,/ Traverse my indolent and passive brain,/ As wild and various as the random gales/ That swell and flutter on this subject Lute!" Despite his guilty babblings, the male poet tropes his identity with that "one intellectual breeze,/ At once the Soul of each, and God of all," but the female voice in the poem is restricted to the repressive and already articulated metaphors of patriarchal Christianity, of the *Nom de Pere;* Sara speaks not for herself but only as a "Meek Daughter in the family of Christ."

The oft-described exploration of nature found in canonical Romantic poetry thus often masks a sexual politics. Nature is usually gendered feminine by these six Romantic poets who adopt the traditional cultural metaphors of Mother Earth, Dame Nature, Lady Bountiful. But by identifying nature as the external objective world which the self-conscious subject must penetrate, possess and interpret, even to the point of "*forcing* some lone ghost/Thy messenger, to render up the tale/ Of what we are" (my italics), as the problematic Narrator of Percy Shelley's *Alastor* puts it in an image that suggests a calculated and violent rape of Mother Nature, these poets often go further than previous poets in denying to Nature her own authority. When Nature was the Book of God, she was read with respect. When she becomes the only obstacle to the poet's assumption of divine creative power, she must be silenced; only the (male) Romantic poet can speak for her. Autumn, a season Keats originally gendered feminine in his letter to Reynolds ("chaste weather—Dian skies"[9]), is rewritten as ambiguously androgynous, as both female gleaner and male reaper, in Keats' great Ode. Keats thus subtly empowers the male poet to utter the music of a female Other, to become the voice of autumn and translate her "mellow fruitfulness" into his own consciousness of mutability and that "ripeness to the core" which enables him to accept the coming winter and his own death. Similarly, the song of the female nightingale, that "light-winged Dryad [or female nymph] of the trees," who expresses her innocent ignorance of her own mortality and her consequent perfect happiness, cannot be translated into his language and must therefore be "buried deep/ In the next valley-glades," leaving the forlorn but speaking poet to interpret her meaning to his male audience, "Here, where men sit and hear each other groan"—"Was it a vision, or a waking dream?"

Even though William Blake dismissed Wordsworth's affirmation in *The Excursion* of "How exquisitely the individual Mind/ . . .to the external World/ Is fitted:—& how exquisitely, too,/ . . .The external World is fitted to the Mind," with the caustic "You shall not bring me down to believe such fitting & fitted. I know better and please your Lordship," he participated in this gender politics. Despite critical claims that Blake anticipated the liberation of women from sexual repression and patriarchal tyranny,[10] Blake shared his culture's denigration of the feminine gender. Identifying the male Los with the artistic imagination and the female Enitharmon with time, space and the natural world, Blake consistently portrayed the female—as poetic metaphor, as a set of human activities, and as a visual image—as secondary to the male. In Blake's symbolic system, males (or the masculine dimension of the psyche) create ideas, forms, designs; females (or feminine states of mind) can desire (and thus inspire) these forms but not create them. Instead the female obediently embodies male-originated ideas and designs in physical forms and perceptible colors. When Los and Enitharmon build Golgonooza, the city of art, Los must first "fabricate forms sublime":

. . .his hands divine inspired began
To modulate his fires studious the loud roaring flames
He vanquished with the strength of Art. . .
And first he drew a line upon the walls of shining heaven
And Enitharmon tincturd it with beams of blushing love
              (*The Four Zoas* VII, 90:20–26; E 356).

In Blake's gendered division of labor, Los and his sons forge, engrave, draw, construct plans; Enitharmon and her daughters then add watercolors, weave coverings ("for every Female is a Golden Loom," [*Jerusalem* 67:4]), and actually build the city, the city that bears a female name, Jerusalem, and serves as the female's ultimate self-realization. For Blake, the human form divine is "A Man" (*J* 96:6) while the female is his "emanation" or "garment," a "Garment of Pity & Compassion" (*Milton* 18:35). Throughout Blake's poetry, the masculine function takes logical and temporal priority over feminine activities.

In Blake's visual art, too, the ideal female is subsumed into the male. Blake's human form divine is typically presented as either a heroic male nude (in the style of Michelangelo) or as a muscular, bearded Christ. Often Blake's Christ wears a long flowing dress with a high waistband that accentuates his breasts, suggesting that this clearly masculine figure has absorbed the female body. This cannibalization of the female form by the male strikingly occurs on Plate 99 of *Jerusalem* where the liberated and naked female

Jerusalem who ecstatically embraces Albion-Urthona is portrayed from the rear so ambiguously that critics have read her both as female and as male.[11] But while the ultimately redeemed Jerusalem has been masculinized, the liberated Albion/Jehovah/Christ has *not* been similarly feminized. The long white mustache and beard of a male remain prominent in the overarching, dominating figure of the old man. Blake's gender politics conform to those of the other Romantic poets: the male imagination can productively absorb the female body, but if the reverse occurs, as when Vala or the Female Will covers the body of Albion in her veil, the image is negatively equated with a fall into death and self-annihilation.[12]

When they insisted on the primacy of human feelings and imaginative creation over the analytical calculations of Enlightenment rationality, the Romantic poets added a new dimension to the literary tradition of gender politics. Historically, the realm of the emotions, love and sensibility had been assigned to the feminine gender; women might not be able to think rationally, but they could love passionately, faithfully, purely. As the abandoned Donna Julia reiterates this view in Byron's *Don Juan*:

Man's love is of his life a thing apart,
  'T is woman's whole existence; man may range
The court, camp, church, the vessel, and the mart;
  Sword, gown, gain, glory, offer in exchange
Pride, fame, ambition, to fill up his heart,
  And few there are whom these cannot estrange;
Man has all these resources, we but one,
To love again, and be again undone.
               (*Don Juan*, Canto I, stanza 194)

When he claimed that poetry is "the spontaneous overflow of powerful feelings" from a man who has "thought long and deeply," Wordsworth and the Romantic poets who followed him effectively stole from women their primary cultural authority as the experts in delicate, tender feelings and, by extension, moral purity and goodness. As Alan Richardson has shown, the male writers of the "Age of Feeling" frequently invoked memories and fantasies of identification with their mothers. They represented themselves either as eagerly nursing infants, filled with both the mother's milk and spiritual wisdom, or as the embodiment of "female softness," or as wise matriarchs (as did Wordsworth in both *The Prelude* and his sonnet *1801*)—in order to "colonize the conventionally feminine domain of sensibility."[13] By taking on the feminine virtues of compassion, mercy, gentleness and sympathy, the male Romantic poets could claim to speak with ultimate moral as well as intellectual authority. Endowed with feminine empathy or what Keats called "negative capability" and Percy Shelley the "instinct and intuition of the poetical faculty," the male poet becomes in Shelley's *Defense of Poetry* a mother while the work of art becomes "a child in the mother's womb." Having given birth to poetry which, according to Shelley, is "the record of the best and happiest moments of the happiest and best minds," the male poet becomes the hero of the modern age. "As he is the author to others of the highest wisdom, pleasure, virtue, and glory, so he ought personally to be the happiest, the best, the wisest, and the most illustrious of men." Finally, such poets "are the unacknowledged legislators of the world."[14] By usurping the mother's womb, life-giving power, and feminine sensibilities, the male poet could claim to be God, the sole ruler of the world.

Foremost among the traditionally feminine qualities colonized by this strain of masculine Romanticism is love. So insistent were all the canonical poets that love was the ultimate, even transcendent, human experience that we have come to equate their idealized version of this emotion with the "romantic love" of Tristan and Isolde. Recall William Blake's affirmation of uninhibited sexual passion which produces "the lineaments of gratified desire," what Oothoon in *The Visions of the Daughters of Albion* hails as "happy happy Love! free as the mountain wind!" (*E* 49). Or Wordsworth's claim, at the end of *The Prelude*, that the self is nourished by fear and love, the sublime and the beautiful, but by love "first and chief," which extends from the infant's first sympathetic intercourse with its mother and nature to that "love more intellectual" which "proceeds/ More from the brooding Soul, and is divine," and which "cannot be" without the imagination (13:143–170). For Coleridge, too, despite his personal relegation to "the poor, loveless, ever-anxious crowd," the capacity to love generated by the "genial spirits" produces that Joy which in *Dejection: An Ode* weds Nature to the "pure of heart" and creates a paradise on earth.

The second generation of male Romantic poets were even more obsessed by erotic love than the first. Byron chose as his hero that mythic lover, Don Juan; many of Keats' finest poems, from *Endymion* and the *Ode on a Grecian Urn* to *The Eve of St. Agnes* and *Lamia*, eloquently explore the delusions and ecstasies of sexual love; and Percy Shelley devoted much of his best-known poetry, from *Alastor* and *Epipsychidion* to the celebration of Asia in *Pro-*

metheus Unbound, to the quest for the perfect soul mate or ideal love.

Given the central role played by passionate love in masculine Romanticism, where love is the means by which the poet attempts to rise on an almost Platonic ladder to the most transcendent and visionary of human experiences, and the explicit valorization of the beloved woman contained within this secular myth, we might expect a recognition of the erotic power and spiritual equality of the female to be essential to their poetry. But when we look closely at the gender implications of romantic love, we discover that rather than embracing the female as a valued other, the male lover usually effaces her into a narcissistic projection of his own self. When Percy Shelley wrote of Mary Godwin, "so intimately are our natures now united, that I feel whilst I describe her excellencies as if I were an egoist expatiating upon his own perfections,"[15] he articulated a fundamental desire of the romantic lover: to find in female form a mirror image of himself, a soul within his soul or second self, what Shelley in his essay *On Love* called the "anti-type." As Shelley here defined love, it is

> the meeting with an understanding capable of clearly estimating our own; an imagination which should enter into and seize upon the subtle and delicate peculiarities which we have delighted to cherish and unfold in secret; with a frame whose nerves, like the chords of two exquisite lyres, strung to the accompaniment of one delightful voice, vibrate with the vibrations of our own; . . . this is the invisible and unattainable point to which Love tends; . . .[16]

This is the quest undertaken by the deceived Poet in *Alastor,* who rejects the village girls and Arab maiden to seek instead his "vision" of the ideal woman whose voice "is like the voice of his own soul" and whose thoughts, of "knowledge and truth and virtue. . ./ And lofty hopes of divine liberty," were the very thoughts "most dear to him" (11:153–161). It is the quest of the poet in *Epipsychidion* who seeks, again unsuccessfully, to become "conscious, inseparable, one" with his beloved Emily:

> Our breath shall intermix, our bosoms bound,
> And our veins beat together; . . .
> The fountains of our deepest life, shall be
> Confused in Passion's golden purity,
> As mountain-springs under the morning sun.
> We shall become the same, we shall be one

Spirit within two frames, oh! wherefore two?
(11:540, 565–6, 571–4)

In these poems romantic love is identified with eros rather than agape, in the tradition of Tristan and Isolde, Romeo and Juliet, and Antony and Cleopatra. Thus the consummation desired by Shelley's narrators can only be achieved through death, through the literal annihilation of the consciousness of division between the lover and his beloved. Similarly, Porphyro and Madeleine flee into the storm, and "are gone"; Lycius' passion for the public possession of his beloved Lamia causes both his death and her disappearance; Manfred's embrace of his sister-bride Astarte—chosen because she "was like me in lineaments—her eyes,/ Her hair, her features, all, to the very tone/ Even of her voice, they said were like to mine;/ But soften'd all, and temper'd into beauty" (Act II, sc ii, 11:106–109)— is fatal; and both the Byronic hero of the Turkish Tales and Don Juan leave in their wake a series of female corpses, from Medora and Kaled to Haidée.

Since the object of romantic or erotic love is not the recognition and appreciation of the beloved woman as an independent other but rather the assimilation of the female into the male (or the annihilation of any Other that threatens masculine selfhood), the woman must finally be enslaved or destroyed, must disappear or die. The "enslav'd" Oothoon offers to bring to Theotormon "girls of mild silver, or of furious gold" rather than to gratify her own desires for numerous lovers; the independent Sara Hutchinson disappears from view on the other side of the mountain at the end of *Dejection: An Ode;* Wordsworth's Margaret cannot survive without her Robert, and his beloved Lucy is in her grave. In matters of love, these poets frequently, and narcissistically, idolized female mirrors of themselves, mirrors inevitably shattered by their biographical experiences of female otherness, whether of Catherine Blake's jealousy, Sara Fricker's contempt, Annette Vallon's inaccessibility, Fanny Brawne's mischievousness, Mary Godwin's depression, or Annabella Milbanke's terrified resistance. This is not to deny the existence of powerful, independent female figures in the poetry of masculine Romanticism, from Blake's Vala to Wordsworth's "Stern Daughter," Duty, from Coleridge's Geraldine to Keats' Moneta, from Shelley's Beatrice Cenci to Byron's Gulbeyaz and Adeline, but only to suggest that the frequent equation of heterosexual love with erotic passion produced a desire for a total union between lover and beloved, a union that necessarily entails the elimination of Otherness.

The most famous Romantic love poems may thus propound a sexism of a most seductive and insidious kind, for the poet claims to cherish his beloved, bright star that she is, above all else. But the love he feels is but self-love: he ignores her human otherness in order to impose his own metaphors, his own identity, upon her, to render her but a clone (or soul mate) of himself. What he most deeply desires is absolute possession of the beloved; but since this desire is never realizable in life, his quest always fails, leaving him frustrated, forlorn, sinking, trembling, expiring, yet still yearning for his impossible ideal.

When we focus on the role that gender plays in masculine Romanticism, we often see the poet appropriating whatever of the feminine he deems valuable and then consigning the rest either to silence or to the category of evil. The female, certainly not the only, but always an inevitable Other, becomes whatever the male poet does not wish to be. The male imagination speaks for female nature; the male lover casts the beloved as a female version of himself; the male poet cannibalizes the feminine emotions of mercy, pity, love; he even becomes a mother, giving birth to his children-poems. Significantly, those poems, once born, often prove limited and hence unsatisfactory, for as Percy Shelley insisted in *A Defense of Poetry*, "the mind in creation is as a fading coal" and "when composition begins, inspiration is already on the decline, and the most glorious poetry that has ever been communicated to the world is probably a feeble shadow of the original conceptions of the poet." [17] The poet's spoken words are thus, as Shelley put it in *Ode to the West Wind*, but "dead thoughts," dead because the static system of linguistic syntax and grammar can never capture the chaotic flux of universal energy. As Byron, given his embracing of both the philosophical and the aesthetic principles of romantic irony, recognized most clearly, Romantic poems that seek to represent the abundant chaos of life can be only self-consuming artifacts.

If we turn from questions of poetic rhetoric to questions of politics, what happens to gender? The masculine Romantic ideology advocated the rights of the common man, demanding the vote and a fair share of the national wealth for the disenfranchised men of the working and lower classes. But what of the rights of the common woman? Blake, Godwin and Shelley wished to eliminate the yoke of marriage for both men and women, but whose interests does free love serve? Shelley has been hailed as a "feminist" for this prophetic vision of liberated women in *Prometheus Unbound:*[18]

> And women, too, frank, beautiful, and kind
> As the free heaven which rains fresh light and dew
> On the wide earth; gentle radiant forms,
> From custom's evil taint exempt and pure;
> Speaking the wisdom once they could not think,
> Looking emotions once they feared to feel,
> And changed to all which once they dared not be,
> Yet being now, made earth like heaven; nor pride,
> Nor jealousy, nor envy, nor ill shame,
> The bitterest of those drops of treasured gall,
> Spoilt the sweet taste of the nepenthe love.
> (*Prometheus Unbound*, III, iv:153–63)

As the final lines suggest, however, the role of liberated women in this utopia is but to love, without jealousy or envy or shame. When in Shelley's poetry a woman does move beyond the domestic realm to enter the public arena as a leader, as Cythna does after Laon's death in *The Revolt of Islam*, she can do so only after she has assumed his name, Laone, and only because she has been taught from childhood by Laon and thus, as Nathaniel Brown revealingly puts it, "has evolved an intelligence and will *similar to his own*"[19] (my emphasis). Neither Shelley nor the other Romantic poets ever imagined a utopia where women existed as independent, autonomous, *different*—but equally powerful and respected—authors and legislators of the world.

When a female character or principle asserts her independence or difference in canonical Romantic poetry, she is all too frequently defined as an evil to be eradicated or overcome. Excessive female sexual or social power is condemned by Blake as "the Female Will" and represented either as the oppressive nurses and barren old maids of the *Songs of Experience* or the corrupting Enitharmons and Valas of the later prophecies. The female power that wins the Ancient Mariner is a leprous "Nightmare," Life-in-Death, while Geraldine's ability to control Christabel's speech is figured in the patriarchal discourse of the Narrator as the poison of a snake. Byron mocks all "ladies intellectual" who have "hen-pecked you all" and portrays a powerful female ruler, Empress Catherine of Russia, as a bloodthirsty whore. By veiling his beloved maidens behind the radiance of his own sexual desire, Percy Shelley subtly suggests that a truly independent woman is not desirable; he sends the "holy and unstained" Beatrice Cenci to her death "wrapped in a strange cloud of crime and shame," subtly tainted by the very act—parricide—that freed her from her father's incestuous embraces. Only Keats insisted at length that a powerful and autonomous woman (like Moneta) may have something to teach the poet, but of this all important yet problematic exception I shall speak at length in Part III.

To the extent that the masculine Romantic ideology entails a commitment to the creative process, to erotic love, to the exploration of self-consciousness, and to an ethic of justice which acknowledges the value and rights of the common man, it also entails a gender ideology which subtly denies the value of female difference. Positive feminine characteristics—sensibility, compassion, maternal love—are metaphorically appropriated by the male poet, while attributes of difference—independence, intelligence, willpower, aggressive action—are denigrated. This form of Romantic sexism is particularly insidious because it denies to women even their traditional gender roles and cultural authority as experts in feeling, love, and maternal care, as the educators and moral guardians of the young, and as the respected rulers of the domestic sphere. After these canonized Romantic poets had stolen their emotions, their intuition, their capacity for imagination and fancy, their romances, and their affinity with nature, what did women have left? If we believe the overt assertions of much male-authored English Romantic poetry and prose, only silence or a willing absorption into the male ego, only madness, death or—which turns out to be equally self-defeating—the lamia-like abandonment or murder of their male lovers.

And yet the gender politics in many canonical English Romantic poems is more complex than their overt plots and characterizations of female figures might at first suggest. The female, both as metaphor and as pronomial gender, has a way of reasserting her strength and priority in the unlikeliest of places. In later chapters, I shall discuss this return of the repressed female in poems by Wordsworth and Keats, but we should be on the lookout for it everywhere. The dialogue and struggle between masculinity and femininity is one that occurs not only *between* the writings of men and women in this historical period but also *within* canonical Romantic poems and prose works,[20] a point I wish to explore in greater detail in my chapters on the Wordsworths and on Keats and Brontë.

PART II

FEMININE ROMANTICISM

2

"A REVOLUTION in Female Manners"

The Enlightenment ideals of the French *philosophes,* of Voltaire, Diderot and Rousseau, opened up a discourse of equality in which women could participate. On Bastille Day, 1789, Mary Wollstonecraft was living alone in London, working as a staff writer for the pro-Jacobin journal *The Analytical Review* published by Joseph Johnson, and meeting daily with the leading freethinkers of the day. In Joseph Johnson's bookshop she eagerly discussed the progress of the American Revolution and the revolutionary events in France with Thomas Paine, Richard Price, William Godwin, Thomas Holcroft, Thomas Christie, and the painters Fuseli and Blake. Seeing in their demands for liberty and equality against the

claims of inherited wealth and aristocratic privilege the possibility
for women's liberation as well, she sprang to the defense of Richard
Price and Thomas Paine in the pamphlet war concerning the origin
of political authority that raged in London in 1790. The war began
with Price's heretical speech before the annual meeting of the London Revolution Society in 1789. This anniversary address, historically intended to celebrate the glorious English revolution of 1688,
became in Price's hands the opening salvo of a fiery attack on the
British monarchy and the established privileges of the English aristocracy. Endorsed by Thomas Paine's *Rights of Man* (1790), which
called upon the common Englishman to throw off the shackles of
monarchy as both the Americans and the French were doing, these
revolutionary ideas inspired a powerful counterattack from Edmund Burke. His rhetorically inspired defense of the French monarchy, of the hereditary principle of succession, of the necessary
alliance between church and state, and of the restriction of political power to men "of permanent property" was published in early
November, 1790, as *Reflections on the Revolution in France, and on
the Proceedings in Certain Societies in London, relative to that Event.*

Responding to Burke's insistence that we "derive all we possess
as an *inheritance from our forefathers*" and that men have equal
rights "but not to equal things," as well as to his inflammatory images of revolutionary France as a female prostitute and of Marie
Antoinette as an innocent and pure young damsel, forced to flee
"almost naked" from her bed, pursued by "a band of cruel ruffians
and assassins," from a palace "swimming in blood, polluted by
massacre and strewed with scattered limbs and mutilated car-
casses,"[1] Mary Wollstonecraft rushed into print in three weeks with
A Vindication of the Rights of Men (November, 1790). Insisting that
all political authority should rest on the grounds of reason and justice alone, she demanded that every person be entitled to enjoy and
dispense the fruits of his or her own labors, that inequality of rank
be eliminated, and that in place of an exaggerated respect for the
authority of "our *canonized forefathers*" be substituted the cultivation of an independent understanding and sound judgment. For
Burke's image of the nation as a ravished wife in need of virile protection, Wollstonecraft substituted the image of the nation as a benevolent family educating its children for mature independence
and motivated by "natural affections" to ensure the welfare of all
its members.[2]

Since she believed that the French Revolution would quickly establish such an enlightened republic, one that would respect the

natural rights of every person, Mary Wollstonecraft was appalled when she read in 1791 that the French minister of education for the new Constituent Assembly had proposed a state-supported system of public education for *Men Only*. She immediately composed a lengthy response to the former Bishop of Autun, Citizen Charles Maurice de Talleyrand-Perigord, and his *Rapport sur L'Instruction Publique, fait au nom du Comité de Constitution* (Paris, 1791). That response, *A Vindication of the Rights of Woman*, went through two editions in 1792. Independently of the French feminist thought of the time, Mary Wollstonecraft perceived that the gender inequality at the core of both the revolutionary French nation and of British society threatened the development of a genuine democracy. She recognized that the denial of education to women was tantamount to the denial of their personhood, to their participation in the natural and civil rights of mankind.

Wollstonecraft therefore attempted to initiate her own revolution, what she explicitly called "a REVOLUTION in female manners."[3] In contrast to a masculine Romantic ideology that affirmed the rights and feelings of the natural man, Wollstonecraft propounded an equally revolutionary but very different ideology, what we might call the feminine Romantic ideology, an ideology grounded on a belief in the rational capacity and equality of woman. Following the lead of Catherine Macaulay's *Letters on Education* (1790), which she had reviewed enthusiastically for the *Analytical Review* two years before, Wollstonecraft explicitly attacked her society's gender definition of the female as innately emotional, intuitive, illogical, capable of moral sentiment but not of rational understanding. Appealing to the Enlightenment rationalists of her day, she grounded her social revolution on a rigorously logical argument, proceeding from the premise that if women are held morally and legally responsible for their sins or crimes (as they were in both England and France), then they must have both souls and the mental capacity to think correctly or ethically. And if women are capable of thinking, they must have a rational faculty. And if they have a rational faculty which is capable of guiding and improving their character and actions, then that rational faculty should be developed and exercised to its greatest capacity.

From this rigorously logical, philosophical argument for the equality of women, Wollstonecraft launched a passionate plea for women's education, for only if women are educated as fully as men will they be able to realize their innate capacities for reason and moral virtue. Calculatedly appealing to male self-interest in order to effect her revolutionary reforms,[4] Wollstonecraft argued that more highly educated women will not only be more virtuous, but they will also be better mothers, more interesting wives and "companions," and more responsible citizens. Wollstonecraft insisted that she was speaking on behalf of *all* women, not just the most talented. As she commented, "I do not wish to leave the line of mediocrity" (50). Therefore she assumed a society in which most men and women would marry, and argued that women would better serve the needs of society, of children, and of their husbands, as well as of their own selves, if they were educated to act more sensibly and judiciously. As Mitzi Myers has emphasized, "the core of her manifesto remains middle-class motherhood, a feminist, republicanized adaptation of the female role normative in late eighteenth-century bourgeois notions of the family."[5]

Because Wollstonecraft assumed a society in which most women would marry, she devoted a large portion of her *Vindication* to describing the ideal marriage, a marriage based on mutual respect, self-esteem, affection and compatibility. It is a marriage of *rational love*, rather than of erotic passion or sexual desire. Wollstonecraft repeatedly insisted in *A Vindication* that sexual passion does not last. She proclaimed,

> one grand truth women have yet to learn, though most it imports them to act accordingly. In the choice of a husband, they should not be led astray by the qualities of a lover—for a lover the husband, even supposing him to be wise and virtuous, cannot long remain. (119)

By identifying the rational woman with the repression, even elimination, of female sexual desire, Wollstonecraft initiated a legacy of female self-denial with which, as Cora Kaplan has forcefully argued, current feminism is still uncomfortably grappling.[6] Yet Wollstonecraft did not sustain an allegiance to a rationality devoid of all sexual or emotional passion, either in her own life or in this very text. As Mary Poovey has shown, the rhetoric and figures of *A Vindication of the Rights of Woman* repeatedly display the tension between Wollstonecraft's effort to deny the idea that women are *essentially* sexual beings and her own conviction that women both desire and need an enduring sexual, as well as emotional, relationship.[7] As we shall see, this very tension between a woman's sexual and emotional needs and her desperate efforts to control, repress or eliminate those desires lest she become a "fallen woman" vibrates through much of the women's fiction of the Romantic period.

In addition to advocating a radically new, egalitarian marriage between two rational and equally respected adults, Wollstonecraft demanded even more revolutionary rights for women: the vote (which she insisted should be given to both working-class men and all women), the civil and legal right to possess and distribute property, and the right to work in the most prestigious professions, including business, law, medicine, education and politics. Above all, she demanded for all children between the ages of five and nine a state-supported, coeducational public school system that would teach reading, writing, mathematics, history, botany, mechanics, astronomy, and general science. After the age of nine, the more gifted girls and boys would receive additional education at state expense. If Wollstonecraft's demands now seem self-evidently practical and just (if a bit demanding for nine-year-olds), it is only because the educational reform she demanded actually happened.

Mary Wollstonecraft not only articulated a utopian vision of the rational woman of the future, she also described in detail the errors and evils of the dominant bourgeois gender definition of the female as the subordinate helpmate of the male. Invoking Milton and Rousseau, she sardonically attacked their portrayals of women. When Milton tells us, she wrote with heavy sarcasm,

> that women are formed for softness and sweet attractive grace [*Paradise Lost* IV:297–99], I cannot comprehend his meaning, unless, in the true Mahometan strain, he meant to deprive us of souls, and insinuate that we were beings only designed by sweet attractive grace, and docile blind obedience, to gratify the sense of man when he can no longer soar on the wing of contemplation. (19)

She saved her bitterest attacks for Rousseau, perhaps because she still cherished Rousseau's political and educational doctrines, his emphasis on the development of both reason and the emotions, and his commitment to individual choice, creative thinking, and the social contract. She was particularly disappointed by the sketch of the ideal woman he drew in *Emile*. Depicting Sophy (Sophia, or female wisdom) as submissive, loving, and ever faithful, Rousseau had asserted that:

> What is most wanted in a woman is gentleness; formed to obey a creature often vicious and always faulty, she should early learn to

submit to injustice and to suffer the wrongs inflicted on her by her husband without complaint.[8]

Rousseau had further defined women's appropriate education as learning to please men:

> A woman's education must. . .be planned in relation to man. To be pleasing in his sight, to win his respect and love, to train him in childhood, to tend him in manhood, to counsel and console, to make his life pleasant and happy, these are the duties of woman for all time, and this is what she should be taught while she is young. (328)

Much of *A Vindication* is devoted to illustrating the damage wrought by this gender definition of women's nature and social roles as essentially sexual. Late eighteenth-century middle- and upper-class English women were taught to be primarily concerned with arousing and sustaining (but never fully satisfying) male sexual desire in order to capture the husbands upon whom their financial welfare depended. They were obsessed with their personal appearance, with beauty and fashion. Encouraged to be "delicate" and refined, many were what we would now recognize as bulimic and anorexic. As Wollstonecraft commented,

> I once knew a weak woman of fashion, who was more than commonly proud of her delicacy and sensibility. She thought a distinguishing taste and puny appetite the height of all human perfections, and acted accordingly.—I have seen this weak sophisticated being neglect all the duties of life, yet recline with self-complacency on a sofa, and boast of her want of appetite as a proof of delicacy that extended to, or, perhaps, arose from, her exquisite sensibility: for it is difficult to render intelligible such ridiculous jargon. (44)

Worse, women were encouraged to be fundamentally hypocritical and insincere. Forced to be flirts and sexual teases, they were encouraged to arouse male sexual desire by allowing their suitors to take "innocent freedoms" or "liberties" with their person, but were forbidden to experience or manifest sexual desire themselves, a situation that left them blushing in unconscious—yet necessarily fully conscious—modesty.[9]

Since they received no rational education, but were taught only what were known as "accomplishments"—singing, dancing, needlework, painting, a smattering of French and Italian, a "taste" for literature (usually French and Gothic romances) and the fine arts—the upper- and middle-class women of Wollstonecraft's society were kept, she claimed, in "a state of perpetual childhood" (9), "created to feel, not to think" (62). They were—and Wollstonecraft like Catharine Macaulay insisted on the term—"slaves" to their fathers and husbands (167), but, in revenge, cruel and petty tyrants to their children and servants. Forced to be manipulative and sycophantic to their masters, they were "cunning, mean and selfish" to everyone else (141). As a result, they became indolent wives and inconsistent mothers, either overly indulgent (to their sons) or hostile (to their infants, often refusing to nurse them), and directly responsible for the high incidence of childhood disease and infant mortality. Wollstonecraft concluded her *Vindication* with a list of common female follies: the belief in fortune-tellers and superstitions, the excessive fondness for romantic love stories, the obsessive concern with fashion and appearance, the selfish promotion of the members of her own family at the expense of others, the mismanaged households and mistreatment of servants, the overindulgence or neglect of children. While some modern feminist readers have been dismayed by Wollstonecraft's evident dislike of the women of her day, we must keep in mind that she blamed these female follies *on men*, on their failure to provide a suitable education for the women for whom they were financially and morally responsible.

Moreover, insisted Wollstonecraft, the historical enslavement of women has corrupted men. She argued that English men have been forced to assume the social role of the master and thus taught to be demanding, self-indulgent, arrogant, tyrannical. Treating their women as inferior dependants has undermined men's ability to understand the needs of others, to act justly or compassionately, to be good leaders. While Wollstonecraft's attack on men is muted (after all, they comprise the audience whom she must persuade), she nonetheless made it clear that the existence of a master-slave relationship between husband and wife creates evils on both sides. "How can women be just or generous, when they are the slaves of injustice?" she asked rhetorically (189).

The revolution in female manners demanded by Wollstonecraft would, she insisted, dramatically change both women and men. It would produce women who were sincerely modest, chaste, virtuous, Christian; who acted with reason and prudence and generosity. It would produce men who were kind, responsible, sensible and just. And it would produce egalitarian marriages based on compatibility, mutual affection and respect. As Wollstonecraft concluded,

> we shall not see women affectionate till more equality be established in society, till ranks are confounded and women freed, neither shall we see that dignified domestic happiness, the simple grandeur of which cannot be relished by ignorant or vitiated minds; nor will the important task of education ever be properly begun till the person of a woman is no longer preferred to her mind. (191)

The rational woman, rational love, egalitarian marriage, the preservation of the domestic affections, responsibility for the mental, moral and physical well-being and growth of all the members of the family—these are the cornerstones of Wollstonecraft's feminism, what we would now define as a "liberal" feminism, one that is committed to a model of equality rather than difference. They are also the grounding tenets of the feminine Romantic ideology. Wollstonecraft's moral vision diverges profoundly from the ideology both of the British Enlightenment and of the Girondist leaders of the French Revolution in its insistence on the rationality and equality of the female and on the primary importance of the domestic affections and the family. By selecting the image of the egalitarian family as the prototype of a genuine democracy, a family in which husband and wife not only regard each other as equals in intelligence, sensitivity, and power, but also participate equally in childcare and decision-making, Wollstonecraft introduced a truly revolutionary political program, one in which gender and class differences could be erased. While Wollstonecraft shared the Enlightenment *philosophes'* affirmation of reason and wit, of sound moral principles, and of good taste grounded on wide learning, her vision of the egalitarian family, in which husband and wife together serve the interests of the family as a whole, undermines both the traditional affirmation of the father as the final social, political and religious authority as well as the concept of a hierarchical universe or social order grounded on the metaphor of the great Chain of Being. Where Enlightenment thinkers and nonconformist writers such as Defoe, Richardson and Paine, challenged the authority of the father in the name of the younger son or the bourgeois capitalist, she heretically demanded the same rights and status for the daughter, the sister and the common woman.

Wollstonecraft's call for a "revolution in female manners" was not the first feminist tract to be published in England. Throughout the previous century a few intrepid women had argued, in print or by example, for the education of women and the elimination of the sexual double standard.[10] In the late Restoration period, Aphra Behn had promoted the equality of women both in the theater and in the home. Mary Astell had seriously proposed to the ladies in 1697 that they withdraw to a nunnery or seminary to pursue an education in both the classics and Christian doctrine. Lady Mary Wortley Montagu, Hester Chapone, Elizabeth Carter, Mary Robinson Montagu, and their bluestocking colleagues had publicly proclaimed the intelligence and wit of women. And Mary Hamilton had heeded Astell's call by writing a feminist utopian fantasy, *Munster Village*, in 1778. In this novel, Lady Frances Munster, upon inheriting her father's estate in Shropshire, immediately uses her wealth to found an academy or private university, in which men and women together learn the arts and sciences, medicine and law and business, combining theoretical knowledge with its practical applications. The success of her efforts is marked in Lady Frances herself, who combines a genuine artistic talent for painting, by which she earns an income sufficient to support herself and her brother's family for several years, with a business acumen that enables her simultaneously to found and run her academy while skillfully increasing the productivity of her landed estates by improving her tenants' cottages and training them to use the latest agricultural and practical methods.

In the 1790s Hannah More, Priscilla Wakefield, Catharine Macaulay, Mary Hays and Anne Frances Randall (Mary Robinson) all advocated extensive practical and intellectual reforms in the education and economic condition of women in England.[11] But Wollstonecraft's *Vindication* was the most favorably reviewed, widely read, and—despite the scandal surrounding Wollstonecraft's death and the publication of Godwin's *Memoirs*—lastingly influential feminist tract of the period.[12] In the following chapters I shall look at the way her revolutionary ideology permeated the writing of such novelists as Maria Edgeworth, Jane Austen, Susan Ferrier, Helen Maria Williams, Ann Radcliffe, Sydney Owenson Morgan, Mary Shelley, and many others. In this necessarily brief overview I will focus primarily on four dimensions of this revolutionary feminine Romanticism: the education of the rational woman, rational love and the politics of domestic responsibility, woman's relation to nature, and the feminine construction of subjectivity.

3

The Rational Woman

The concept of the rational woman promoted during the latter half of the eighteenth century by Mary Astell, the bluestockings, Hannah More and Mary Wollstonecraft had an enormous impact upon the women writing in England between 1780 and 1830. Maria Edgeworth, Helen Maria Williams, Mary Hays, Susan Ferrier, Mary Brunton and Jane Austen all wrote novels designed to advocate the revolutionary idea that women must think as well as feel, that they must act with prudence, avoid the pitfalls of sexual desire, and learn from their mistakes. In focusing our attention upon a heroine who develops in intellectual and moral stature, these novelists explicitly corrected a tradition of eighteenth-century writing by women which Jane Spencer in *The Rise of the Woman Novelist—From Aphra Behn to Jane Austen* has called "the didactic tradition" of "reformed heroines."[1] In these didactic novels the author functions as moral teacher, tracing the development of her heroine from fallible youth to a mature acceptance of the status quo and the role of dutiful wife. Inspired by the conduct-books of female propriety and the insistence of "Sophia," in her *Woman's Superior Excellence over Man* (1751), that women can become as sensible and virtuous as men, such female *Bildungsromane* as Mary Davy's *Reform'd Coquet* (1724), Eliza Haywood's *History of Miss Betsy Thoughtless* (1751), and Frances Burney's *Evelina* (1778) portrayed the heroine as one capable of learning the errors of her overly impulsive or selfish ways from her lover-mentor.

Mary Wollstonecraft and the novelists directly influenced by the revolutionary feminine Romanticism promoted in *A Vindication of the Rights of Woman* and other feminist tracts transformed this tradition by putting forth a subtle critique of masculinity, of the flaws in intelligence and moral virtue demonstrated by the male as well as the female characters, and of the dangers of romantic love and the creative imagination for both men and women. By focusing as much on the failures of traditional marriages as on the heroine's acquisition of a meritorious husband, these romantic novelists significantly challenged the conservative tendencies of a Hannah More—who in *Coelebs in Search of a Wife* (1808) and elsewhere argued that the rational woman, however powerful at home, should uphold the doctrine of the separate spheres and acknowledge the superiority of her husband in the public realm—with a revolutionary criticism of the authority of the father and husband, a demand for more egalitarian marriages, and an insistence on the domestic affections as the basis of all public and private virtues and happiness.

In her unjustly neglected but extremely well-written and compelling novel, *Belinda* (1801), Maria Edgeworth paints the portrait of the new Belinda, the woman who will replace Pope's "fairest of mortals" as the envy of her age. Belinda Portman, an attractive young woman of sound sense, wide reading, prudence, personal modesty and a loving heart, is sent to London by her matchmaking aunt to live with Lady Delacour, the acknowledged leader of high society. As the witty, shrewd and vivacious Lady Delacour exposes her to the intrigues, deceptions and hidden miseries of the fashionable world, Belinda is subtly drawn into a network of hypocrisy and double-dealing. But Belinda acts quickly to preserve her honor. When Lady Delacour borrows two hundred pounds from Belinda to buy a pair of horses, but instead uses the money to purchase a carriage, allowing Belinda's admirer Clarence Hervey to buy the horses, supposedly at Belinda's request, Belinda refuses to let the matter drop and arranges for Lord Delacour to pay for both the horses and the carriage. And when rumors circulate that Belinda is angling for Lord Delacour's affections even before his wife's anticipated death, she immediately leaves their house to reside with the benevolent and sincere Percival family at Oakley Park.

While the fascinating Lady Delacour with her sprightly dialogue, zest for fashion and intrigue, and private suffering (she is convinced, wrongly, that she is dying of breast cancer, is alienated from her husband, and refuses to see her daughter) provides one seductive but cautionary female role model for Belinda, Lady Delacour's former friend Harriet Freke provides another. A self-professed champion of the rights of woman who seeks to end the "slavery" of women to a false "delicacy" by having both sexes call things by their right names, Harriet Freke—her name, "freak," in the late eighteenth century meant, not a "monstrosity" but rather "a capricious humour, a whim, a vagary" (*Oxford English Dictionary*)—goes in Edgeworth's opinion too far. By wearing men's clothing, participating in a duel which seriously injures Lady Delacour, and playing cruel practical jokes on both Lady Delacour and the West Indian servant Juba, Harriet Freke undermines her campaign for the liberty of women. She assumes the worst aspects of masculinity—tyranny over the weak, cruelty, infidelity, physical violence—rather than fusing, as Belinda does, the positive qualities of both genders. In her man's riding boots, hitting her crop against the table, arguing loudly but without sense against Mr. Percival, roaming the countryside alone at night stirring up trouble, Harriet Freke is an early image of what we might now call the macho woman.

In introducing her as a "freak" or caprice of nature, Maria Edgeworth points to a more moderated and balanced feminism, one that would combine the positive characteristics of each gender.[2] As Edgeworth testified in her *Letters for Literary Ladies* (1799), she was not "a champion for the rights of woman"—which she narrowly defined as "a vain contention for superiority" by women over men—but was rather concerned "to determine what is most for our general advantage."[3] Belinda Portman preserves the sensibility and modesty associated with femininity, but combines these with shrewd judgment, a personal sense of honor, sound moral principles based on careful reasoning and extensive observation, earned self-esteem, and a generous capacity for loyalty and love. While she is emotionally and sexually attracted to Clarence Hervey, she curbs her responses to his admiring advances until she is convinced he is not committed to another woman. She admits Mr. Vincent's addresses at the advice of her friends, the judicious Percivals, but gives him no deceptive encouragement and breaks off the relationship as soon as she learns that he is a gambler. She has a clear sense of the proper relation of the sexes in marriage—

"surely," she tells Lady Delacour, "your ladyship does not think that a wife is a being whose actions are necessarily governed by a husband."[4] She seeks a marriage of equality and compatibility, with a man "of superior genius and virtue, with a temper and manners suited to her taste" (122). She thus represents the transition from what Beth Kowaleski-Wallace has called "older-style patriarchy with its emphasis on paternal prerogative, hierarchy and the exercise of force" to "new-style patriarchy with its appeal to reason, cooperation between the sexes and the non-coercive exercise of authority."[5]

Edgeworth paints Belinda's marital aspirations against the negative backdrop of the Delacour marriage—a match of interest, convenience, and vanity—and in harmony with the positive example of the Percival marriage—an egalitarian marriage where each partner understands and participates in both the serious occupations and the affections of the other, where each values and esteems the good sense and benevolence of the other. She thereby illustrates the virtues of the rational woman and the rational marriage. At the same time Edgeworth offers a trenchant critique of those men who fail to take women seriously and who act on impulse rather than sound judgment. Irritated by his wife's superior intelligence and wit, and the rumor that he "is governed by a woman," the foolish and vain Lord Delacour becomes a drunkard and a lout, indulging in food, gaming and a mistress, rather than attempting to remain friends with his wife. Sir Philip Baddeley cannot speak three words to a woman without resorting to swearing. Even the generous and loyal West Indian, Mr. Vincent, lacked "the power and habit of reasoning" (198) and is ruined by his desire for excitement and risk which leads him ever back to the gambling tables until both fortune and Belinda are lost.

Edgeworth saves her most damning criticism for the young man whom Belinda eventually marries, but not until after he has learned by experience the errors of his ways. Intelligent, charming, wealthy, witty, Clarence Hervey has grown tired of the artifices of the world of fashion. Inspired by Rousseau's program of female education in *Emile* (as was Richard Lovell Edgeworth's friend Thomas Day[6]), Hervey has determined to educate an unspoiled child of nature to be his wife. Finding a beautiful, innocent orphan girl in the woods, he keeps her in solitary retirement in Twickenham, ensuring that she remains entirely artless, sincere, amiable, and gratefully dependent. As Rachel, renamed Virginia in homage to Bernardin de St. Pierre's *Paul et Virginie,* grows older, Hervey learns to his dismay that, although honor-bound to marry her, he finds her increasingly boring:

> In comparison with Belinda, Virginia appeared to him but an in-sipid, though innocent child: the one he found was his equal, the other his inferior; the one he saw could be a companion, a friend to him for life, the other would merely be his pupil, or his play-thing. Belinda had cultivated taste, an active understanding, a knowledge of literature, the power and the habit of conducting herself; Virginia was ignorant and indolent, she had few ideas, and no wish to extend her knowledge; she was so entirely unac-quainted with the world, that it was absolutely impossible she could conduct herself with that discretion, which must be the combined result of reasoning and experience. (344)

Clarence Hervey is saved from a life-long error, marriage with an incompatible woman, only by the successful interference of Lady Delacour, who locates both Virginia's long-lost father and the man whom she has long loved in secret, Captain Sunderland.

Maria Edgeworth's *Belinda* is a textbook example of the new feminine Romantic ideology. Belinda succeeds in establishing a marriage of equality and compatibility because she has remained true to her moral and rational principles, cemented by the solid example of the benevolent and egalitarian Percival marriage. Clar-ence Hervey achieves the same only after he has recognized that the truly valuable relationship is with a woman who is not his in-ferior or grateful dependent but his equal in intellectual and moral achievements. And their combined goodwill and tactful interven-tion finally succeed in reconciling Lady Delacour with both her husband and her daughter.

The fact that almost every commentator has preferred Lady Delacour—the witty lady of high society whose cleverness and se-cret miseries, whose capacity for both powerful affection and in-tense jealousy, all endear her to the reader—over Belinda suggests that the same unreconciled tension between female sexual passion and female self-control that lies at the heart of Wollstonecraft's *Vindication* also vibrates through Edgeworth's novel. Edgeworth herself confessed to her cousin Sophy after reading of the passion-ate loves of Miss Milner and Matilda in Elizabeth Inchbald's *Simple Story,* "I really was so provoked with the cold tameness of that stick or stone Belinda, that I could have torn the pages to pieces."[7] But Edgeworth is even more critical of Lady Delacour, whose faults the novel never lets us forget: her jealousy, her spite against her enemy Mrs. Luttridge, her callous disregard of her servants' feelings and needs, her cruelty to her daughter and husband, her addiction to opium, and her willingness to risk her own and her husband's reputation in her dalliance with Colonel Lawless, who is killed for her sake in a duel. Even though some critics have argued that the novel endorses Lady Delacour's view of Belinda as cold and heartless,[8] Lady Delacour is not the voice of the author: the unreliability of her narration is focused in the excessively theatrical and artificial tableau which she constructs at the end of the novel. As Edgeworth makes clear, and as Belinda knows, it takes *time* to develop a genuine love based on mutual knowledge and esteem, time which the impatient Lady Delacour, in her desire to arrange all her friends' destinies at once, is reluctant to accommodate. Edgeworth's lack of sympathy for Lady Delacour, and the intensity of passion and sexual desire she embodies, is registered in the violent transformation Edgeworth imposes on Lady Delacour at the end of the novel: she becomes "Lady Delacour Reform'd" and acknowledges that lasting spiritual and emotional comfort can be found only in "domestic happiness."

That sustained domestic happiness is Edgeworth's highest value, as opposed to a passionate romantic love or that "liberty" which uneducated girls define "as escape from habitual restraint to exercise their own will, no matter how," is documented both in her life—Maria Edgeworth declined her only proposal of marriage (from the Swedish diplomat Edelcrantz, a man with whom she was "exceedingly in love"[9]) to remain with her father and siblings in Ireland—and in her *Letters for Literary Ladies* (1799). In the "Letters of Julia and Caroline," she portrays the dangers and penalties that befall a girl who, like Julia, defines herself as an ardent advocate of intense romantic love, of Byronic sensation for its own sake ("All that I dread is that *apathy* which your philosophers call tranquillity" [119]), and who chooses "the eager genius, the exquisite sensibility of enthusiasm" over "the even temper, the poised judgment, the stoical serenity of philosophy" (121). Preferring the lot of the woman of feeling ("great pleasure, and great pain—great virtue, and great defects—ardent hope, and severe disappointment—extasy and despair") to that of the rational philosopher ("calm happiness unmixt with violent grief, virtue without heroism—respect without admiration, and a length of life, in which to every moment is allotted its proper portion of felicity" [121]), Julia impulsively marries Lord V—. He is a man who shares none of her tastes for literature but who desires "public diversions and public admiration, dissipation, and all the pleasures of riches and high rank," who has a "taste for show and expense, his family pride, and personal vanity," and whose "easiness of temper and fondness" for Julia will give her "entire command at home and abroad" (146). Within five years, Julia is thoroughly bored by the fashionable world and separates from her demanding husband. Living alone, she falls easy prey to the advances of her admirers, elopes with one to France, is abandoned, and finally returns to London a year later, penniless and dying, broken in spirit, and filled with remorse.

In contrast, the prudent Caroline achieves Edgeworth's ideal of a non-eroticised domestic life, defined by "a Gentleman" (modelled on her father, Richard Lovell Edgeworth) in *Letters for Literary Ladies* as "the pleasure which men of science and literature enjoy in an union with women, who can sympathise in all their thoughts and feelings, who can converse with them as equals, and live with them as friends; who can assist them in the important and delightful duty of educating their children; who can make their family their most agreeable society, and their home the attractive centre of happiness" (114). Ignoring Wollstonecraft's revolutionary call for all women to enter the public realm as workers and voting citizens, Maria Edgeworth does not imagine a life for women outside the home. But she does share Wollstonecraft's conviction that men as well as women must commit themselves to the domestic affections and find their greatest fulfillment in an egalitarian marriage and the education of their children.

The dangers of excessive sensibility and of prohibited sexual passion for men as well as for women are spelled out in Helen Maria Williams' *Julia* (1790). A woman's answer to Goethe's *Werther*, this novel tracks the enormous emotional havoc wreaked by a young man who cannot repress his passion. Julia, modelled on Rousseau's *Nouvelle Héloïse*, is a young woman of refined sensitivity, poetic tastes, modest genius, and affectionate disposition, who prefers the "satisfactions of home" to the frivolous joys of dissipation in London society. She is joined by her closest friend and cousin, Charlotte, a sweet-tempered girl who worships Julia. When Charlotte goes on a tour of Italy with her father, she meets and falls in love with Frederick Seymour, a young diplomat who combines a good understanding and fine taste with noble ambition, an "enthusiasm . . . awake to every generous impression" with a "warmth of feeling." Frederick is moved by Charlotte's modest simplicity and good-heartedness, so different from the vain and silly society women he has hitherto encountered, and soon proposes to her. She accepts with perfect joy.

But when the engaged lovers return to London, Frederick meets Julia, whose superior beauty attracts his eye and whose intelligence can understand the subtleties of his thought and wit in ways that Charlotte cannot. His passion is aroused; despite his pledge to Charlotte, he is overwhelmed with love for Julia. And even though, in other circumstances, Julia might have returned his passion, her intense affection for her cousin and her uncle effectively stifles her sexual response; as Williams tells us, her "exquisite sensibility was corrected by the influence of reason."[10] Despite several encounters in which Frederick once saves her life and frequently manifests his love, Julia preserves her self-control. Frederick, honor-bound, marries Charlotte, but cannot hide his passion for Julia from prying eyes. During her first pregnancy, Charlotte is finally informed of Frederick's love for Julia, confirming her own sense of his distance and distraction from her. Charlotte, in misery, turns away from Julia, who intensely suffers this loss of her earliest and best friend in painful silence. His constitution weakened by his emotional turmoil, Frederick dies of a winter cold on the night of his son's birth, in unrelieved misery caused by his hopeless and uncontrolled desire, which has destroyed not only his happiness, but that of his wife and his beloved Julia.

As opposed to Goethe and the masculine Romantic *Sturm und Drang* school, Williams explores the damage done by a prohibited and irrational passion, the cruelty it wreaks on innocent bystanders, the ways in which it destroys a potentially happy family. When Julia sees a painting of "Charlotte at Werther's Tomb," which anticipates Frederick's death, she comments that *Werther* "is well written, but few will justify its principles" (259). In *Julia*, passion destroys Frederick. But Williams insists that such erotic desire is even more dangerous for women:

> Women have greater reason than men to fortify their hearts against those strong affections, which, when not regulated by discretion, plunge in aggravated misery that sex, who, to use the words of an elegant and amiable writer [John Gregory in *A Father's Legacy to His Daughters*, p. 12], "cannot plunge into business, or dissipate themselves in pleasure and riot, as men too often do, when under the pressure of misfortunes; but must bear their sorrows in silence, unknown and unpitied; must often put on a face of serenity and cheerfulness, when their hearts are torn with anguish, or sinking in despair." Though a woman with recti-

tude of principle, will resolutely combat those feelings which her reason condemns; yet, if they have been suffered to acquire force, the struggle often proves too severe for the delicacy of the female frame; and, though reason, virtue, and piety, may sustain the conflict with the heart, life is frequently the atonement of its weakness. (279–80)

As did Wollstonecraft and Edgeworth, Williams firmly endorsed the enduring domestic affections over unlicensed sexual passion as the basis of true love and benevolence. "Our affections are not constantly active, they are called forth by circumstances; and what can awaken them so forcibly, as the renewal of those domestic endearments which constitute the charm of our existence?" (44). Julia's lifelong affection for her father, uncle and cousin lead to the numerous acts of charity she eagerly performs for those in need—an old soldier, hungry peasants, a young child, even wounded animals. And it constitutes the basis of the happy family unit she and Charlotte finally construct after Frederick's death, a unit that includes Charlotte's father and son as well as the two women. Williams clearly implies that heterosexual passion may not contribute to domestic love; she firmly excludes it from her happy family.

The ardent disciple of both Godwin and Wollstonecraft, Mary Hays tried to mediate—and not very successfully—between the conflicting demands of masculine and feminine Romanticism. In her epistolary novel, *The Memoirs of Emma Courtney* (1796), she celebrated passionate love and the power of individual feelings, but at the same time offered a vivid demonstration of how much damage such uncontrolled passion could do, both to men and to women. Emma, an enthusiastic, innocent, sweet-tempered young woman, conceives an intense attachment to the son of her much-loved elderly friend, Mrs. Harley. Encouraged by his mother and inspired by his portrait, Emma falls in love with Augustus Harley before she meets him. For over two years she openly pursues him. She initiates a fervent correspondence in which she insists upon the depth of her love and admiration for him, and finally offers herself to him without the sacrament of marriage—only to have her persistent and increasingly demanding overtures rejected by the alternately friendly and stern Harley. Finally informed of his prior commitment to another woman, a secret marriage, she collapses into despair, contemplates suicide, is wracked by fever, and recovers only because of the wise counsel of her father's friend Mr. Frances and the attentions of a young man, Dr. Montague, who has long loved her. Emma finally agrees to marry Montague, and comes to realize that a marriage grounded on a "rational esteem, and a grateful affection," rather than on the "romantic, high-wrought, frenzied emotions," the "enthusiasm" and "fanaticism" of a "distempered imagination,"[11] is the basis of an enduring friendship and mental tranquillity, of genuine personal happiness.

But even as Emma foreswears the gratification of individual desire to embrace Wollstonecraft's concept of marriage as companionship, her husband remains tormented with jealous rage that Emma loves him less than she loved Harley. After Harley's death at their doorstep, during which he confesses that he had reciprocated Emma's love but refrained from telling her so to protect both her and his honor, and Emma's insistence on adopting Harley's orphaned son, Montague in revenge takes a mistress, impregnates her, tries first to abort and then in fact murders his illegitimate child, and finally commits suicide. His masculine pride and impassioned love for Emma have caused even more wretchedness than her love for Harley. Although Mary Hays' novel is clearly autobiographical, and traces the nuances of her own unregulated, openly confessed and one-sided sexual passion for William Frend, it finally adopts an ironic distance from its heroine, cautioning the reader in a few strategically placed footnotes to beware of Emma's unbridled enthusiasms and sublime sentiments. Having learned at the school of hard knocks, Mary Hays finally endorses a life of useful work, prudence, and sustained rational reflection for women, a life which they must create for themselves since their education and exposure to the fiction of sensibility have provided no useful guidance.

Susan Ferrier's *Marriage* was begun in 1810 by a woman who had attended James Stalker's Academy (one of the first coeducational schools in Scotland[12]) and who was well acquainted with the Enlightenment thinkers of late eighteenth-century Edinburgh, the "Athens of the North." *Marriage* can be read as a fictional translation of Wollstonecraft's *Vindication*. Ferrier begins by detailing the damage wrought when Lady Juliana, seduced by sentimental romances, refuses the aristocratic marriage arranged by her tyrannical father the Earl of Courtland. Caring only for the increase of economic and political influence, the Earl has chosen a rich, ugly, elderly Duke for his daughter; Juliana, willfully rebelling, insists that she will marry only for love, an emotion her father condemns as "plebeian" and "confined to the lower orders."[13] Instead Juliana elopes with Henry Douglas, a handsome but penniless Scots

Guardsman. But this marriage, founded only on mutual sexual desire, proves disastrous.

> Educated for the sole purpose of forming a brilliant establish-
> ment, of catching the eye, and captivating the senses, the culti-
> vation of [Juliana's] mind, or the correction of her temper, had
> formed no part of the system by which that aim was to be accom-
> plished. (6)

Spoiled, selfish, unable to tolerate the rough manners or coarse
food of her Scots in-laws, Juliana finally abandons her husband to
return to London to live parasitically upon her brother's shallow
goodwill. Unable to divorce her husband, who has been sent to military service in India after being freed from the debtor's prison to
which his wife's expensive and vitiated tastes have condemned
him, Juliana's life is devoted to her pet dogs and fashionable society, and only secondarily to raising her daughter Adelaide. Lady
Juliana embodies Wollstonecraft's portrait in *A Vindication* of the
selfish, spoiled, ignorant, neglectful society lady (modelled on
Wollstonecraft's employer, Lady Kingsborough) who cares more
for her pug dog than for her own daughters, and whose marriage,
based on no more than a passing sexual passion, has destroyed the
emotional happiness of both husband and wife.

Lady Juliana gives birth to twin daughters, Adelaide and Mary,
who function in the novel as exemplars of faulty and successful female education. Adelaide, in London, learns by example to be
"heartless and ambitious"; even more cold and selfishly calculat-
ing than her mother, she decides to marry the elderly, obstinate,
but very wealthy Duke of Altamont. She then finds his dogged refusal to satisfy her whims intolerable and runs off with her cousin
Lindore, only to find his sexual ardor rapidly cooling into "indifference" and herself condemned to "guilt and infamy" (495).

In contrast, Mary Douglas is raised by her "rational, cheerful,
sweet-tempered" aunt, a woman with a "noble and highly gifted
mind" who has voluntarily given up her first passionate love when
it met with her guardian's disapproval and instead married a man
whom she has found enduringly compatible and sensible. Inspired
by her aunt's benevolence, rationality and devotion to Christian
principles of charity and moderation, Mary learns to control her
emotions, to feel intense sympathy for the poor and needy, and to
worship devoutly. As Nancy Paxton rightly observes, "Mary has
been educated as if she were a boy; her reason has been cultivated

by study, she has been taught modern languages, and has been encouraged to think for herself."[14] Even in London, she insists on attending church despite her mother's ban, on taking care of the blind and lonely Mrs. Lennox, and on refusing the marriage with Lord Glenallen that her mother arranges for her. Her prudence and sympathy for the dying Mrs. Lennox win her the devotion of Charles Lennox, a wise, handsome, loving young Colonel who respects Mary's virtues and shares her capacity for benevolence and an enduring love.

While Ferrier's novel overtly endorses the "happy Marriage" of Mary Douglas and Charles Lennox as providing "as much happiness as earth's pilgrims ever possess" (513), it encodes a more subversive and revolutionary ideology than that suggested by Mary's insistence that she will "never marry, unless I marry a man on whose judgment I could rely for advice and assistance, and for whom I could feel a certain deference that I consider due from a wife to her husband" (419–20). The novel insistently associates this "happy" marriage with death—Mary and Captain Lennox plight their troth over the deathbed of his mother, Sir Sampson dies on their wedding day, leaving them the inheritance they need to live. And the idealized Captain Lennox is portrayed in such a bland, stereotypical way that the reader knows he has failed to capture Ferrier's imagination. As Mary Cullinan shrewdly asks, "Was Ferrier trying to depict the tedium of a perfect union by boring readers past endurance?"[15]

The novelist's own sympathies—and the modern reader's—lie not only with Mary but also, and perhaps more intensely, with her cousin Emily Lindore. Raised within the dissipated household of her vain, apathetic father and Aunt Juliana, she has remained "insupportably natural and sincere" (196), becoming at the same time independent and willful, clever and insightful. While she lacks the religious training and consequent benevolence and sympathy that Mary has learned from her Aunt Douglas, Emily engages us by her wit and her refusal to submit to her Aunt Juliana's petty tyrannies. Emily has long loved her cousin Edward Douglas, despite what she clearly sees are his faults: "he was handsome, brave, good-hearted, and good-humored, but he was not clever" (486). Their marriage is one of greater equality than is Mary's, for Edward's patriarchal privileges will be more than matched by Emily's superior intelligence. To Mary's belief that a woman must defer to her husband, Emily responds:

Now, I flatter myself, my husband and I shall have a more equitable division; for though a man is a reasonable being, he shall
know and own that woman is so too—sometimes. All things that
men ought to know better, I shall yield: whatever may belong to
either sex, I either seize upon as my prerogative, or scrupulously
divide. . . . (420)

While Mary is the ostensible heroine of the novel who wins all her
arguments with Emily and attains the husband that Emily half desired, Emily is the voice of shrewd, worldly female intelligence and
honest, bold wit. While she lacks Mary's moral scruples and religious devotion, primarily because her Aunt Juliana failed to intro-
duce her to the Bible when she was young, Emily's utterances
sparkle with an energy and comic wit that suggest she is in part a
projection of the author herself.[16] And her choice of a husband
whose faults she knows and can tolerate, a husband who remains
devoted to her and admires her, suggests that other kinds of happy
marriages are possible than those described by Hannah More.

Perhaps the most subtle and yet most compelling representation
of the crosscurrents in feminine Romanticism occurs in the fiction
of Jane Austen. A full consideration of Austen's writing—so well
analysed by so many—is beyond the scope of this book. But it is
crucial to see that Austen is neither the eighteenth-century conservative so many critics have long described, nor the radical feminist Margaret Kirkham and others have recently claimed.[17] Jane
Austen espoused a value system firmly grounded on a belief in
women's capacity for intellectual and moral growth, in the desirability of egalitarian marriages based on rational love and mutual
esteem, and in the prototype of domestic affection and responsibility as the paradigm for national and international political relations. Her fiction, as Claudia Johnson and Alison Sulloway have
persuasively argued,[18] is that of a moderate feminist, solidly progressive in its measured examinations both of the failures of the
patriarchy and the landed gentry and of the potential for moral
and intellectual equality between the sexes.

Inspired by Mary Wollstonecraft and the several women writers
in the late eighteenth century who had attempted to encourage
women's capacities for rational and ethical development,[19] Jane
Austen portrayed the heroines of her novels, *not* as the women of
passionate sensibility celebrated by Rousseau, by the male Romantic poets, and by such Jacobin novels as Henry Mackenzie's *Julia de Roubigné* or Elizabeth Inchbald's *A Simple Story*. Instead,

Jane Austen's heroines are women of *sense*, women like Elinor Dashwood and Anne Elliot who refuse to be overcome by sexual passion. Even those heroines who are initially seduced by Gothic romances and fairy tales of romantic love, like Catherine Morland in *Northanger Abbey*, are capable of recognizing the errors of their youthful delusions—even as they come to understand the more subtle ways in which men like General Tilney can oppress and torment the women in their family.

Indeed, all of Austen's novels are novels of female education, novels in which an intelligent but ignorant girl learns to perceive the world more accurately, to understand more fully the ethical complexity of human nature and society, and to gain confidence in the wisdom of her own judgment. Emma Woodhouse—Jane Austen's fantasy figure of unrestricted female power, benevolence and authority[20]—must still recognize how unfairly she has criticised Jane Fairfax, how insensitively she has manipulated Harriet Smith, how her vanity and pride have led her to misjudge both Robert Martin and Frank Churchill, and how cruelly she has insulted Miss Bates, before she can justify her claim to be the "first in Highbury" and demonstrate that she is the equal in intelligence and good breeding—and the superior in generosity—of Mr. Knightley. Above all, Emma must curb her romantic imagination, must cease being an "imaginist" like Cowper before his fire in *The Task*, "Myself creating what I saw,"[21] and learn to perceive others more correctly and compassionately, before she can fully emerge as Jane Austen's ideal woman of independent power and responsible authority, the queen of both Hartfield and Donwell Abbey.

Similarly, Elizabeth Bennet must overcome both her proud confidence in her own ability to distinguish simple and intricate human characters and her prejudiced and inaccurate assessment of Mr. Darcy, through a process of painful mortification, self-analysis, and learning, before she can recognize that Mr. Darcy is the man best suited to be her husband. Elizabeth Bennet's marriage to Fitzwilliam Darcy in *Pride and Prejudice* exemplifies Mary Wollstonecraft's ideal marriage, a marriage based on rational love, mutual understanding, and respect. It is Jane Austen's version of the utopian feminist ideal, first put forth in Mary Hamilton's *Munster Village* (1778), the novel from which Jane Austen borrowed the names of "Eliza" and "Bennet" and "Bingley."[22] In Munster Village, Lady Frances combines a superior female education with a strong commitment to the domestic affections and the judicious management of her landed estates. In order to pass on this inheritance to her niece Eliza and nephew Edward, she established the first coeducational academy (or university) as well as a public hospital, and undertakes economically feasible land and business reforms which benefit both workers and managers.

Although Lady Frances has complete control over Munster Village, Elizabeth Bennet does not attain such independence. In *Pride and Prejudice* it is a further sign of Elizabeth Bennet's intelligence that the overriding emotion she feels for Darcy, as Jane Austen repeatedly states, is "gratitude." A contested word in the discourse of sentiment in the Romantic period, "gratitude" was described by Maria Edgeworth as the appropriate feeling of a daughter for a father, of a student for her tutor, but not of a lover or wife. As Clarence Hervey confesses in *Belinda*,

> Nothing could be more absurd than my scheme of educating a woman in solitude to make her fit for society. I might have foreseen what must happen, that Virginia would consider me as her tutor, her father, not as her lover, or her husband; that with the most affectionate of hearts, she could for me feel nothing but *gratitude*. (428)

But Dr. John Gregory, in his influential conduct-book *A Father's Legacy to his Daughters*, had recognized that, since a modest woman feels no sexual desire, she *would* choose her husband on this basis: "What is commonly called love among you is rather *gratitude*, and a partiality to the man who prefers you to the rest of your sex." [23]

Why does Elizabeth Bennet feel "above all, above respect and esteem," the emotion of gratitude for Darcy? To calculate the reverberations of this term in *Pride and Prejudice*, we should recall that the Oxford English Dictionary defines gratitude as "the condition of being grateful or thankful, of having a warm sense of appreciation for a kindness received." We are also grateful when we are not given something unpleasant, like a punishment, that we deserved or expected to receive. I suggest that gratitude is an emotion most often felt by people who are, at least momentarily, in a humbled or subordinate position. Children feel grateful to their parents for being kind to them or for not punishing them; slaves or workers feel grateful to a master or employer who does not brutalize them or rewards them with unexpected bonuses; we all feel grateful to people who give us presents or favors we did not expect. At the same time, we may feel overwhelmed by their generosity, indebted, and perhaps even a bit inferior, to them.

In *Pride and Prejudice*, it is *women* who most feel gratitude. When

Elizabeth first rejects Darcy's proposal, she acknowledges that "It is natural that obligation should be felt, and if I could *feel* gratitude, I would now thank you. But I cannot."[24] Nonetheless, as she reflects on his proposal after his departure, she admits that "it was gratifying to have inspired unconsciously so strong an affection" (134). Again, when she receives his letter of explanation and self-justification, "His attachment excited gratitude; his general character respect; but she could not approve him" (147). After Elizabeth encounters the still cordial Darcy at Pemberly, "it was gratifying to know that his resentment had not made him think really ill of her" (175). Finally, that night, as she examines her feeling for Darcy, she recognizes that

> there was a motive within her of good will which could not be overlooked. It was gratitude.—Gratitude, not merely for having once loved her, but for loving her still well enough, to forgive all the petulance and acrimony of her manner in rejecting him, and all the unjust accusations accompanying her rejection. (181)

Jane Austen wants us to understand that rational love, for a woman, *must* be based on gratitude. In a society where every woman is in want of a husband with a good fortune, where marriage is, as Charlotte Lucas reminds us, a woman's "pleasantest preservative from want" (86), and where women have the option of refusing but never of initiating a marriage proposal, a woman must above all be grateful to the man who rescues her from the financial deprivations of spinsterhood. As the never-married Jane Austen wrote caustically to her unmarried sister Cassandra, "Single Women have a dreadful propensity for being poor—which is one very strong argument in favour of Matrimony."[25] And for no woman more than for Elizabeth, whose family estate is entailed on Mr. Collins and whose own dowry, inherited only after her mother's death, cannot exceed eight hundred pounds. Darcy might, like his sex, have preferred to triumph; he might have refused to requite her love; he might have withheld his "valuable" affection and declined to make her mistress of Pemberley. Elizabeth is fully conscious that she has received from Darcy more than she could give him; as she reflects,

> it was an union that must have been to the advantage of both; by her ease and liveliness, his mind *might* have been softened, his manners improved, and from his judgement, information, and

knowledge of the world, she *must* have received benefit of *greater* importance. (214, my emphasis)

Elizabeth's—or women's—gratitude is carefully differentiated by Jane Austen from male gratitude in affairs of the heart. Whereas female gratitude derives from financial need and women's restricted access to "knowledge of the world," male gratitude is based on little more than vanity. As Jane Austen tells us in *Northanger Abbey*, although Henry Tilney sincerely loved Catherine Morland,

> I must confess that his affection originated in nothing better than gratitude; or, in other words, that a persuasion of her partiality for him had been the only cause of giving her a serious thought. It is a new circumstance in romance, I acknowledge, and dreadfully derogatory of an heroine's dignity,

she continues parodically, "but if it be as new in common life, the credit of a wild imagination will at least be all my own" (*Northanger Abbey*, ch. 30). Where men proceed from gratitude to love and esteem, women move from love and esteem to gratitude.

Even after her marriage, Elizabeth remains grateful, and subservient, to Darcy. Discussing his friendship with Bingley,

> Elizabeth longed to observe that Mr. Bingley had been a most delightful friend; so easily guided that his worth was invaluable; but she checked herself. She remembered that he had yet to learn to be laught at; and it was rather too early to begin. (256)

Elizabeth must censor her comments to Darcy; she cannot now—and may never be able to—mock him. As Joseph Allen Boone has shrewdly commented, "The impulse to give Darcy time to grow, of course, is both endearingly human and humane, but it subtly reinforces Elizabeth's future role, as wife, to wait rather than initiate."[26]

Elizabeth's dependency on Darcy is sharply defined, as always in Jane Austen's fiction, in terms of money.[27] Even though Elizabeth is Darcy's wife, she has only a very small personal income at her disposal. When Lydia asks her to get Wickham a place at court, she refuses. However, "such relief as it was in her power to afford, by the practice of what might be called economy in her own private expenses, she frequently sent them" (267). Elizabeth in effect receives an "allowance" from Darcy; she remains a dependent in his household.

Those who have read the romance of Darcy and Elizabeth as all "light and bright and sparkling," as a fairy tale consummation of female equality, independence and personal happiness in marriage,[28] have not paid enough attention to the darker nuances of Jane Austen's words. Darcy and Elizabeth may live happily ever after, but only if Darcy *permits* his wife to "take liberties" with him. For as Jane Austen tells us on the last page of the novel, Georgianna Darcy, who had always stood in awe of her much older brother,

> had the highest opinion in the world of Elizabeth; though at first she often listened with an astonishment bordering on alarm at her lively, sportive, manner of talking to her brother. . . . By Elizabeth's instructions she began to comprehend that a woman may take liberties with her husband, which a brother will not always allow in a sister more than ten years younger than himself. (268)

But as Jane Austen's precisely chosen words remind us, Darcy still has the power *not* to allow either his sister or his wife to "take liberties" with him. He remains the master of Pemberly, controlling the "liberties" of all the women enclosed within—even as they, like all middle-class eighteenth-century women, must allow their suitors to "take innocent liberties" with them (recall that Wickham almost succeeded in raping Georgianna Darcy). Jane Austen advocates a marriage of genuine equality between husband and wife— and has seduced many readers into believing that such is the case with Darcy and Elizabeth—but she is honest enough to remind us that such marriages may not yet exist in England.

Except perhaps in the Navy. In *Persuasion*, Austen's last and most socially progressive novel, Admiral Croft and his sensible, strong-willed wife have a marriage that can accurately be described as a partnership of equals. Although we never learn what Mrs. Croft actually did while living on shipboard and aiding the Admiral in the command of his fleet, beyond the mending, we do see that on land, their decisions are made jointly and with full mutual respect and affection. All household purchases and domestic arrangements, all social activities, all professional decisions, are shared equally by both, whether driving the landau, conversing with other naval families in Bath, arranging the lease of Kellynch Hall, or determining the Admiral's patronage. The Croft marriage is clearly the prototype for the other successful marriages in the novel, whether the Harvilles, the elder Musgroves, the Benwicks, the Hayters, or the long awaited one of Anne Elliot and Captain Wentworth, a marriage that judiciously balances prudence and warmth, "fortitude and gentleness," the "resolution of a collected mind" with the intensity of an enduring love.

Jane Austen's conviction that the survival of women inside and out of marriage depends upon rational resolution is perhaps clearest in *Mansfield Park*, where we are asked to endorse the cautious modesty of Fanny Price rather than the energetic imagination of Mary Crawford. Fanny is the voice of prudence in the novel, of sound moral and intellectual sense, a voice that sustains the organic growth of the family within a clean, well-lighted home, a voice that is finally beyond price.[29] In contrast, the women of *Mansfield Park* who are foolishly educated all end badly. The "accomplished" Bertram sisters can recite by rote but they cannot recognize the insincerity of Henry Crawford, the stupidity of Mr. Rushworth, or the shallowness of Mr. Yates. Seduced by erotic desire, Maria Bertram Rushworth ends her days in banishment from both the husband she abandoned and her family home at Mansfield Park, condemned to the selfish and manipulative company of Aunt Norris. Mary Crawford, whose imagination, wit and charm identify her with revolutionary masculine Romanticism in the novel, rebels against the discipline of logic and morality and is finally depicted as little better than a prostitute, beckoning seductively from a doorway. Despite her cleverness and capacity for genuine affection, Mary Crawford cannot have the stable, enduring affection of Edmund Bertram but must settle instead for the company of her restless, self-indulgent, and irresponsible brother.

That women must exercise good sense and self-control in order to survive respectably is the calculated argument of *Mansfield Park*, Jane Austen's least likable novel. As Margaret Kirkham has told us, its title was carefully chosen—Lord Mansfield's famous legal judgment in the case of Somerset versus Stewart in 1772 proclaimed that while the slave trade might be appropriate for the colonies (significantly, Sir Thomas Bertram owns a slave plantation in Antigua, where his manager is having trouble controlling his slaves), nonetheless England "is a soil whose air is deemed too pure for slaves to breath in it."[30] Like Mary Wollstonecraft and Catharine Macaulay, Jane Austen insisted that the English women of her day were little better than domestic slaves, bought and sold on the marriage market, and kept at home by fathers and husbands under "restraint."[31] For Jane Austen, becoming a governess, the main economic alternative to marriage for respectable middle-class women, was no better. Jane Fairfax bitterly compares the "governess-trade" to the slave trade: "There are places in town—Offices for the sale—not quite of human flesh—but of human intellect." She admits that the two trades are "widely different certainly as to the guilt of those who carry it on; but as to the greater misery of the victims, I do not know where it lies."[32] The best that Jane Austen's "enslaved" middle-class countrywomen could attain was a generous master, one who must be cautiously and wisely chosen, one who would allow his wife to "take liberties" with him.

Modern readers will want to resist Jane Austen's too-easy identification of middle-class women with West Indian slaves. As I shall discuss in the next chapter, feminine Romanticism was distinctly class-biased in favor of the middle class, treating the lower classes as "children" to be governed, controlled, and reformed, and incorporating the heroic virtues previously assigned to the aristocracy into the middle class. Even the names of Jane Austen's heroes, Knightley and Darcy, inscribe her assumption that virtue and nobility are linked.

Given the economic dependence of women upon men, it follows that women cannot obey the impulses and dictates of their feelings. Sexual desire and passionate love too easily lead women into unhappy marriages, as we see when Lydia Bennet is punished for her "high animal spirits" and promiscuous desire by the indifferent contempt of Wickham. Or they can threaten a woman's life, as when Marianne Dashwood almost dies after Willoughby cruelly rejects her ardent love. Or worse, they can condemn women to the perpetual disgrace and ostracism endured by Maria Bertram and the two Elizas in *Sense and Sensibility.*

In opposition to Romantic poems such as *The Eve of St. Agnes, Don Juan* and *Epipsychidion* that leave open the possibility that erotic love and passionate feeling can enable us to experience a heaven on earth, the leading women writers of the day followed Wollstonecraft in urging their female readers to foreswear passion—which too often left women seduced, abandoned, disgraced—and pregnant, with only the career of prostitution remaining to them. Of course, many male-authored texts of the Romantic period also portray the dangers of erotic seduction, for *men*—one thinks of Keats' wretched Knight and Lycius, of the poet-narrators of *Alastor* and *Endymion*, of Manfred and the guilt-ridden heroes of Byron's Turkish Tales. But all these poems endorse the desirability of a *wholly reciprocal* sexual passion. For male writers, the fear is never that of pregnancy, parenthood and prostitution, but rather of abandonment, loss of self-control, madness and even a death caused by that frustration and despair. The exception, perhaps, is Wordsworth's Vaudracour, whose unsanctioned, passionate love for Julia finally commits her to a convent and him to the responsibilities of parenting their bastard son. But that child soon dies, "by some mistake/ Or indiscretion of the Father" (*The Prelude*, 1805, IX:906–7), and Vaudracour lives, to know not the shame of social opprobrium but rather the emptiness of "an imbecile mind."

Denouncing sexual passion, women writers urge their readers to embrace reason, virtue, and caution. The spontaneous overflow of passionate feeling in a female who has *not* thought long and deeply can be disastrous for the welfare of women. Whether we read Wollstonecraft or Austen, Maria Edgeworth's *Belinda* or Susan Ferrier's *Marriage*, Helen Maria Williams' *Julia* or Mary Hays' *Memoirs of Emma Courtney*, Mary Brunton's *Self-Control* or Hannah More's *Strictures on the Modern System of Female Education*, we hear a call, not for sensibility but for sense, not for erotic passion but for rational love, a love based on understanding, compatibility, equality and mutual respect.

Cautious, sensible love based on esteem is all the more necessary for women in a society where women are economically dependent on men, yet where men cannot be trusted to behave wisely or well. The female novelists of the Romantic era agree in stressing the evils of a patriarchal culture which oppresses them. Few go so far as Mary Wollstonecraft, in *Maria, or the Wrongs of Woman,* or the female Gothic novelists in depicting the physical tyrannies of a legal or religious system which permits the imprisonment, torture, and even murder of women who do not obey their fathers, husbands or priests. But all draw attention to the myriad ways in which men fail to perform their moral and financial duties as leaders of their families and the nation. Edgeworth portrays the sufferings inflicted on Irish tenants by irresponsible absentee British landlords as well as the dissipations and uselessness of such London aristocrats as the Delacours and Sir Philip Baddeley. Ferrier draws attention to the amorality of the governing class in her portraits of the enervated Lindores and the wasteful, self-indulgent Colonel Delmour, while Elizabeth Inchbald depicts the mental oppressiveness of the authoritarian former priest, Lord Dorriforth, in *A Simple Story.*

Nowhere are the claims of the aristocracy to patronage, prestige and power scrutinized with more care than in the fiction of Jane Austen. Those who have assigned her to the Tory party of anti-Jacobin conservatism have singularly failed to see the ways in which she questions the moral and political practices of both the aristocracy and the landed gentry, even as she engages in a subtler form of gender politics by asserting the rights of women to a social status and an intellectual and moral development equal to that of men. Perhaps influenced by the American and French Revolutions, she envisions a more egalitarian and gender-free society in which the best attributes of the middle classes shall prevail and women shall be as powerful as men. Jane Austen's allegiance remains solidly with the middle classes, those who *earn* their living; she never engages the plight of the working classes or the homeless poor, save as objects of charity or fear, as when the gypsies threaten Emma and Harriet.

The amorality, irresponsibility and selfish greed of men from the aristocratic, landed gentry and professional classes is everywhere portrayed in Austen's fiction. Sir Walter Elliot is so profligate, self-centered and vain that he has squandered his inheritance, been forced to lease his ancestral estate, Kellynch Hall, and condemned to end his days in rented rooms in Bath; a "foolish spendthrift baronet," he has no sense of responsibility for his children or tenants and thus can "feel no degradation in his change" and sees "nothing to regret in the duties and dignities of the resident land-owner" (*Persuasion*, 152). Sir Thomas Bertram is a slaveowner whose Antiguan plantation is badly managed; nor does he exercise effective moral control over his English household. His oldest son blithely gambles away half his inheritance, including his brother's living, while his oldest daughter marries a man she detests merely to escape her father's "restraint," and then sacrifices her reputation by eloping with Henry Crawford. Mr. Woodhouse is a self-absorbed hypochondriac, forcing his guests to forego food and drink in order to conform to his invalid's vitiated appetite, while he excessively indulges his favorite, Emma. Only Mr. Knightley and Mr. Darcy have a clear sense of financial and personal responsibility for their estates, staff, and dependents; but they exercise their power with a firmness that can be oppressive to women. As Mr. Knightley acknowledges to Emma, "I have blamed you, and lectured you, and you have borne it as no other woman in England would have borne it" (*Emma*, 417). Mr. Darcy, however amiable he may be to his housekeeper, will not permit his younger sister to "take liberties" with him. These two landlords may not be quite the "redeemer/ jailors" that Nina Auerbach sees,[33] but they both have a strong sense of pride and personal dignity that will brook no insults from those they regard as their inferiors.

Jane Austen does not confine her criticism of the aristocracy to the patriarchs that control it. Female aristocrats, emulating their menfolk, display the same arrogance of power, if somewhat less effectively. Lady Catherine de Bourgh, Elizabeth and Mary Elliot, and even the good-natured Lady Russell are all snobs, incapable of perceiving genuine human merit when class inferiority is present, and exercising their power over their relatives with insensitivity and selfishness. Even Emma Woodhouse manifests traits of unwarranted class pride in her attitudes to Robert Martin, the Coles, Mr. Elton and the rambunctious Mr. Weston, and in her failure to appreciate the plight of the impoverished gentlewoman,[34] although she eventually learns to value merit more highly than birth.

Jane Austen is equally critical of the greed and moral hypocrisy of the professional classes. Mr. Collins and Mr. Elton, her representations of the clergy in action, are sycophantic, foolish, self-serving men, eager to advance their own standing in the community by pleasing a patroness or marrying wealth. Only Edward Ferrars and Edmund Bertram hold out the promise of becoming responsible clergymen, living in their own parish, and genuinely caring for the spiritual and financial needs of their congregation, but we never see them actually performing their duties. Lawyers in Austen's work are a greedy, selfish, irresponsible lot, whether we observe Mr. Phillips encouraging his nieces to consort with Wickham and the Dragoons, or the peevish John Knightley, concerned only to preserve his home-fire comforts, or more tellingly, John Dashwood, all too easily persuaded by his wife to keep his half sisters' inheritance for his son. Only doctors are presented positively, working long hours and bringing welcome relief, whether to hypochondriacs, as Mr. Perry does to Mr. Woodhouse, or to the seriously ill, as Mr. Harris does to Marianne Dashwood. The wealthy wives and widows of the professional class exercise their power with even more vanity, cruelty and irresponsibility than do their husbands: Mrs. John Dashwood eagerly impoverishes her mother- and sisters-in-law, Mrs. Edward Ferrars almost ruins her oldest son's life by failing to find a useful profession for him, while Mrs. Churchill forces her adopted son Frank into a life of deceptions by her incessant demands for service and attendance.

Jane Austen, as has often been noted, is positively disposed to the military, and portrays her naval officers in *Persuasion* and William Price, the young midshipman in *Mansfield Park*, with unqualified approval of their industry, courage, and domestic virtue. But she is far more critical of the army, depicting the evils of a standing army, embodied in Wickham in *Pride and Prejudice* or Frederick Tilney in *Northanger Abbey*, in ways that echo Mary Wollstonecraft's condemnation of a standing army in *A Vindication:*

> A standing army . . . is incompatible with freedom; because subordination and rigour are the very sinews of military discipline; and despotism is necessary to give vigour to enterprizes that one will directs. . . .
>
> Besides, nothing can be so prejudicial to the morals of the inhabitants of country towns as the occasional residence of a set of idle superficial young men, whose only occupation is gallantry, and whose polished manners render vice more dangerous, by concealing its deformity under gay ornamental drapery. . . . A man of rank or fortune, sure of rising by interest, has nothing to do but to pursue some extravagant freak; whilst the needy *gentleman*, who is to rise, as the phrase turns, by his merit, becomes a servile parasite or vile pander. (17)

While Jane Austen does not follow Wollstonecraft in troping the parasitical military as negatively "feminine" in their "womanly indolence, polished manners, and love of ornamental dress," as Elissa Guralnick puts it,[35] she does insist on the abuse of authority practised by army men. In General Tilney, she represents the despotism of power.[36] While he has not murdered his wife, "his temper injured her" and he imposes an oppressive "restraint" on his children. He effectively imprisons his daughter Eleanor in his Gothic castle, tyrannically turning her friend out of doors on seven hours' notice, and refusing her the liberty to marry the man she loves, until that man suddenly acquires a peerage and a fortune.

Jane Austen wants us to see the myriad ways in which patriarchal power—especially the possession of money—can corrupt both men and women. Her ideal figures, whether male or female, are those who use their wealth to forward benevolent ends, whether employing at just wages the workers on their estates (Pemberley, Donwell Abbey) or performing continuous acts of charity for the needy in their neighborhoods (as Emma makes sure Miss Bates has enough to eat and regularly visits the sick and poor—or, at the opposite end of the social scale, the crippled and impoverished Mrs. Smith in *Persuasion* knits what she can sell to help those in even direr straits). Her satirized characters all succumb to the greed of commercial capitalism, seeking to benefit themselves at the expense of others. At the level of economics, Jane Austen's critique of patriarchal power emerges through her celebration of a partial levelling of the classes, an affirmation of the middle-class virtues of industry, thrift, benevolence, responsibility, and generosity embodied in the Gardiners (who were in trade) and the Crofts. Hence, she typically presents marriages in which the upper and lower classes merge with the middle class, whether the baronet's daughter and the originally portionless naval captain (*Persuasion*), the landed and the unlanded gentry (*Pride and Prejudice*), the clergyman with a handsome living and the lower-class daughter of an alcoholic ex-sailor (*Mansfield Park*).

In her critique of abused patriarchal power, of capitalist greed and aristocratic snobbery, Jane Austen endorses Wollstonecraft's argument that the master-slave relationship embedded both in the English class system and in gender roles damages both masters and slaves. Her focus on the lives of middle-class women effectively undermines the status quo by detailing the many ways in which existing patriarchal social institutions do not serve women well, whether we think of marriage, primogeniture, the authority of the father, or the greater freedom and experience of men. In a society where men can choose and women only refuse, women do not have the opportunity to realize to the full their own capacities for thought and action. They can only develop the rational ability to make the best of what they are offered, if not with the cold calculation of a Lucy Steele, then certainly with the pragmatic common sense of a Charlotte Lucas. The feminine Romantic ideology propounded in the fiction of the 1790s and early 1800s systematically revealed the faults of the fathers and brothers and lovers even as it urged its heroines to develop sound moral principles, those habits of virtuous thought and prudent behavior capable of withstanding the temptations of sexual desire, excessive sensibility, or immediate personal gratification. Here, as we shall see more clearly in the next chapter, feminine Romanticism is a direct descendant of the eighteenth-century tradition of enlightened protestant dissent, as well as of the growth of the bourgeois subject and of a capitalist economic system grounded in thrift, the accumulation of savings, moderation, and hard work.

4

Family Politics

Feminine Romanticism differs markedly from masculine Romanticism in its attitude to the political process. In opposition to the revolutionary Promethean politics urged by the young Wordsworth and Coleridge, by Blake, Godwin and Percy Shelley, a program that advocated radical social change and utopian transformations of the social and political order, the women writers of the Romantic era offered an alternative program grounded on the trope of the family-politic, on the idea of a nation-state that evolves gradually and rationally under the mutual care and guidance of both mother and father. Frequently invoking Edmund Burke, they endorsed his concept of the organic development both of the mind and of the political body under benevolent parental control as the model for a successful human community, although, as we shall see, at the same time they challenged Burke's patriarchal sexual politics.

Mary Shelley articulated this concept of the family-politic in a passage in *Frankenstein* that functions ironically both as her personal credo and as a statement of feminine Romanticism's primary commitment to the preservation of the domestic affections and the family unit. I say ironically because the following words are spoken by the non-nurturer Victor Frankenstein to his bored listener, Walton. Both Walton's boredom and Frankenstein's immediate dismissal of this credo as mere "moralizing" in the sentence that follows this passage function dialectically and subversively in the context of this novel to call into question not the credo itself, but the self-absorbed ambition of these two male characters.

> A human being in perfection ought always to preserve a calm and peaceful mind, and never to allow passion or a transitory desire to disturb his tranquillity. I do not think that the pursuit of knowledge is an exception to this rule. If the study to which you apply yourself has a tendency to weaken your affections, and to destroy your taste for those simple pleasures in which no alloy can possibly mix, then that study is certainly unlawful, that is to say, not befitting the human mind. If this rule were always observed; if no man allowed any pursuit whatsoever to interfere with the tranquillity of his domestic affections, Greece had not been enslaved; Caesar would have spared his country; America would have been discovered more gradually; and the empires of Mexico and Peru had not been destroyed.[1]

Invoking the "domestic affections" as the model for all political action, the women writers of the Romantic period proposed a new political program, one that would inexorably change the existing systems of patriarchy and primogeniture. Domestic affections should flow equally and mutually among all members of the family unit. Inherent in this feminine Romantic ideology is a commitment to the equality of the sexes and the incalculable value of each family member. The oldest son is no better—or worse—than the youngest daughter; both are to be cherished equally. At the level of sexual politics, the trope of the family-politic entails a democracy in which women and men have equal rights and responsibilities.

At this point the women writers of the age parted company from Edmund Burke. Burke's model of the organic nation would preserve the patriarchal control of the all-knowing, omnipotent father. Mary Shelley insisted instead, as did her mother Mary Wollstonecraft, as did such women writers as Helen Maria Williams, Mary Hamilton, Maria Edgeworth, Susan Ferrier, and Jane Austen, on the equality—and perhaps even the superiority—of the female in creating and sustaining the domestic affections and, by extension, the health and welfare of the family-politic.

Mary Wollstonecraft's *A Vindication of the Rights of Men* (1790), written to counter the attack against liberalism mounted by Edmund Burke's *Reflections on the Revolution in France* (1790),[2] specifically denounced Burke's three main arguments: that all legal and political authority is derived from the past, through a process of succession and inheritance; that religion is the basis of civil society and an alliance between the established church and the civil government necessary for the maintenance of social order; and that the class system is "natural" and requires that positions of civil authority should be held only by men who have earned or inherited significant property. Appealing to reason as the highest virtue and moral guide, Wollstonecraft repeatedly insisted that the rights of the individual, "those rights which men inherit at their birth, as rational creatures,"[3] are denied by the legal precedents of primogeniture and arranged marriages designed to preserve family estates, and that social progress can be produced only by liberty and equality, for "Inequality of rank must ever impede the growth of virtue, by vitiating the mind that submits or domineers" (116).

Burke had insisted that the love of country develops from the domestic affections:

> To be attached to the subdivision, to love the little platoon we belong to in society, is the first principle (the germ as it were) of public affections. It is the first link in the series by which we proceed toward a love to our country and to mankind.[4]

Burke went further, to derive the authority of the government itself from the institution of the patriarchal family. As Burke put it, "We procure reverence to our civil institutions on the principle upon which nature teaches us to revere individual men; on account of their age; and on account of those from whom they are descended" (39). In opposition to Burke's deference to "our canonized forefathers," Wollstonecraft promoted a more rational model of political authority also based on the paradigm of the family, but on the *egalitarian* rather than the patriarchal family: "that first source of civilization, natural parental affection, that makes no difference between child and child, but what reason justifies by pointing out superior merit" (46). Invoking the parent's obligation to educate the child to a condition of maturity and self-reliance, she argued against Burke:

> The preponderance of inconsistencies, when weighed with precedents, should lessen the most bigotted veneration for antiquity, and force men of the eighteenth century to acknowledge, that our *canonized forefathers* were unable, or afraid, to revert to reason, without resting on the crutch of authority; and should not be brought as a proof that their children are never to be allowed to walk alone. (40–41)

The ideal state, like the ideal family household, would care for rich and poor alike, for the poor "have a right to more comfort than they presently enjoy" (144). She ended her *Vindication of the Rights of Men* with a utopian vision of a new Eden, created by the division of large estates into small farms and by the development of communities where "the clergyman would superintend his own flock, the shepherd would . . . love the sheep he daily tended; the school might rear its decent head" (147). Above all, "domestic comfort, the civilizing relations of husband, brother, and father, would soften labour, and render life contented" (147).

Here Wollstonecraft, responding to a man, deliberately inverted her society's construction of gender and imagined a male political community grounded on the domestic affections usually attributed to women. In her extended defense of the French Revolution, written in 1795, she again reversed traditional gender expectations and claimed for the female the finest successes of the political developments in France. Whatever the failures and cruelties of the revolution, she argued, it had forever destroyed the vitiated tyrannies of the *ancien régime* and liberated a new vision of democracy. As she rhapsodized,

> a new spirit has gone forth, to organise the body-politic; and where is the criterion to be found, to estimate the means, by which the influence of this spirit can be confined, now enthroned in the hearts of half the inhabitants of the globe? Reason has, at last, shown her captivating face, beaming with benevolence; and it will be impossible for the dark hand of despotism again to obscure its radiance, or the lurking dagger of subordinate tyrants to reach her bosom. The image of God implanted in our nature is now more rapidly expanding; and, as it opens, liberty with *maternal* wing seems to be soaring to regions far above vulgar annoyance, promising to shelter all mankind. (my italics)[5]

This extraordinary passage assigns a female gender not only to reason and liberty, but also—by implication—to God. The ideal state is one grounded on the ethic of care, one in which the rights of all are respected, one in which "all mankind" (by which Wollstonecraft means humanity) finds maternal shelter and sustenance. As she insists, "Nature having made men unequal, by giving stronger bodily and mental powers to one than to another, the end of government ought to be, to destroy this inequality by protecting the weak" (7).

Defining patriotism as "the expansion of domestic sympathy,

rendered permanent by principle" (89), she sees the growth of democracy as inevitable, for "equality, indeed, was then first established by an universal sympathy; and men of all ranks joining in the throng [which marched to Paris on July 13, 1789], those of the first could not be discriminated by any peculiar decency of demeanour, such public-spirited dignity pervaded the whole mass" (169). Despite the violence of the revolutionary leaders, the inevitable result of lives lived in servitude, corrupted by suspicion and intrigue—and Wollstonecraft attacks the use of the guillotine as passionately as she denounces the evils of the *ancien régime*—she remains convinced that the revolution in France has been progressive. "It was a revolution in the minds of men" (396), a triumph of reason over "the strongholds of priestcraft and hypocrisy" that future generations will complete by constructing "a new system of government to be adapted to that change" (12, 396). In these political tracts, Wollstonecraft both implicitly and explicitly promoted the trope of the egalitarian family as the basis of good government, for as she insisted, the origin of civilization lies in "the family affections, whence all the social virtues spring" (309).

This trope was adopted both by her daughter and by other women writers of her age. In *The Last Man*, Mary Shelley explicitly invoked and then attacked Burke's celebration of the organically developing body-politic (in which the patriarchal father serves as the head of body, family and state, producing a constitutional monarchy and a highly regulated class system) by showing that the body-politic can become diseased and die.[6] In *Lodore*, she replaced Burke's model of the patriarchal body-politic with a celebration of the egalitarian family as the basis of the successful nation-state. Only after Lady Lodore sacrifices her place in the class system, only after she gives up her wealth, her social position, and her claims to aristocratic privilege, in order to provide for her impoverished daughter and son-in-law, does she find personal happiness and a sense of well-being. Her new success is signalled by her marriage to Horatio Saville, a man of empathy and benevolence, who acknowledges that the claims of a child can take precedence over the claims of a husband. When Lady Lodore agreed to marry Saville, "she told him that her first duties were towards Ethel [her daughter]—and that he took a divided heart, over the better part of which reigned maternal love. Saville, the least egoistic of human beings, smiled to hear her name that a defect, which was in his eyes her crowning virtue" (III:306). In this passage, Mary Shelley subtly follows her mother's revolutionary political vision by implying that the primary claim upon both a woman's and a man's heart and mind is not the authority of the father or husband but the welfare of the child.

Sharing Wollstonecraft's and Shelley's concern above all for the nurturance of human relationships *over time*, Helen Maria Williams nonetheless offered a very different reading of the French Revolution. The most prolific female political commentator in the Romantic period, Williams embraced the events in France as the manifestation of the gradual evolution of social justice. Her criticism of those who, like William Wordsworth, turned away from political action to celebrate instead mental and spiritual revolution, is recorded in her poem "To Dr. Moore." Here she condemns Wordsworth by explicitly identifying the possession of "the philosophic mind," not with the conviction of personal immortality proclaimed in his *Ode: Intimations of Immortality from Recollections of Early Childhood*, but instead with an enduring commitment to work for the rights and liberties of the common people of France. Writing in 1823, acknowledging her disillusionment with Napoleon, she nonetheless sees in the France of her day a time of increased political justice:

> For now on Gallia's plain the peasant knows
> Those equal rights impartial heav'n bestows.[7]

As Williams praises her absent friend, Dr. Moore, she notably erases comment upon her self, focusing instead on the virtues of another. Recalling her two decades as an English observer of the political events in France, she concludes,

> For me, the witness of those scenes, whose birth
> Forms a new era in the storied earth;
> Oft, while with glowing breast those scenes I view,
> They lead, ah friend belov'd, my thoughts to you!
> Still every fine emotion they impart
> With your idea mingles in my heart;
> You, whom I oft have heard, with gen'rous zeal,
> With all that truth can urge, or pity feel,
> Refute the pompous argument, that tried
> The common cause of millions to deride;
> With reason's force the plausive sophist hit,
> Or dart of folly the bright flash of wit;
> And warmly share, with philosophic mind,
> The great, the glorious triumph of mankind.
>   (II:65–78, pp. 232–3)

Living in France from 1790 till the end of her life, Helen Maria Williams consistently refracted the political turmoil in France through the lens of her own ideological ethic of care, insisting that she could recognize in the historic events of the revolution a gradual, if painful, progress toward greater social equality, justice and compassion. On her arrival with her sister in Paris on 13 July 1790, Helen Maria Williams attended the great anniversary celebration of the Federation at the Champs de Mars on July 14. Described in detail by Mona Ozouf,[8] this *fête* was a carefully choreographed exercise in revolutionary propaganda, designed to manifest to the citizens of France their universal participation in the community of man, without distinction of rank, age or sex. The festival overwhelmed the enthralled Helen Maria Williams by its communality, its seriousness of purpose, its sheer grandeur. Impressed by the absence of all social distinctions, by the fusing of the people and the King, by the festival's rationally ordered processions and spatial configurations—in which the National Assembly and royalty together wound through the level field and then ascended to the top of the pavilion—Williams enthused,

> How am I to paint the impetuous feelings of that immense, that exulting multitude? Half a million of people assembled at a spectacle, which furnished every image that can elevate the mind of man, which connected the enthusiasm of moral sentiment with the solemn pomp of religious ceremonies; which addressed itself at once to the imagination, the understanding, and the heart.[9]

Even though she was a foreigner, Williams was at once swept up in a wave of emotion, experiencing what seemed to her an almost sacred bonding with the mass of humanity around her, convinced then and for all the years to come that the French Revolution had brought genuine freedom to the people of France. So committed was she to this revolutionary ideal that she eagerly volunteered to play the role of liberty at a private *fête* celebrated three months later at the chateau of her friend Madame du Fossé. She appeared in the last scene as the Statue of Liberty, wearing a Phrygian cap; she was then draped with a tricolor scarf, the signal for the audience to break into a rousing chorus of *ça ira*. Thus, she records in her *Letters from France*,

> do the French, lest they should be tempted, by pleasure, to forget one moment the cause of liberty, bind it to their remembrance in the hour of festivity; with fillets and scarfs of national ribband;

> connect it with the sound of the viol and the harp, and appoint it
> not merely to regulate the great movements of government, but
> to mould the figure of the dance. (I:205–6)

Seeing in both these festivals the visible and transparent representation of the achievements of the National Assembly and the beginning of a golden era of French democracy, Helen Maria Williams
encoded in her very body the founding ideology of the revolution,
the belief in liberty, equality, fraternity. As an icon of *female* liberty,
however, she implicitly claimed that women as well as men had
achieved a new freedom and dignity under the revolutionary Republic.

We should recognize here that Williams was naive: she failed to
see the ways in which the representation of Liberty as female could
function to oppress women. As Joan Landes and others have
pointed out,[10] this iconography enabled the male leaders of the
French revolution to control their female compatriots by making
them the objects of masculine representation rather than active,
equal partners in the building of the new nation. Liberty, or Marianne, became the *mother* of the new France, explicitly reinscribing contemporary French *citoyennes* within the private, domestic
sphere. Despite this subtle and, as the career of Olympe de Gouges
suggests, finally effective repression of women by the leaders of the
French Revolution, Williams continued to affirm the overt rhetoric
of the revolution. She argued passionately that women could work
side by side with men in the public arena for the welfare of the
entire nation, just as both sexes could benefit from a more equitable distribution of goods and services.

Her eight volumes of *Letters from France*, describing the events
in France from July 1790 through 1795, unfold a narrative of spec-
tacular if necessarily uneven triumph over tyranny. She grounds
her affirmation of the revolution simultaneously in her sense of
communion with the freed workers of France and in her direct experience, through her friends the du Fossé's, of the evils of the *ancien régime*. More aware of the sufferings inflicted on the French in
the past and hence more accepting of present excesses than Mary
Wollstonecraft or Mary Shelley, Williams presents the tale of the
du Fossé family as the paradigm of the political tyranny of the *ancien régime*, enforced collectively by church and monarchy in both
the private and the public realm.

In brief, Augustin Francois Thomas du Fossé, the eldest son of
the wealthy Baron du Fossé, fell in love with the virtuous daughter

of a local bourgeois farmer, the paid companion of his mother. Their relationship, founded on mutual esteem and extensive knowledge of each other's character and temperament, promised the highest domestic happiness. But the snobbish Baron du Fossé objected to the match and issued a *lettre du cachet*, which authorized the imprisonment of his oldest son and heir, to prevent the marriage. The young couple, now secretly married, fled to England where they barely survived by giving French lessons. Augustin, now a father unable to feed his growing family, was persuaded to return to France by the promise of a reconciliation with his father and an allowance. As soon as he entered his father's house, he was arrested and imprisoned in the monastery of Les Frères de Sainte Charité where he was held, unable to communicate with his wife and daughter, for three years. He finally managed to escape from prison, seriously injuring himself in a leap from the monastery walls, and would have been reinterred had not the townspeople of Beauvais protected him from the priests and his father and shipped him back to London. Reunited at last with his family, sick, in dire poverty, he was eeking out a minimal existence when the Williams sisters, eager to learn French, hired him as their teacher. The day after the fall of the Bastille, du Fossé returned to France with his family, claimed his rightful share of his inheritance, gave up his aristocratic title, and became—with the Williams sisters— an ardent supporter of the revolution. His history became for Helen Maria Williams the narrative of the *ancien régime* itself, a story of unrelenting and arbitrary political cruelty. This evil ended only with the advent of revolutionary freedom and the new regime instituted in the du Fossé household, a regime of mutual benevolence, rational action, gender equality, justice and "domestic felicity" (II:2).

The du Fossé story was also for Williams the narrative of the abuses of patriarchy, of the excessive power of the father in the domestic sphere. Repeatedly she portrayed the cruel behavior of Baron du Fossé as the dereliction of paternal responsibility. Commenting on Augustin's imprisonment, she exclaimed:

> Is it not difficult to believe that these sufferings were inflicted by a father? A father!—that name which I cannot trace without emotion; which conveys all the ideas of protection, of security, of tenderness; that dear relation to which, in general, children owe their prosperity, their enjoyments, and even their virtues!—Alas, the unhappy Mons. du Fossé owed nothing to *his* father, but that

> life, which from its earliest period his cruelty had embittered, and which he now condemned to languish in miseries that death only could heal. (I:156–7)

The arbitrary authority of the father over his sons and daughters would, in Williams' view, end with the revolution. Although she does not contest the obligations of children to a *good* father, Williams, like Wollstonecraft, saw the revolution as providing an opportunity for women to share equally in governmental power, in both the public and the private sphere. She enthusiastically applauded those female aristocrats who with "a spirit worthy of Roman matrons" willingly gave up "titles, fortune and even personal ornaments, so dear to female vanity, for the common cause" and who became the "secret springs in mechanism, by which, though invisible, great movements are regulated" (I:27, 37–8). She commented approvingly on the French practice of instructing the wife of a merchant in arithmetic and insisting that she act as her husband's first clerk in his countinghouse, thus training her to carry on the business in his absence or after his death. In addition, she urged the English to adopt the new French institution of the *Lycée*, a place where bourgeois men and women of Paris gathered to hear lectures by the most celebrated professors on natural philosophy, chemistry, natural history, botany, history, and *belles lettres*, and where Greek, Italian, French and English languages were taught (II:130–1). Like Wollstonecraft, Williams saw in the practices of the new revolutionary era in France a model for the equality of women, for the education and vocational training of females on a par with males.

Helen Maria Williams suffered the reign of Robespierre and the Jacobins in an extreme form; under the edict which forbade all foreigners to remain in Paris, she was arrested and incarcerated in Luxembourg Prison for six months. But even here, her enthusiasm for the possibilities of the revolution remained undiminished; she comments feelingly on the numerous acts of bravery, sacrifice, generosity and personal courage manifested by the other prisoners, whether former aristocrats, Girondists, or innocent bystanders like herself.[11] Despite her fear, disgust and outrage at Robespierre and the Montagnards, and her horror at the unending massacre, in which the guillotine becomes "the minister of finance" (I:224), beheading innocent persons solely so the Convention could appropriate their property, she remained convinced that the noble ideals of the revolution would finally win out. As she commented, no people ever travelled to the temple of Liberty by a path strewed with roses; nor has established tyranny ever yielded to reason and justice, till after a severe struggle. I do not pretend to justify the French, but I do not see much right that we at least have to condemn them." (IV:227)

She ended her first account of the events in France with the death of Robespierre (in her eyes the ultimate betrayer of revolutionary ideals), the joyous release of all those unjustly imprisoned by the Convention, the defeat of the Jacobin factions in the countryside, the successes of the French armies fighting at the borders, and an affirmation of the new constitution, the Declaration of the Rights of Man. Unlike Wollstonecraft, who returned to England revulsed by the September massacres and the reign of Terror, Williams remained in France for the rest of her life, committed to the new French nation and the sophistication of its culture. Writing from abroad for an English audience, she preserved during the ministries of Pitt and Burke the enthusiasm of the Enlightenment *philosophes* for a democratic government and of Olympe de Gouges for the equality of women.

Living with another English emigré John Hurford Stone, raising two nephews, and earning a modest income from her writing, Helen Maria Williams became famous for hosting parties at which the ideals of the Girondists were kept alive. At first she ardently supported Napoleon Bonaparte, believing that he possessed not only the desire and the will to unify France under the democratic ideals of the revolution, but also the soul of a poet. In 1798 she publicly hailed Bonaparte as "the benefactor of his race converting the destructive lightning of the conqueror's sword into the benignant rays of freedom."[12] Not until the coronation of Napoleon the Great, Emperor for Life, by Pope Pius VII, on December 2, 1804, did Helen Maria Williams undergo the crisis of the true believer. In her *Narrative of the Events which have taken place in FRANCE*, published in London in 1816, Williams tracked not only the career and downfall of Napoleon Bonaparte after April, 1815, but also the path of her own disillusion. Chronicling Napoleon's hypocrisies, vanities, cruelties to women (whom he forced into marriages financially advantageous for himself), and military defeats, she sardonically portrayed the too easily duped French as the instruments of a malevolent despot.

So outraged was she by Napoleon that she could finally portray the restoration of the Bourbon monarchy as "the pure effusion of real happiness,"[13] a happiness registered in the faces of the Parisians themselves. Although she remained a devotee of political liberty and continued to call for the establishment of a Congress of Europe that would create a constitutionally guaranteed democracy not only for France, but for all the countries invaded by Napoleon, this second narrative subtly reveals that her primary values were those of domestic tranquillity and the preservation of the civilized arts.[14] As she detailed the disposition of the works of art captured by Napoleon, temporarily housed in the Louvre, and finally reclaimed by their respective homelands, she passionately decried the damage done to Venice's winged lion and Titian's *Transfiguration* during the process.

Her deepest emotions appeared when she was asked to describe the future fate of France.

> Are the French people, after all the mazy wanderings of the Revolution, are they approaching an asylum . . . ; are they going home at last?—This is indeed a momentous question. It is not made by me, as perhaps it may be by yourself, in the spirit of speculative investigation; to me it comprehends all that can awaken solicitude, all that can interest the heart; all chance of personal tranquillity towards the evening of a stormy life, and all hope of felicity for the objects most dear to me, and to whom life is opening. France is to me also the country of my friends—of persons endeared to me by the tie of common suffering. We have passed through the tempest, to use the words of M. de Boufflers, "*sous la même parapluie.*" How should I have lived so many years among the French without loving that amiable people, to apply the term in their own sense, who so well know the art of shedding a peculiar charm over social life! How much better than others they understand the secret of being happy! happy at a cheap rate, and without being too difficult, and too disdainful as we are in England, about the conditions; while they bear misfortunes with a cheerful equanimity, which if it does not deserve the proud name of philosophy, is of far more general use; the former being common property, belonging to all, and not, like the latter, the partial fortune of an enlightened few. (302–4)

Here we can see the basic social tenets of feminine Romanticism: a commitment to the domestic virtues, to home, to the equality of men and women, to the living of a good and happy life at modest expense.

In her *Tour in Switzerland* in 1798, Williams had singled out for

praise the Swiss institution of the *jour de famille* which once a week
brought together the extended kinship network:

> There is something respectable, and even affecting in these *pa-
> triarchal* meetings; they seem a means of drawing closer those
> ties of consanguinity which are the best refuge against human
> ills; in which the purest affections of the heart mingle themselves
> with the wants and weakness of our nature; guiding with watch-
> ful tenderness the wanderings of youth, and supporting with un-
> wearied care the feebleness of age. (I:15, my italics)

Despite the devastations and sufferings of the Terror and the Na-
poleonic campaigns, Williams remained convinced that the French
had sustained a capacity to value that which is truly worthwhile, a
humanitarian impulse for benevolent social relationships. Where
Wollstonecraft and Mary Shelley could see the French Revolution
only as denying an ethic of care, Williams could see it rather as the
final triumph of an ethic of care, a recognition of the right of every
citizen to the protection of the state. Thus, despite their directly
opposing attitudes to the revolution itself, all these women writers
sustained the same ideological commitment to the egalitarian
family as the model of good government.

As Williams' specific affirmation of Swiss "patriarchal" families
alerts us, however, implicit in Romantic women writers' reliance
on the trope of the family-politic is the acceptance of a hierarchical
order in which, if not the father exclusively, then both parents
equally, have authority and control over their children. Recall that
in her credo, Mary Shelley had asserted that "if no man allowed
any pursuit whatsoever to interfere with the tranquillity of his domestic affections, . . . America would have been discovered more
gradually" (51). Shelley does *not* say that America would *not* have
been discovered, but only that the colonization of America would
have occurred more slowly. She here casts America in the role of a
newborn-child-continent that should have been more carefully
nurtured and developed by its European explorer-rulers. Shelley's
program of gradual reform and colonization, grounded on the
preservation of the loving family-politic, inevitably replicates the
inequalities inherent in the hierarchical structure of the bourgeois
family, inequalities based no longer on gender, but now on age. In
other words, implicit in her ideology of the polis-as-family is the
construction of certain political groups (or countries) as "children"
who must be governed. Her affirmation of this class system is tellingly revealed both in her personal revulsion from the lower

classes, particularly those of foreign nations—the German peasants whose "horrid & slimy" faces she found so disgusting during
her honeymoon voyage along the Rhine in 1814 that her "only wish
was to absolutely annihilate such uncleansable animals"—and in
her unquestioned assumption that she belonged to the landed gentry of her husband's ancestors rather than to the artisanal and dis-
senting lower middle classes of her own parents.[15]

This problematic aspect of the politics of feminine Romanticism
is vividly displayed in the writings of Maria Edgeworth. Collabo-
rating with her father in the promulgation of his educational theories—they published *Practical Education* in 1798—and helping
him to manage Edgeworthtown, a landed estate in northern Ireland, Maria Edgeworth rhetorically assigned both her Irish peasant tenants and black West Indian slaves to the category of children, who needed to be well treated, with justice and benevolence
and understanding, to be educated in honesty, Christian morality
and especially obedience, but who could not yet be granted the
freedoms and responsibilities of adulthood. What Michael Hurst
has rightly called her "Colonial Office mentality"[16] is glaringly revealed in her didactic tale for young readers, *The Grateful Negro.*[17]
Edgeworth here contrasts the practices of the irresponsible West
Indian slaveowner Jefferies and his vicious overseer Durant, who
regularly use "the most cruel and barbarous methods for forcing
the slaves to exertions beyond their strength" (4), to the benevolent
practices of Mr. Edwards and his humane overseer Abraham Bay-
ley. Mr. Edwards

> treated his slaves with all possible humanity and kindness. He
> wished that there was no such thing as slavery in the world; but
> he was convinced, by the arguments of those who have the best
> means of obtaining information, that the sudden emancipation of
> the negroes would rather increase than diminish their miseries.
> His benevolence, therefore, confined itself within the bounds of
> reason. He adopted those plans for the amelioration of the state
> of the slaves which appeared to him the most likely to succeed
> without producing any violent agitation or revolution. For in-
> stance, his negroes had reasonable and fixed daily tasks; and
> when these were finished they were permitted to employ their
> time for their own advantage or amusement. If they chose to em-
> ploy themselves longer for their master they were paid regular
> wages for their extra work. (5–6)

Moreover, Mr. Edwards managed his plantation with such thrift
and prudence that neither his slaves nor the produce of their pri-

vate gardens (or "provision-grounds") were ever seized to pay his debts.

When Mr. Edwards buys Mr. Jefferies' best slave, Caesar, and at the same time purchases his fiancée Clara, giving them both a re-modelled cottage and even a sharp knife to prune the nearby trees and vines, Caesar vows to serve him "faithfully." Caesar refuses to join his best friend Hector in his conspiracy to exact revenge on all the slaveowners of Jamaica, defying both Clara and the Obeah woman Esther who has entranced Clara. Although Caesar's "heart beat high at the idea of recovering his liberty, . . . he was not to be seduced from his duty" (43). He reveals the plot to burn all the plantations and kill all the white people on the island to Mr. Edwards in time to save all but the Jefferies estate, and thus earns Edgeworth's moral approbation, "THE GRATEFUL NEGRO" (64).

Explicit in this story is Edgeworth's conviction that the enlightened members of the ruling class, whether white slaveowners or, by extension to Ireland, the Anglo-Irish Protestant Ascendancy, have the right as well as the obligation to control the lower classes. As Hurst suggests, "she saw her role as something between a colonial civil servant and a missionary rescuing the masses from inferior material and spiritual practices. Priestly witch-doctors [or the Obeah woman Esther] and the mumbo-jumbo of the old Irish language she regarded with the same scorn as [Thomas] Macaulay did the customs of the 'Hindoos'."[18] That Maria Edgeworth equated the position of West Indian slaves with those of nineteenth-century Irish tenant-farmers is clarified in her *Essay on Irish Bulls* where she quotes with approval Voltaire's comment in his *Age of Louis XIV* that:

> Some nations seem made to be subject to others. The English have always had over the Irish the superiority of genius, wealth, and arms. The *superiority which the whites have over the negroes.*[19]

In her novel *The Absentee*[20] Edgeworth roundly condemns the irresponsible practices of absentee English landlords in Ireland, whom she explicitly likens to slaveowners in Jamaica (130), but at the same time she supports a "union" between England and Ireland in which, as in the very temperament of her hero Lord Coulambre, "English prudence governed, but did not extinguish, his Irish enthusiasm" (6). The "good agent" who wisely manages Coulambre's estates is named, with explicit reference to Edmund Burke and his "little platoon," Mr. Burke.[21] At this point, Edgeworth's racial politics intersect with her gender politics. The sanctified "union" of England and Ireland is troped in *The Absentee* as the marriage of the Anglo-Irish Lord Coulambre with the Irish Grace Nugent, a union in which his masculine wisdom and experience will be supported by her feminine intelligence, loyalty and "civil courage" (125). The happy bourgeois family thus becomes the model for colonizer-colonized relationships.

A book should be written about the shifting roles of race, class and gender in Edgeworth's writing. By displacing her concern with the education and governance of the Irish peasantry onto figures of black slaves, she rhetorically mounted a more scathing condemnation of contemporary Anglo-Irish absentee landlords than other writers on the subject who saw no analogy between West Indian slavery and Irish tenant-farming. Moreover, she frequently assigned to her black characters a moral insight and strength of character notably missing from her white characters. In her comic drama, *The Two Guardians* (1817), for instance, it is the black serving boy Quaco who is the voice of innocent virtue in the play: he generously gives his own wages to the impoverished gentlewoman Widow Beauchamp, and, unlike his youthful West Indian master, St. Albans, he "can't love" the spoiled, selfish but beautiful Juliana. Edgeworth presents black characters as moral exemplars, but she also images them as foolish and irresponsible children: the black servant Juba in *Belinda* is prey to irrational superstitions and his master Mr. Vincent compulsively gambles away both his estate and Belinda's esteem. Even Quaco, granted his "freedom" from slavery when he reaches British soil in *The Two Guardians*, immediately chooses a position of submission: if he can't be "massa's slave alway," he will be his "servant" (160). We have circled back, as always in Edgeworth's writing, to the figure of the grateful Negro (and the grateful wife). Edgeworth's commitment, like most romantic women writers, was to a family-politic in which a liberal and universal educational reform instituted by enlightened rulers would *gradually* improve the social order without the political turmoil or financial and personal costs of a military revolution. Racial and gender integration and equality could be achieved, they believed, without changing the hierarchical structure of the existing class system.

Family Politics and the Domestic Ideology

Social historians now agree that a significant change in the ideological construction of the family, and especially in the cultural evaluation of the role of the mother, occurred during the eighteenth century in England. Lawrence Stone, Randolph Trumbach, Leonore Davidoff and Catherine Hall, Alice Ryerson and most recently Barbara Gelpi have all argued powerfully for the emergence during this century of a more emotionally charged "affective" nuclear family and an idealised mother who remained at home in more sustained and intimate contact with her children—"breast feeding them, supervising and participating in their play, guiding them in the use of language, socializing, cleansing, amusing, and instructing them," as Gelpi summarizes.[22] The increased cultural demand that mothers breast-feed their own infants, prominently advocated by Rousseau and promulgated in the conduct-books and medical treatises of the eighteenth century, was widely reflected in the texts of the male Romantic writers. Gelpi has tracked the image of the eroticised breasts of the mother, especially the nursing mother, in British magazine illustrations and in the poetry of Percy Shelley during this period, and Alan Richardson has shown how the male Romantic poets appropriated the idealised image of the nursing mother to themselves as a figure of procreativity.[23] If we accept that a more highly charged ideology of maternity evolved just before and during the Romantic period, how did the women writers of this era respond to it?

Again, an entire book could and should be written on this subject; what follows are but exploratory, merely suggestive remarks. The demand for female education and the family-politic endorsed by the leading romantic women writers insisted upon the role of the mother as *educator* of her young children, as the one who taught them to read, write, maintain habits of cleanliness and good health, and exercise moral duty, self-discipline, and religious observance. However, the figure of the breast-feeding mother (or her eroticised breasts) rarely, if ever, occurs in the female-authored texts of the Romantic period that I have read. The only possible exceptions that I can think of are in Wollstonecraft's *Maria, or the Wrongs of Woman*, where Maria, in prison, is tormented by the image of her absent infant: "She heard her half speaking half cooing, and felt the little twinkling fingers on her burning bosom—a bosom bursting with the nutriment for which this cherished child might now be pining in vain. From a stranger she could indeed receive the maternal aliment, Maria was grieved at the thought— but who would watch her with a mother's tenderness, a mother's self-denial?"[24] And in Amelia Opie's tale, *The Father and Daughter*, the seduced, impregnated and abandoned Agnes Fitzhenry first appears struggling through a storm with a moaning infant clutched to her bosom as she returns to her father's house. Here, of course, the existence of the infant at her breast is a sign of shame, the icon of the fallen woman, which Agnes must redeem.

But these examples—both problematic insofar as they register sites of conflict in the mother-infant relationship—only highlight the absence of the nursing mother in the major female-authored texts of the romantic period. Barbara Gelpi has defined the dominant "plot" of maternity, culled from such women's magazines as *La Belle Assemblée* and *The Lady's Magazine* as this:

> a blameless wife and mother, morally superior to her scapegrace husband, finally distances herself from his ribald and irresponsible practices in order to devote total, loving attention to her child, usually a daughter. The husband, moved to repentance by her example, returns to a domestic life ordered under her direction.[25]

This is, of course, the "plot" of the *lives* of several Romantic women writers, most notably Charlotte Smith and Felicia Hemans, with one all-important exception: Benjamin Smith did not repent and return to the maternally controlled home, nor did Felicia Hemans' estranged husband, Captain Hemans, come back from Italy. The leading women Romantic writers did not construct this plot because they did not believe it; in their fiction and poetry, abandoned wives and mothers make their way alone, or with the help of friends, relatives and second husbands.

The absence of idealised *nursing* mothers in women's writing suggests that the Romantic women writers wished to rest their concept of maternity not on biological essentialism but on social construction. The most successful mother in Susan Ferrier's novels is an *adoptive* mother, Mrs. Douglas in *Marriage*—although adoptive mothers can also be irresponsible, as is Mrs. St. Clair in Ferrier's *Inheritance*. Jane Austen's biological mothers are for the most part morally defective (Mrs. Bennet, Lady Catherine de Bourgh, Mrs. Price, Lady Bertram, Mrs. Ferrers) or absent, as in *Emma* and *Persuasion*—her heroines receive their most reliable guidance from such mother-substitutes as Mrs. Gardiner, Lady Russell, and Mrs. Croft. Although the educating mother is everywhere present in Maria Edgeworth's tales for children, in her novels she portrays mothers as either absent (in *Belinda* and *The Absentee*) or concerned but ineffective (as in *Helen*). Mary Shelley consistently presents her heroines as either unmothered (in *Falkner*, *Lodore* and *Matilda*), or badly mothered (in *The Last Man*), even monstrously so, as in Victor Frankenstein's failure to mother his child. Even those female writers who present positive portrayals of mothers, as do Frances Burney (although the mother of the heroine of her best novel, *The Wanderer,* died in child-birth) and Felicia Hemans, also represent those mothers as unable to protect their daughters from misery.

I would tentatively suggest, then, that the ideology of maternity is represented in very different ways in male- and female-authored texts in the Romantic period. Male writers focus on biological maternity, on the body of the mother (and especially on her milk-filled breasts), as the source of life itself, while female writers concern themselves with the various ways in which the socially constructed role of motherhood can be *performed.* They celebrate the mother as educator and moral guide, as the provider of spiritual and emotional comfort. But they do not eroticise the mother or endorse the notion that a woman's sexual desires are aroused and satisfied by nursing her infant. By breaking the tie of maternity to breast-feeding, they open the possibility that men as well as women can and should fulfill the role of responsible motherhood.

Behind this social construction of mothering as a learned rather than an instinctual practise lies a powerful challenge to the domestic ideology itself. Throughout this book, I wish to contest the seamless account of the triumph of a hegemonic domestic ideology in England between 1750 and 1850 put forth in Mary Poovey's *The Proper Lady and the Woman Writer,* Nancy Armstrong's *Desire and Domestic Fiction* and Davidoff and Hall's *Family Fortunes.* Basing their conclusions primarily upon conduct books and religious tracts written by men and women, including the *Spectator* of Addison and Steele, they have described the ways in which women writers were forced to accommodate themselves to, indirectly subvert, or gain power wholly within an ideological construction of the proper lady as the modest, domesticated woman, one confined to the private sphere. While such accommodations and subversions undoubtedly occurred in writing by Romantic women—as Poovey has documented and for which I offer further support in Chapter 6—there was an equally powerful Romantic female literary tradition that openly contested and corrected this domestic ideology in significant ways. Some Romantic women writers rejected the public sphere altogether as irredeemably brutal, corrupt, and self-destructive. They constructed the ideal male as one who is finally entirely absorbed into the feminine, private sphere, as did Charlotte Smith in *The Old Manor House* or Mary Shelley in

Lodore and *Falkner*. Alternatively, they offered images of all-female families or communities as sites of personal fulfillment, such as Ann Radcliffe's convent of Santa della Pieta in *The Italian* or the female family of choice (Mrs. Pemberton, Mrs. Mowbray and Savannah) that takes on the responsibility of rearing the motherless Editha at the conclusion of Amelia Opie's *Adeline Mowbray*.

More powerfully, they contested the patriarchal doctrine of the separate spheres by articulating a very different domestic ideology, what I have been calling feminine Romanticism. Here I wish to stress, employing Rita Felski's terminology in *Beyond Feminist Aesthetics*, that feminine Romanticism ideologically constitutes an alternative "counter-public sphere." Many women writers of the Romantic era—including Mary Wollstonecraft, Mary Hays, Jane Austen, Maria Edgeworth, Susan Ferrier, Mary Shelley, Helen Maria Williams and others discussed in this chapter—explicitly or implicitly advocated "family politics" as a political program that would radically transform the public sphere. They proclaimed the value of rational love, an ethic of care, and gender equality as a challenge both to a domestic ideology that would confine women within the home and to a capitalist laissez-faire system that would set the rights of the individual, free-will or rational choice, and an ethic of justice above the needs of the community as a whole. Their "counter-public sphere" has much in common with socialist theories of the equitable distribution of public goods and services, and should be recognized as a viable alternative political ideology.

5

Domesticating the Sublime

Masculine English Romanticism has long been associated with a love of nature, or more precisely, with the epistemological relationship of the perceiving mind to the object of perception. When the fully conscious poetic mind grasps a nature that is entirely unmediated by language—or wholly constructed by its own linguistic tropes—it experiences what the Romantic writers called "the sublime." This concept of the sublime promoted by eighteenth-century theorists and the male Romantic poets, as well as by their myriad modern commentators, from Samuel Monk and Marjorie Hope Nicolson to Geoffrey Hartman and Thomas Weiskel,[1] is distinctly, if unwittingly, gendered. The sublime is associated with an experience of masculine empowerment; its contrasting term, the beautiful, is associated with an experience of feminine nurturance, love and sensuous relaxation. This gender differentiation was implicit in the most famous treatise on the sublime published in the eighteenth century, Edmund Burke's *Philosophical Inquiry into the Origin of Our Ideas of the Sublime and the Beautiful* (1757). Grounding his aesthetic categories on a psychology of pain and pleasure, Burke identified the experience of the sublime with the idea of pain or the annihilation of the self, at a time when one also knows that one's life is not genuinely threatened. As Burke wrote:

> Whatever is fitted in any sort to excite the ideas of pain and danger; that is to say, whatever is in any sort terrible, or is conversant

about terrible objects, or operates in a manner analogous to terror, is a source of the *sublime;* that is, it is productive of the
strongest emotion which the mind is capable of feeling.[2]

Such emotion can only be produced, Burke argued, by a power
greater than oneself:

I know of nothing sublime, which is not some modification of
power. . . . pain is always inflicted by a power in some way superior, because we never submit to pain willingly. So that strength,
violence, pain and terror, are ideas that rush in upon the mind
together (112).

Burke then characterized as the height of the sublime in literature
those passages in Homer or the Old Testament where man, encoun-
tering the divine, the voice in the whirlwind or the commands of
Athena, was made painfully aware both of his own mortality and
of his chosen election. Thinking of the visual arts, he further speci-
fied the qualities of the sublime in a landscape: a greatness of dimension that gives rise to the idea of infinity; obscurity (which
blurs the definition of boundaries); profound darkness or intense
light, and hence dark or intensely bright colors and sudden, sharp
angles. Confronted with such overwhelming natural phenomena
as the Alps, huge dark caves, a blinding sunset, or a towering
gloomy ruin, the human mind first experiences terror or fear and
then—as our instinct for self-preservation is gradually relaxed—
astonishment, admiration, reverence and respect. Thus, Burke
concluded, from the contemplation of a sublime landscape, one is
led to a sensible impression of the Deity by whose power such magnificent scenes are created.

During the eighteenth century, painters consciously represented
such sublime landscapes as the locus of the divine. The most
widely known and imitated of these was the Italian painter Salvator Rosa, who peopled his scenes of Alpine desolation either with
gaunt, fervently praying or crucified saints or with *banditti* lurking
to attack innocent travellers. Such English and German landscape
artists as Joseph Wright of Derby, John Martin, Caspar David Friedrich and Philippe de Loutherbourg extended the landscape of the
sublime to Welsh and Scottish mountains, the Baltic sea and the
frozen Arctic, and to such Biblical and classical scenes of destruction as the Deluge, the fall of Nineveh, the burning of Troy, Pande-
monium and the Day of Judgment.

In opposition to the sublime experience of terror and awe, Burke argued that man's most pleasurable sensations are derived from love and the sensuous enjoyment of life. Hence, those "qualities in things which induce in us a sense of affection and tenderness" and which arouse our sexual instinct to procreation are defined as the beautiful. Burke identified the qualities of the beautiful as smoothness, gradual variation and flowing lines, smallness, delicacy, and "clean and fair" colors in their "milder" shades (220). The "ideal" or beautiful landscape was everywhere associated with the undulating lakes, harmonized foregrounds and backgrounds, glowing golden or silvery tonalities, and securely framed compositions of Claude Lorrain and his British imitators Richard Wilson and Paul Sandby.

As Isaac Kramnick persuasively argued in his psychohistorical study of Burke's life and works,[3] the sublime has for Burke the qualities he associated with his powerful, demanding, violent, unloving father: it is vast, dark and gloomy; "great, rugged and negligent"; "solid and ever massive"; awesome in its infinite power; capable of rousing fear, terror and abject admiration. In contrast, the beautiful has the qualities Burke associated with his gentle, shy, devoted mother: it is "small," "smooth and polished," "light and delicate," gently undulating, regular. The maternally nurturant as well as the erotic aspects of the beautiful are clear in the passage in which Burke summed up his concept of beauty:

> Most people have observed the sort of sense they have had, on being swiftly drawn in an easy coach on a smooth turf, with gradual ascents and declivities. This will give a better idea of the beautiful, and point out its probable cause better than almost any thing else. (300)

Although Kant differed from Burke in his conceptualization of the sublime, grounding it not on a psychology of the emotions but on an epistemology, he also implicitly gendered the sublime as an experience of masculine struggle and empowerment. In his *Critique of Judgment* (1790), Kant defined the sublime experience as one in which the mind or reason (*Vernunft*) successfully detaches itself from participation in the phenomenological world, the world of understanding (*Verstand*), and in this act of transcendental contemplation and self-analysis, achieves intellectual mastery over the power of nature.

> Consider bold, overhanging and, as it were, threatening rocks, thunderclouds piling up in the sky and moving about accompa-

nied by lightning and thunderclaps, volcanoes with all their destructive power, hurricanes with all the devastation they leave
behind, the boundless ocean heaved up, the high waterfall of a
mighty river, and so on. Compared to the might of any of these,
our ability to resist becomes an insignificant trifle. Yet the sight
of them becomes all the more attractive the more fearful it is,
provided we are in a safe place. And we like to call these objects
sublime because they raise the soul's fortitude above its usual
middle range and allow us to discover in ourselves an ability to
resist which is of a quite different kind, and which gives us the
courage [to believe] that we could be a match for nature's seeming omnipotence.[4]

Kant denies Burke's claim that the experience of the sublime is
necessarily accompanied by fear or terror. As Kant insists, reason
can transcend the realm of bodily sensation and physical nature.

For it is a law (of reason) for us, and part of our vocation, to esti-
mate any sense object in nature that is large for us as being small
when compared with ideas of reason; and whatever arouses in us
the feeling of this supersensible vocation is in harmony with that
law. (Section 27:115)

It is vital to recognize that Kant's effort to establish a triumphant
transcendental ego entails the detachment of this ego from the
body, from the emotions, from physical nature—all realms traditionally associated with the feminine. Moreover, Kant's affirmation
of reason excludes difference: the transcendental ego finally stands
alone, uncontaminated by contact with other people. As Kant comments,

we also regard *isolation from all society* as something sublime, if
it rests on ideas that look beyond all sensible interest. To be sufficient to oneself and hence have no need of society, yet without
being unsociable, i.e. without shunning society, is something ap-
proaching the sublime, as is any case of setting aside our needs.
(Section 29:136)

In Kant's formulation of the sublime, corporeal distinctions—of
sex, race, age, physical abilities—vanish. In his quest for pure reason, Kant erases the body, and hence the female, altogether. The
subtle sexual politics at work in Kant's definition of the sublime is
unmasked by his association of the sublime and its capacity to
withstand fear and danger with the (male) warrior, who in compar-

ison with the statesman "deserves the superior respect" of the pop-
ulace, "even in a fully civilized society" (Section 29:121). Kant finally affirms war itself "which has something sublime about it if it
is carried on in an orderly way and with respect for the sanctity of
the citizens' rights," in contrast to "a prolonged peace" which
"tends to make prevalent a mere[ly] commercial spirit, and along
with it base selfishness, cowardice, and softness, and to debase the
way of thinking of that people" (Section 28:122). Kant's contempt
here for peace and "softness" reveals his hostility to an ethic of care
(his own moral system, based on the categorical imperative, is an
ethic of justice).

Coleridge and Wordsworth radically transformed the Burkean
and Kantian sublime by insisting that the experience of infinite
power is attended, not by fear and trembling, but rather by a deep
awe and a profound joy. When Coleridge, in *This Lime-tree Bower
My Prison*, sends his friends on a walking tour that culminates in
the experience of the sublime, he represents the sublime as an emotional experience of spiritual fusion with the "one Life within us
and abroad," together with a linguistic omnipotence which
Thomas Weiskel has defined as characteristic of the "positive" sublime (in which the mind substitutes its own discourse for what
Derrida would define as a necessarily absent presence or ontological being).[5] For Coleridge, the sublime is troped as a joyous apprehension of a world "less gross than bodily," as the cognition of a
holy Spirit or mental power that animates both the natural landscape and man. This union of man and God is linguistically figured
in Coleridge's repetition of the word "Spirit" to refer both to God
("Almighty Spirit") and to human beings ("Spirits").[6] Similarly,
when Wordsworth encounters the sublime in *The Prelude* (1805),
after crossing the Gondo Gorge in Book VI and at the climax of his
ascent of Mount Snowdon in Book XIII, the confrontation arouses
not terror but rather an awestruck and joyful recognition of the
"glory" of his own Soul (VI:532), of the power of his own creative
imagination which produces both "sovereignty within" and
"chearfulness in every act of life" (XIII:114, 117).

It is crucial to see that the powerful pleasure produced by the
experience of the sublime for both Coleridge and Wordsworth in
these poems rests on their capacity to erase the difference between
the self and the other. In *This Lime-tree Bower My Prison*, in which
Coleridge acknowledges that he is speaking for someone else and
thus interpreting an absent text,[7] he nonetheless denies the boundaries between here and there, between past and present and future,

between his imprisoned self and the separated other, Charles Lamb. In a linguistic trope that rejects rational distinctions, Coleridge asserts that we can "contemplate/ With lively joy the joys we cannot share" and thus experience a pleasure we are not experiencing. In the final section of the poem, Coleridge asserts both his emotional union with Lamb ("and I am glad/ As I myself were there!") and the spatial identification of their two bodies ("So my friend . . . may stand, as I have stood"). Insisting on his capacity to *be* Lamb, to participate in that Nature who "ne'er deserts the wise and pure," Coleridge annihilates the very difference that divides the self from the other, the human from the divine, and, implicitly, the male from the female. This last implication is revealed in Coleridge's revision of the poem. The original version of *This Lime-tree Bower My Prison* sent to Robert Southey ended by invoking "my Sister & my Friends";[8] the final version focuses uniquely upon the "gentle-hearted Charles . . . to whom/ No sound is dissonant which tells of Life." Erasing the female other, Coleridge establishes Charles Lamb alone as his authentic self in the poem, feeling what Coleridge feels, responding as Coleridge responds.

Wordsworth also eliminates the distinction between the self and the other in his confrontations with the sublime in *The Prelude* (1805). His imagination and the features of Nature become the workings of "one mind" (VI:565), that "mighty Mind" of female Nature which Wordsworth claims as the "Brother" of his own at the end of the poem (XIII:89). In both these masculine Romantic constructions of the sublime, a male poet finally speaks of, for and in the place of a nature originally gendered as female. Keats, too, despite what we shall see is a far greater engagement in feminine Romanticism, portrayed the sublime encounter—the confrontation of the Apollonian poet of *The Fall of Hyperion* with the face of Moneta—as a successful masculine envoicement of a silenced female divinity. As Blake put it more aggressively in *Jerusalem*, in the fallen world we inhabit, "no more the Masculine mingles/ With the Feminine, but the Sublime is shut out from the Pathos" (i.e. the Beautiful; *J* 90:10–11).

How did the women writers of the Romantic period respond to this engendering of the sublime as a masculinized experience of empowerment, of the beautiful as a feminized experience of nurturing and sensuous love? To answer this question, we must look first at those writers who consciously exploited landscape in their writings as both metaphor and metonymy. The representation of the sublime in feminine Romanticism takes two distinct, but re-

lated forms. One group of writers, those familiar to us as the authors of Gothic fiction, accepts the identification of the sublime
with the experience of masculine empowerment. But they explicitly equate this masculine sublime with patriarchal tyranny. Their
novels expose the dark underside of the doctrine of the separate
spheres, the sexual division of labor, and the domestic ideology of
patriarchal capitalism. The father, whether as patriarch or priest,
is unmasked as the author of violence against women, as the per-
petrator of sadistic tortures and even incest, and thus as the viola-
tor of the very bonds of affection and responsibility that constitute
the bourgeois family. His crimes almost always occur among Alpine landscapes or ruined Gothic towers, the loci of the masculine
sublime. By moving the exercise of sublime power into the household, the female Gothic domesticates the sublime as paternal
transgression—represented as father-daughter incest—that is
everywhere most monstrous and most ordinary.

To see this paradigm clearly, we have only to look to the novels of
the acknowledged leader of the female Gothic, Ann Radcliffe. A
devotee of Salvator Rosa, she repeatedly invokes his landscapes as
the settings of her novels. Emily St. Aubert and her father, seeking
health and psychic restoration among the mountainous regions of
the French Pyrenees in 1584 in *The Mysteries of Udolpho*, encounter
the following landscape:

> The scene of barrenness was here and there interrupted by the
> spreading branches of the larch and cedar, which threw their
> gloom over the cliff, or athwart the torrent that rolled in the vale.
> No living creature appeared, except the izard, scrambling among
> the rocks, and often hanging upon points so dangerous, that fancy
> shrunk from the view of them. This was such a scene as *Salvator*
> would have chosen, had he then existed, for his canvas; St. Au-
> bert, impressed by the romantic character of the place, almost
> expected to see banditti start from behind some projecting rock,
> and he kept his hand upon the arms with which he always trav-
> elled.[9]

Similarly, in *The Italian*, when Ellena Rosalba is kidnapped by
Schedoni's hired ruffians, she is taken to a convent in the Puglia in
the northernmost Italian Alps, which is explicitly set in a Salvator
Rosa landscape:

> It was when the heat and the light were declining that the car-
> riage entered a rocky defile, which shewed, as through a telescope

reversed, distant plains, and mountains opening beyond, lighted up with all the purple splendor of the setting sun. Along this deep and shadowy perspective a river, which was seen descending among the cliffs of a mountain, rolled with impetuous force, fretting and foaming amidst the dark rocks in its descent, and then flowing in a limpid lapse to the brink of other precipices, whence again it fell with thundering strength to the abyss, throwing its misty clouds of spray high in the air, and seeming to claim the sole empire of this solitary wild. Its bed took up the whole breadth of the chasm, which some strong convulsion of the earth seemed to have formed, not leaving space even for a road along its margin. The road, therefore, was carried high among the cliffs, that impended over the river, and seemed as if suspended in air; while the gloom and vastness of the precipices, which towered above and sunk below it, together with the amazing force and uproar of the falling waters, combined to render the pass more terrific than the pencil could describe, or language can express. Ellena ascended it, not with indifference but with calmness; she experienced somewhat of a dreadful pleasure in looking down upon the irresistible flood; but this emotion was heightened into awe, when she perceived that the road led to a slight bridge, which, thrown across the chasm at an immense height, united two opposite cliffs, between which the whole cataract of the river descended. The bridge, which was defended only by a slender railing, appeared as if hung amidst the clouds. Ellena, while she was crossing it, almost forgot her misfortunes.[10]

As these two passages suggest, the landscapes of the sublime function in a double way in Radcliffe's novels.

On the one hand, Radcliffe uses Rosa's landscapes of dark nights, mountainous peaks and chasms, raging torrents and fierce storms, to establish an environment in which human cruelty and physical violence can flourish. Her sublime landscapes are characteristically peopled by *banditti*, fierce gypsies, hired assassins and pirates. Travelling peacefully along the road to Rousillon, Emily St. Aubert and her father must skirt at night a blazing fire around which a predatory group of gypsies are dancing. Count de Villefort and his daughter Blanche, seeking respite from a raging midnight storm among the French Alps, find themselves the prisoners of a gang of thieves, assassins and pirates. And Vivaldi and Paulo, looking for Ellena among the mountainous regions of the Puglia, find themselves "among scenes, which seemed abandoned by civilized society to the banditti who haunted their recesses."[11]

Radcliffe's purpose, however, is not to reinscribe Burke's or Rosa's representations of the sublime landscape as one in which one fears for one's life at the hands of both natural and human elements. Instead, as Kate Ellis has suggested, Radcliffe believes that sublime horror originates not from nature but rather from man. She calculatedly moves the terror of the sublime from the outside into the home, the theoretical haven of virtue and safety for otherwise "unprotected" women.[12] In *The Mysteries of Udolpho, banditti* not only rove among the savage Alps but actually *inhabit* the homes of the female characters.

Montoni, for example, is the husband of Emily St. Aubert's aunt and her legal guardian, but he is also the leader of a fierce band of *condottieri*, paid mercenaries who function as little more than bandits and murderers. Montoni's status as one of the *banditti* is underlined by his willingness to protect Orsini, a confessed assassin, and by the persistent rumor that he has murdered his cousin, Signora Laurentini, in order to inherit the Castle of Udolpho. Within the Castle itself, Montoni reenacts the role of the legendary Bluebeard, tormenting his wife, imprisoning her when she is ill, refusing her medicine and care, until he can sneeringly rejoice at her early death. And he regards his niece by marriage as his personal property, to dispose of in marriage as he chooses, or, when she resists, to abandon to the metaphoric wolves, withdrawing his "protection" so that the rapist Verezzi may pursue her. Radcliffe's point is clear: the deepest terror aroused by the masculine sublime originates in the exercise of patriarchal authority within the home.

Radcliffe underlines this point by showing just how easily such tyrants can gain access to vulnerable young women. Montoni is Emily's legal guardian. Blanche de Villefort's chateau has been penetrated through a secret passageway by cruel pirates, pirates who kidnap her faithful guard Ludovico. More subtly, Radcliffe draws a parallel between Valancourt, the noble and heroic young man with whom Emily St. Aubert has fallen in love, and her captor Montoni. Emily's father first assumes that Valancourt is a highwayman and actually wounds him in the belief that he is a bandit about to attack them. Both Valancourt and Montoni are gamblers who have lost their fortunes in play. Both spend time in prison. Both marry real or putative inheritors of the St. Aubert estates. Although Valancourt is "redeemed" at the end of *The Mysteries of Udolpho* by his enduring love for Emily, his remorse, his generosity, and his innocence of the additional crimes of whoremongering and blackmail, it is actually Emily who, as Kate Ellis has argued,[13] has been responsible for preserving the virtue of the home. By refusing to marry Valancourt when he has lost her esteem, she aggressively upholds a standard of moral purity and rational prudence that the novel endorses and from which Valancourt lapses. Despite the novel's final assertion that "the bowers of La Vallee became, once more, the retreat of goodness, wisdom and domestic blessedness" (672), the marriage of Emily and Valancourt may appear to the reader to rest on less secure foundations; having fallen once, Valancourt may all too easily fall again into violent passion, a lack of self-control, and criminal excess.

The vulnerability of the Edenic home to the "snake" of patriarchal power is underlined in *The Italian* where the "father" is a priest as well as the murderer of his brother, the rapist of his brother's wife, and the man who both encourages and almost carries out the desire of the Marchioness di Vivaldi to murder her putative daughter-in-law. Ellena Rosalba is saved from both incest and death at the hands of her villainous uncle only because he mistakenly concludes at the last moment that he is her biological father and has more to gain from her marriage to Vivaldi than from her murder. Radcliffe here drives home her argument that the greatest evil women must fear comes from *within* the sanctified family, both the patriarchal family and the supposed institutional protector of that family, the Catholic church.

By displacing the horror of the Burkean sublime from nature into the home, which in her novels is repeatedly described as the "prison" of women—whether it is the Castle of Udolpho (227), or the peasant cottages by the sea where Schedoni and Montoni entrap their victims, or the convent of San Stefano (84)—Radcliffe subverts the bourgeois domestic ideology of the late eighteenth century, the sentimental vision of the private home as an earthly paradise of virtue, love and peace. The home may be a man's castle, but women are no more secure there than in the savage wilds of nature where *banditti* roam freely.

On the other hand, Radcliffe constructs an alternative, more positive representation of the sublime. Whereas Burke had insisted that the experience of the sublime originates in the fear for one's life, aroused by the instinct for self-preservation, and then mounts a platonic or aesthetic ladder from astonishment to a recognition of divine power, Radcliffe anticipates Coleridge and Wordsworth in suggesting that one can reach this consciousness of the power and glory of divine creation without fear and trembling. Significantly, her heroines respond to the magnificence of Alpine scenery with pleasure rather than fear. For Emily St. Aubert and her father, the grandeur of the Pyrenees "soften, while they elevate, the heart, and fill it with the certainty of a present God" (28).

Radcliffe parts company from Coleridge's treatment of the sublime, however, by grounding the experience of the positive sublime on a recognition of the *distance* of the perceiving self from the other. For Radcliffe, the experience of the sublime in nature is one that is finally *beyond* language, one that impresses the finite self with the presence of an inexpressible other. At the same time, this confrontation with the divine elevates the perceiving self to a sense of her or his own integrity and worth as a unique product of divine creation. Rather than assuming Wordsworth's stance of the *spectator ab extra*, Radcliffe presents this heightened self-esteem as leading the single self to a renewed appreciation of the equal value and dignity of other people. This quintessentially *democratic* dimension of the Radcliffean sublime is articulated by Emily St. Aubert.[14] Consoling her father for his financial ruin, she argues:

> poverty cannot deprive us of intellectual delights. It cannot deprive you of the comfort of affording me examples of fortitude and benevolence; nor me of the delight of consoling a beloved parent. It cannot deaden our taste for the grand, and the beautiful, or deny us the means of indulging it; for the scenes of nature—those sublime spectacles, so infinitely superior to all artificial luxuries! are open for the enjoyment of the poor, as well as of the rich. Of what then have we to complain, so long as we are not in want of necessaries? Pleasures, such as wealth cannot buy, will still be ours. We retain, then, the sublime luxuries of nature, and lose only the frivolous ones of art. (60).

Grounded in self-esteem, the Radcliffean experience of the positive sublime can produce a sympathy or love that connects the self with other people. A shared enthusiasm for the grandeurs of Alpine scenery is what draws Emily and Valancourt together in love; the memory of those shared experiences unites them through their separate sufferings, whenever they enact their commitment to think of each other as the sun sets; and Emily's inability to forget those shared moments keeps alive her love for Valancourt even after she has prudently rejected an offer of marriage from her dishonored lover.

The positive Radcliffean sublime both inspires and sustains love by giving each individual a conviction of personal value and significance. It thus enables the women who experience it to effect a mental escape from the oppressions of a tyrannical social order.

Imprisoned by Schedoni in the convent of San Stefano, Ellena climbs to a turret balcony above her bedroom:

> a landscape spread below, whose grandeur awakened all her heart. The consciousness of her prison was lost, while her eyes ranged over the wide and freely-sublime scene without. .... To Ellena whose mind was capable of being highly elevated, or sweetly soothed by scenes of nature, the discovery of this little turret was an important circumstance. Hither she could come, and her soul, refreshed by the views it afforded, would acquire strength to bear her, with equanimity, thro' the persecutions that might await her. Here, gazing upon the stupendous imagery around her, looking as it were, beyond the awful veil which obscures the features of the Deity, and conceals Him from the eyes of his creatures, dwelling as with a present God in the midst of his sublime works, with a mind thus elevated, how insignificant would appear to her the transactions, and the sufferings of this world! How poor the boasted power of man, when the fall of a single cliff from these mountains would with ease destroy thousands of his race assembled on the plains below! How would it avail them, that they were accoutred for battle, armed with all the instruments of destruction that human invention ever fashioned? Thus man, the giant who now held her in captivity, would shrink to the diminutiveness of a fairy; and she would experience, that his utmost force was unable to chain her soul, or compel her to fear him, while he was destitute of virtue. (90–91)

For Burke and Rosa, the contemplation of the sublime roused an Oedipal anxiety caused by the overwhelming power of the father. For Coleridge, Wordsworth and Kant, the joy of the sublime experience is dependent upon the annihilation of Otherness, upon the erasure of the female. For Radcliffe and other women Gothic writers, the contemplation of sublime nature first produces the recognition that the self is separated from the Other. If that other is an oppressor, the sublime arouses a sense of personal exaltation, a consciousness of virtue and self-esteem, and hence of tranquillity, a mental freedom from the tyrannies of men and women who are now reduced to impotent insignificance. If the other is beloved, then the experience of the sublime mediates a renewed connection between the lovers grounded in individual integrity, self-esteem, and mutual respect.

The second tradition of the feminine sublime is located in those women writers who grew up in Scotland or Ireland or Wales, surrounded by the mountainous landscapes explicitly celebrated as sublime by numerous English writers and painters. For these writers—and I am thinking particularly of Sydney Owenson, Susan Ferrier, and Helen Maria Williams—sublime landscapes are home scenery, the location of blissful childhood memories. Confronting magnificent mountains and lakes, their characters experience a heightened sensibility, not of anxiety, but of love, reverence, and mutual relationship. Often their protagonists respond to a mountainous landscape or a radiant sunset with the same loss of ego or consciousness-of-self that Thomas Weiskel identified as characteristic of the masculine "negative" sublime, where an excess of presence or metonymical meaning in nature negates the mind, emptying it of all self-awareness. But for these women writers, this experience brings with it no Oedipal anxiety, no recognition of human frailty or mortality. Instead, they represent it as a flowing out, an ecstatic experience of co-participation in a nature they explicitly gender as female. For them, this female nature is not an overwhelming power, not even an all-bountiful mother. Instead nature is a *female friend*, a sister, with whom they share their most intimate experiences and with whom they cooperate in the daily business of life, to the mutual advantage of each.

Hence the experience of the sublime for this tradition of women writers is rarely solitary. If alone, the female protagonist feels comforted, even addressed by, female nature, with whom she communes either in words or in song. More often, the protagonists share their experience of the sublimity of female nature and the heightened sensibility it stimulates with another person, most often a cherished lover.

This tradition of the feminine sublime is epitomized in *The Wild Irish Girl*, written in 1806 by the thirty-year-old Anglo-Irish Sydney Owenson, who in 1812 became Lady Morgan, the name under which she is now known. A spirited defense of all things Irish against a host of British imperialist prejudices, this novel is constructed as a series of letters from a benighted but quickly enlightened young English gentleman, heir to his father's Irish estates, to a sceptical friend in London. The novel begins with the narrator's arrival in Ireland, where he soon encounters, as he travels to the West Country, a characteristically sublime landscape:

To him who derives gratification from the embellished labours of art rather than the simple but sublime works of nature, *Irish* scenery will afford little interest; but the bold features of its varying landscape, the stupendous altitude of its "cloud-capt" mountains,

the impervious gloom of its deep-embosomed glens, the savage
desolation of its uncultivated heaths and boundless bogs, with
those rich veins of a picturesque champagne, thrown at intervals
into gay expansion by the hand of nature, awaken, in the mind of
the poetic or pictorial traveller, all the pleasures of tasteful enjoyment, all the sublime emotions of a rapt imagination. (6–7)[15]

Thinking in categories, Morgan goes on to specify the aesthetic
conventions employed here:

if the flowing fancy of Claude Lorraine would have dwelt enrap-
tured on the paradisaical charms of English landscape, the superior genius of Salvator Rosa would have reposed its eagle wing
amidst scenes of mysterious sublimity with which the wildly
magnificent landscape of Ireland abounds. (7)

That Morgan was conversant with Burke's aesthetic classifications of the sublime and the beautiful, as well as with the gender
implications of Burke's distinctions, is evident in her later biography of Salvator Rosa. She explicitly identified Rosa's fiercely independent temperament and heroic rebellion against both secular
and religious authorities with the landscapes he chose to paint, the
volcanoes and mountains of La Puglia and the Abruzzi in central
Italy, which were inhabited, she claimed, by "beings full of the restless energy and uncompromising independence which form the
moral attributes of mountainous regions."[16] She then contrasts Rosa's sublime landscapes with the beautiful pastoral landscapes of
Claude and Poussin, in terms that support Burke's tropings of the
beautiful as an experience of loving (feminine) nurturance, the
sublime as an experience of heroic (masculine) struggle with
the infinite. In the art of Claude and Poussin, Morgan claimed,

Nature, in her tranquil beauty, always appears the benefactress
of man, not his destroyer; the source of his joys, not the tomb of
his hopes and the scourge of his brief existence.[17]

In opposition to Claude and Poussin, she argued, Rosa portrayed
female nature as a terrifying enemy that challenged the masculine
ego to a fight to the death:

he painted her the inevitable agent of human suffering, mingling
all her great operations with the passions and interests of man,
blasting him with her thunderbolt! wrecking him in her storms!
burying him in her avalanches! and whelming him in her torna-

does! . . . His deep and gloomy forest . . . is only given as the shelter of the formidable bandit. . . . The long line of stony pathway cut through masses of impending rock, is but the defile in which the gallant cavalier, bent on some generous enterprise, is overtaken by the pitiless outlaw—or, by the rush of storms, which seem to threaten destruction at every step his frighted steed advances.[18]

Having invoked the category of the Burke/Rosa sublime in landscape in *The Wild Irish Girl*, Morgan subversively frustrates the narrator's (and our) expectations by undercutting the aesthetic conventions of this genre. Instead of the unrelieved desolation of Rosa's rocky, barren landscapes, her protagonist Horatio M——, alias Henry Mortimer (significantly we never learn his patronymic), encounters among the mountains both "a gloomy bog" and "the perpetual pasturage which satisfies the eye of the interested grazier" however it "disappoints the glance of the tasteful spectator" (7). In place of Rosa's life-threatening *banditti* and outlaws, Horatio encounters first a group of women spinning, led in their Irish songs by an improvisatrice who celebrates the harmony between their work and female nature; then a helpful English-speaking guide; and finally, on the high road, instead of a murdering highwayman, a destitute but dignified peasant who shares his meagre home and food with the traveller, with a "manly courteousness" (21) that puts Horatio to shame. Morgan here suggests that in Ireland the confrontation with a sublime female nature inspires, not fear and trembling, but a life of dignity and natural grace, lived in peaceful harmony with one's fellow human beings, however difficult it may be to eke a living from the "rigid soil."

Horatio then experiences a moment of transcendent exaltation, a moment which can be compared with Wordsworth's portrayal of his poetic election in Book IV of *The Prelude*. Recall Wordsworth returning at dawn from a festive dance, surrounded by the sublime, boundary-denying sunrise of a "magnificent" morning:

> The Sea was laughing at a distance; all
> The solid Mountains were as bright as clouds,
> Grain-tinctured, drench'd in empyrean light.
> (IV:333–35)

At this moment, Wordsworth comes to know his vocation:

> My heart was full; I made no vows, but vows
> Were then made for me; bond unknown to me

Was given, that I should be, else sinning greatly,
A dedicated Spirit. On I walk'd
In blessedness, which even yet remains.
                    (IV:341–45)

Wordsworth feels that he has been chosen by a power beyond his comprehension, as Samuel was chosen for the priesthood: here his experience of the sublime paradoxically entails both a recognition of the limits of his own consciousness and the conviction of his own blessed creative power, the certainty that his spirit is one with that of the divine creator.

Morgan's narrator, returning at sunset from Catholic vespers, moves through a sublime landscape to a significantly different consciousness.

> I cast my eyes around; all still seemed the vision of awakened imagination—surrounded by a scenery, grand even to the boldest majesty of nature, and wild even to desolation—the day's dying splendours awfully involving in the gloomy haze of deepening twilight—the grey mists of stealing night gathering on the still-faintly illuminated surface of the ocean, which, awfully spreading to infinitude, seemed to the limited gaze of human vision to incorporate with the heaven, whose last glow it reflected—the rocks, which on every side rose to Alpine elevation, exhibiting, amidst the soft obscurity, forms savagely bold, or grotesquely wild, and those finely interesting ruins, which spread grandly desolate in the rear, and added a moral interest to the emotions excited by this view of nature in her most awful, most touching aspect.
>
> Thus, suddenly withdrawn from the world's busiest haunts, its hackneyed modes, its vicious pursuits, and unimportant avocations—dropt as it were amidst scenes of mysterious sublimity—alone—on the wildest shores of the greatest ocean of the universe—immersed amidst the decaying monuments of past ages—still viewing in recollection such forms, such manners, such habits, (as I had lately beheld,) which to the worldly mind may well be supposed to belong to a race long passed beyond the barriers of existence, with "the years beyond the flood"—I felt like the being of some other sphere, newly alighted on a distant orb. . . . My soul, for the first time, had there held commune with herself: the "lying vanities" of life no longer intoxicating my senses, appeared to me for the first time in their genuine aspect, and my heart still fondly loitered over those scenes of solemn interest, where some of its best feelings had been called into existence. (42)

Horatio here moves through the stereotypical landscape of the Burkean/Kantian sublime—sunset, rocks, infinite ocean, "wild" forms, ruins. And in this landscape, he shares Wordsworth's sense of being lifted out of time and space ("the being of some other sphere"). But he does not equate that experience with one of dedication or divine election, of being singled out from other people to act as their leader, priest or savior-poet: "Others will love; and we may teach them how," as Wordsworth put it. Nor does he experience it as a struggle with a nature that tries to overwhelm or destroy him. Instead he sees it as a completely human experience, as a coming to know what is best *within* himself—"My soul . . . held commune with herself." Moreover, it is an experience inspired not solely by the grandeurs of nature but also by the rituals of a human community, here the religious practices of Irish Catholic vespers which Horatio has just witnessed. Stimulated by the contemplation of the interaction of social forms, manners and habits with the natural environment in which they occur, the sublime becomes for Horatio an experience that brings him into more sincere communion with other people; forsaking the "lying vanities" of city life, he will now live with greater honesty, humility and benevolence, sharing his thoughts and feelings with the nobility and peasants of Ireland.

For Wordsworth, the experience of the sublime entails isolation, a struggle for domination, exaltation, and the absorption of the other into the transcendent self. Only then does Wordsworth turn to another, to Coleridge or the shepherds that people the later books of *The Prelude,* in an effort to move from apocalypse to what Geoffrey Hartman has described as a state of *akedah*, a "tying to" nature. For Morgan, the sublime produces self-knowledge and an immediate dialogue with others. Her narrator's meditation is interrupted by the music of an Eolian lyre, trembling like Coleridge's with the harmonies of one life, and accompanied here by "the voice of a *woman!*" (43) Thus Morgan introduces her heroine Glorvina, the wild Irish girl with whom Horatio will fall passionately in love. More important to my argument, however, is Morgan's consistent association in this novel of the sublime with the differentiated but harmonized notes of music, with the interactions of human love, with friendship, with a negotiated communion and voluntary bonding—both of one's soul with itself and of one soul with another, equally complete soul.

Morgan's subversion of the masculine sublime can take a comic turn. Just before hearing the seductive song of Glorvina, Horatio had indulged a desire to conquer and possess the landscape upon which he gazed ("I raised my eyes to the Castle of Inismore, sighed, and almost wished I had been born the lord of these beautiful ruins, the prince of this isolated little territory, the adored chieftain of these affectionate and natural people" [42]). Entranced by Glorvina's siren song, he eagerly climbs the ruined walls, only to lose his footing and fall precipitously into the castle yard. His fall is metaphoric: the male's desire to master both female nature and the female voice is humorously, if rather brutally, undercut. Here Morgan's narrator usurps the role of one of Rosa's *banditti*, but he is clearly harmless.

The reverse may not be true, however. With broken arm and leg and severely gashed forehead, Horatio is taken into the Castle and falls into a delirious slumber:

> I dreamed that the Princess of Inismore approached my bed, drew aside the curtains, and raising her veil, discovered a face I had hitherto guessed at, than seen. Imagine my horror—it was the face, the head, of a *Gorgon!* (51)

Again, the terror of the Burkean sublime—here gender-encoded as a masculine fear of female sexuality, power, and his own castration—is parodically undercut:

> I cast my eyes through a fracture in the old damask drapery of my bed, and beheld—not the horrid spectre of my recent dream— but the form of a cherub hovering near my pillow—it was the Lady Glorvina herself! (51)

For Morgan, the sublime is characteristically the entryway into a love founded not on the male psyche's narcissistic absorption of his female anti-type or soul mate that characterizes Shelley's *Epipsychidion* or Byron's *Manfred*, but on the recognition both of difference and of compatibility. Recovering from his injuries, the welcome guest both of Glorvina and of her father, the Prince of Inismore, Horatio is ever more attracted to Glorvina, an attraction that is consistently mediated by Rosa's sublime landscapes.

> We both arose at the same moment, and walked in silence towards the window. Beyond the mass of ruins which spread in desolate confusion below, the ocean, calm and unruffled, expanded its awful waters almost to apparent infinitude; while a body of dark sullen clouds, tinged with the partial beam of a meridian

sun, floated above the summits of those savage cliffs, which skirt this bold and rocky coast, the tall spectral figure of Father John, leaning on a broken column, appeared the very impersonation of philosophy moralizing on the instability of all human greatness.

What a sublime assemblage of images!

"How consonant," thought I, gazing at Glorvina, "to the tone of our present feelings!" Glorvina bowed her head affirmatively, as though my lips had given utterance to the reflection.

How, think you, I felt, on this involuntary acknowledgment of a mutual intelligence? (65–66)

Where Rosa or Burke would have represented Father John solely as a *memento mori*, in Morgan's rewriting this spectral presence instead inspires two people to enter into an unspoken dialogue that finally produces a shared feeling not of fear but of love. For Morgan, the heightened awareness of the self produced by the sublime leads not to self-absorbed reflection but to communication with other selves, to a "mutual intelligence" between two equally independent, sensitive people. Her association of the experience of the sublime with a *shared* love is articulated by Father John, Glorvina's kindly and devoted mentor:

> this sacred sympathy between two refined, elevated, and sensible minds, in the sublime and beautiful of the moral and natural world, approaches nearer to the rapturous and pure emotion which uncreated spirits may be supposed to feel in their heavenly communion, than any other human sentiment with which we are acquainted. (147)

In this feminine Romantic tradition, the sublime combines with the beautiful to produce, not the experience of *sehnsucht*, of solitary, visionary transcendence sought (however futilely) by several male Romantic poets, but an experience of communion between two different people, that very "sympathy" or *domesticated* sublimity which Morgan hails on the last page of her novel as the essence of "reason and humanity" (255).

The Scottish novelist Susan Ferrier takes this tradition of the feminine, domesticated sublime one step further. In her fiction, sublime nature is specifically equated with human morality. As Vineta Colby has observed, Ferrier's "characters show their real natures—and the quality of their early education—by the way in which they respond to the Scottish landscape."[19] For Ferrier, as for Morgan, the experience of a sublime landscape should produce a sense of participation in a human community, here a community grounded on the natural benevolence and dignity displayed both by the Highland chiefs and their enlightened descendants. Those characters capable of responding positively to the awesome grandeur of the Scottish highlands are also capable of valuing rational discourse, disciplined behavior, the domestic affections, the equality of women, and the dictates of an enlightened Christianity, the hallmarks of Ferrier's feminine Romanticism.

When confronted with the magnificent scenery of Scotland, Mary, the heroine of Ferrier's first novel *Marriage*, rises above the terror and consequent melancholy caused by her first encounter with mortality, the sudden death of her beloved grandfather, to a renewed sense of participation in a providentially ordered universe:

> Though summer had fled, and few even of autumn's graces remained, yet over the august features of mountain scenery the seasons had little control. Their charms depend not upon richness of verdure, or luxuriance of foliage, or any of the mere prettinesses of nature; but, whether wrapped in snow, or veiled in mist, or glowing in sunshine, their lonely grandeur remains the same; and the same feelings fill and elevate the soul in contemplating these mighty works of an Almighty hand.[20]

Mary's sensitive response to sublime nature is paralleled by her moral capacity for prudence, self-discipline and loyalty, qualities that win her a marriage with the wise and good Captain Lennox. In contrast, her mother and twin sister, who are bored or disgusted with rugged alpine scenery and flee to London, are morally shallow and easily corrupted into lives of dissipation, selfishness and betrayal. Again, in Ferrier's *Inheritance*, the generous and enthusiastic, if badly educated, Gertrude can sincerely appreciate the beauties of the Scottish landscape, even as she wrongly conceives them as properties to be possessed:

> Gertrude gazed with ecstasy on all around, and her heart swelled with delight as she thought this fair scene she was destined to inherit; and a vague poetical feeling of love and gratitude to Heaven caused her to raise her eyes, swimming in tearful rapture, to the Giver of all good.[21]

Not until Gertrude has lost her worldly inheritance will she be entitled to her spiritual inheritance, the greater good of coming to appreciate the ultimate values of natural beauty, of a wise and loving husband, and most important, of "the calm radiance of piety and virtue."[22] In contrast, her supposed mother, the deceitful and finally unmasked Mrs. St. Clair, is miserable and alienated amidst the rugged beauty of Scotland. And in *Destiny*, Ferrier's last novel, the superiority of the simple, loving Edith to her worldly cousin Florinda is registered in their differing responses to nature: Edith prefers the "firs and heathers of my own native land" while the self-ish and shallow Florinda responds only to the changeable tropical nights of southern Italy.[23]

In addition to offering an alternative definition of the sublime as an experience that produces an intensified emotional and moral participation in a human community, this tradition of Romantic women writers specifically condemned Burke's and Wordsworth's representations of the sublime as a moment of masculine empowerment over female nature. A commitment to the welfare of others and an ethic of care necessarily involves accepting limitations upon the powers and gratifications of the individual self. Helen Maria Williams, responding directly to Wordsworth's celebration of the "philosophic mind" as a triumph over that "homely Nurse," the earth, insisted that the greatest moral and intellectual achievement lay not in the conscious apprehension of the immortality of the human mind, but rather in the daily practice of friendship and the domestic affections, however mutable they may be.

Her critique of the Wordsworthian sublime is recorded in two poetic commentaries on his *Ode: Intimations of Immortality from Recollections of Early Childhood*. In *To James Forbes, Esq., on His bringing me flowers from Vaucluse, and which he had preserved by means of an ingenious process in their original beauty*, Williams suggests that it is not the "thoughts that do often lie too deep for tears" that reconcile human beings to their mortal sufferings but rather the demonstrated connections of love that make life bearable. Receiving James Forbes' bouquet, Williams responds:

> I love the simplest bud that blows,
> I love the meanest weed that grows:
> Symbols of nature—every form
> That speaks of her this heart can warm; . . . [24]

For Williams, the "meanest flower that blows" brings, not self-absorbed meditations on mortality and the enduring power of the creative mind, but rather a simple pleasure in the daily delights of everyday nature. It is Williams' heart rather than her mind that is touched; for her the outward manifestations or "symbols" of nature are reminders of the myriad opportunities for human affection and service to others.

Hence the deliberately "occasional" nature of the title and content of this verse: life is a series of opportunities or occasions for the expression of affection, and only such expressions can truly "warm" the heart. The value of this bouquet to Williams is enhanced by the fact that these flowers grew in the Vaucluse "where *Petrarch* mourned, and *Laura* trod"; nature is more meaningful when associated with human events, especially those events which record the existence of an enduring, passionate human love. And finally, these flowers are most valuable to Williams because they are a *gift*, because

> with love and fame
> This wreath entwines a milder name;
> Friendship, who better knows than they
> The spells that smooth our length'ning way.

In the domesticated, feminine sublime, the meanest flower that blows is significant, not because it arouses a consciousness of our complicity in the eternal cycles of life and death, but because it can provide us with both the literal occasion and the figural sign for friendship, a demonstration of the enduring ties that bind human beings to nature, and one person to another, *within* time.

6

Exhausting the Beautiful

Up to this point, I have been tracking the manifestations of Wollstonecraft's "revolution in female manners," the ways in which writing by women in the Romantic period constructed a new version of the ideal woman, one who was rational rather than emotional or sexual, one who participated in an egalitarian marriage that became the model for good government, one who cooperated ecologically with a Nature troped as a loving sister. Wollstonecraft's construction of femininity explicitly challenged the dominant gender ideology of her culture, the concept of the female promoted by conservative and radical thinkers alike, from Burke to Rousseau. In this chapter I want to pursue the question: what happens when a Romantic woman writer chooses to inhabit rather than reject the hegemonic construction of the ideal woman?

Returning to Edmund Burke's *Philosophical Inquiry into the Origin of our Ideas of the Sublime and the Beautiful* (1757), let me explore in greater detail just how Burke conceptualized the beautiful, the category that in his view opposed the masculine sublime. Burke attributed the origin of the aesthetic experience of the beautiful to the feeling of pleasure aroused by love, by that "sympathy" or procreative desire that leads to the "multiplication of the species" (63). Although Burke acknowledged that men, animals, landscapes and physical objects could be beautiful, he consistently identified the qualities of the beautiful with the feminine, even with "the *sex*" (66; "the" sex, in the eighteenth century, referred to the female sex alone). Burke summed up the qualities of the beautiful thus:

> First, to be comparatively small. Secondly, to be smooth. Thirdly, to have a variety in the direction of the parts; but, fourthly, to have those parts not angular, but melted as it were into each other. Fifthly, to be of a delicate frame without any remarkable appearance of strength. Sixthly, to have its colours clear and bright, but not very strong and glaring. Seventhly, or if it should have any glaring colour, to have it diversified with others. (222)

Burke's aesthetic classifications participated in, and helped to support, a powerful hegemonic sexual politics. As he constructed the category of the beautiful, Burke also constructed the image of the ideal woman, as his illustrative remarks reveal. Beauty is identified with the "softer virtues" (205), with easiness of temper, compassion, kindness and liberality, as opposed to the higher qualities of mind, those virtues which cause admiration such as fortitude, justice and wisdom, and which Burke assigned to the masculine sublime. Beauty is associated with "the mother's fondness and indulgence" (207), with "the soft green of the soul on which we rest our eyes" (206). In taste, beauty is the sweetness Burke explicitly identifies with breast-milk, "the first support of our childhood" (297). The beautiful, then, is that which both embodies and produces "affection and tenderness" (85).

Beauty, for Burke, is identified not only with the nurturing mother but also with the erotic love-object, the sensuous and possessible beloved. Identifying beauty with the small, the diminutive, pointing out that "it is usual to add the endearing name of *little* to every thing we love" (211), Burke revealingly commented that "we submit to what we admire, but we love what submits to us" (212). The ideal woman, then, is one who engages in a practice of what today we would call female masochism, willingly obeying the dictates of her sublime master. The smoothness of beauty is further associated by Burke with the "smooth skins" of "fine women" (213), while the Hogarthian S-line of beauty, the quality of "gradual variation," is explicitly located, in a passage that unmasks Burke's erotic investments, in a woman's breast:

> Observe that part of a beautiful woman where she is perhaps the most beautiful, about the neck and breasts; the smoothness; the softness; the easy and insensible swell; the variety of the surface,

which is never for the smallest space the same; the deceitful maze, through which the unsteady eye slides giddily, without knowing where to fix, or whither it is carried. (216)

Burke specifies two further dimensions of this ideal, eroticised, maternal beauty: she is "delicate," even to the verge of sickliness (although never disfigured by the overt signs of ill health)—manifesting a "weakness" whose appropriate accompanying quality of mind is "timidity" (219). And when the beautiful woman speaks, it is with a voice that is soft, sweet, clear, even, smooth—never shrill, harsh, deep or loud. The characteristic effect that the beautiful voice or music produces is "that sinking, that melting, that languor," which excites above all the passion of "melancholy" (235).

Hundreds of upper- and middle-class women in England in the Romantic era aspired to become the languorous, melting beauty that Burke envisioned. And Rousseau, in his portrait of the education of Sophy in Book V of *Emile*, taught them how.

A woman's education must . . . be planned in relation to man. To be pleasing in his sight, to win his respect and love, to train him in childhood, to tend him in manhood, to counsel and console, to make his life pleasant and happy, these are the duties of woman for all time, and this is what she should be taught while she is young. (328)

To be pleasing to men: this for Rousseau is the ultimate social role of women, one for which they are suited by their "natural" modesty or *pudeur*, which arouses man's sexual desire but at the same time relieves him, as Ruth Yeazell has perceptively noted,[1] from both the embarrassment of sexual impotence and the nightmare of being too aggressively pursued.

The consequence of this "sexual education," as Mary Shelley called it in her novel *Lodore*, is the cultural production of a woman who defines her subjectivity solely in relation to a man, who can conceptualize her own existence only as the object and creator of love. As Byron put it in *Don Juan*, "Man's love is of his life a thing apart,/ 'Tis woman's whole existence" (I:194). Together, Burke, Rousseau and Byron define the hegemonic domestic ideology of the Romantic period: the construction of the ideal woman solely as daughter, lover, wife and mother, one who exists only to serve the interests of male children and adults, and whose value is equated with her beauty, submissiveness, tenderness and affection.[2]

Taking the poetry of Letitia Elizabeth Landon and Felicia Hemans as illustrative, we can begin to explore the gains and losses
for a woman poet who situated her self and her work wholly *within*
the Burkean-Rousseauian categories of the beautiful and the domestic. As Isobel Armstrong has suggested,[3] we can best understand the poetry of Letitia Landon if we consider it in relation to
Burke's concept of the beautiful. Landon constructed both her life
and her poetry as an embodiment of Burke's female beauty. Her
poetry first appeared under the modestly discreet initials
"L. E. L."—a signature whose cultural significance her young male
admirers immediately grasped. As Edward Bulwer-Lytton later recalled in his review of her novel *Romance and Reality:*

> We remember well when she first appeared before the public in
> the pages of *The Literary Gazette.* We were at that time more ca-
> pable than we are now of poetic enthusiasm; and certainly that
> enthusiasm we not only felt ourselves, but we shared with every
> second person we then met. We were young, and at college, lav-
> ishing our golden years, not so much on the Greek verse and mys-
> tic character to which we ought, perhaps, to have been rigidly
> devoted, as
>   'Our heart in passion and our head in rhymes.'
> At that time poetry was not yet out of fashion, at least with us of
> the cloister; and there was always, in the Reading Room of the
> Union, a rush every Saturday afternoon for *The Literary Gazette,*
> and an impatient anxiety to hasten at once to that corner of the
> sheet which contained the three magical letters of "L. E. L." And
> all of us praised the verse, and all of us guessed at the author. We
> soon learned it was a female, and our admiration was doubled,
> and our conjectures tripled. Was she young? Was she pretty?
> and—for there were some embryo fortune-hunters among us—
> was she rich?[4]

Bulwer-Lytton and his peers eagerly identified the "magical" letters L. E. L. with a feminine youthful beauty and a wealth that
might be *possessed* by a male Oxford undergraduate.

Landon supported this construction of her "self" as desirable
beauty both visually and verbally. She became friends with the
painter Daniel Maclise, who painted at least four individual portraits of her as well as including her in his famous group portrait
of "Regina's Maids of Honour."[5] Maclise consistently portrayed
Landon as the icon of female beauty: she gazes demurely down or
sideways, her hair chastely drawn back or topped with a hair-knot
in the shape of a girlish bow, and her elegant dress designed to ac-

centuate her waspishly small waist, her delicate wrists, and above all, her arching neck, voluptuously white shoulders, bared chest and half revealed swelling breasts.

This commercial production of her self as an acquirable artifact of beauty reached its apotheosis when Landon agreed to write the first volume of *Heath's Book of Beauty* in 1833. Since the appearance of Rudolph Ackermann's *Forget Me Not, a Christmas and New Year's Present for 1823*, the vogue for annual gift-books composed of handsomely illustrated stories and verse had increased, catering especially, as Anne Renier comments, to an audience of young ladies who preferred them to the more severe conduct-books; they could respectably accept them from a devoted admirer, and still avoid "the dreaded stigma of appearing a bluestocking." [6] Growing in size from the original pocketbook format of *Forget Me Not, The Gem* and *The Amulet,* to the octavo format of *The Keepsake* and *Fisher's Drawing Room Scrap-Book,* these gift-books shamelessly recruited famous writers and aristocratic editors (Lady Emmeline Stuart Wortley took over the editorship of *The Keepsake* in 1840, while Countess Blessington replaced Landon as the editor of *Heath's Book of Beauty* in 1835) and included highly idealized portraits of the English nobility as well as topographical landscapes focussing on stately homes and castles or exotic scenes visited only by the very wealthy—all in an effort to enhance their snob-appeal for the upwardly aspiring middle classes. Bound in gilt-edged leather or ornately gilded cloth (damask, silk, satin, plush, brocade), including embossed presentation plates, often available in ornamental slipcases (as was *Forget Me Not*), these annual gift-books functioned simultaneously as expressions of feeling (an act of friendship, of gift-giving) and as cultural signs of education, taste and wealth. Accessible to the middle-classes, they represented the chance to experience the pride of ownership, "a bourgeoise semblance of aristocratic self-possession," as Sonia Hofkosh shrewdly puts it. [7]

Here I wish to focus on the gender rather than the class implications of these early versions of the modern coffee-table book. Designed for women, these best-sellers systematically constructed through word and picture the hegemonic ideal of feminine beauty. As ideological propaganda, they proved more seductive—and perhaps more effective—than the more serious conduct-books. In steel engravings of exceptionally high quality, they promoted an image of the ideal woman as specular, as the object rather than the owner of the gaze. The women in these illustrations typically look down, up or sideways, but rarely straight ahead; they are looked at but they do not see (the viewer, the world before them). They are presented as chaste but nonetheless erotically desirable—with a consistent highlighting of bare white arching necks and broad shoulders and half uncovered breasts. Or they are imaged as the mother, devotedly attending the infant (usually titled) upon her lap.

As the author of the contents of the first edition of *Heath's Book of Beauty,* as the contributor of numerous verses to *Fisher's Drawing Room Scrap-book, The Keepsake,* and *Friendship's Offering,* as the supplier of the following epigram that graces the titlepage of the first three volumes of the *Forget Me Not:*

> Appealing, by the magic of its name,
> To gentle feelings and affections, kept
> Within the heart like gold,

Letitia Landon commodified herself as a purchasable icon of female beauty. It was a beauty defined not only by visual image but also by word. Writing to order—Landon was commissioned to write all the stories and verses to accompany the preexisting engravings for the first edition of *Fisher's Drawing Room Scrap-Book* in 1832 as well as to provide regular contributions to most of the other gift-books throughout the 1830s—Landon created the verbal equivalent of Burke's visual beauty. Her verses on "Mrs. Wombwell" move from a description of outward specular Beauty, the product, to an analysis of the temporal process by which it was produced:

> Ah Beauty! what a charm hast thou! . . .
> Young, fair, thou art; oh, very fair!
>   Still, on that face appears
> The sadness deeper memories·wear,
>   The tenderness of tears.
>   (lines 1, 28–31;
>   *Heath's Book of Beauty,* 1838)

Inspired by Burke, Landon's writings construct the interior life or subjectivity of the beautiful woman as one defined by love, fidelity, sensitivity—and melancholy. In her book for children, *Traits and Trials of Early Life* (1837), she included a story, "The History of a Child," that was immediately read as Landon's fictive autobiography, as the fate of female genius: the story of a lonely, sensitive, bookish, unloved girl, rejected even by her adored nurse—"What a tiresome child it is!" Suffering numerous "mortifications," experiencing "the bitterness of neglect and the solitude of a crowd," this girl grows up devoted to her dog, who dies, her only friend Lucy, who dies, and her father, who alone responds to her affectionate embraces. Landon concludes: "I have told the history of my childhood, childhood which images forth our life. Even such has been mine—it has but repeated what it learnt from the first, Sorrow, Beauty, Love, and Death."[8]

This story is a fiction, as numerous of Landon's contemporaries commented in exasperation (her own childhood was a happy one of constant companionship with her brother Whittington and numerous school-friends[9]), but her readers seized upon it as the necessary narrative of the origins of female beauty and hence of both Landon's life and poetry. Landon was thus entirely complicit in her culture's construction of female beauty, rewriting her own life and subjectivity to conform to preexisting categories. Sorrow, Beauty, Love, Death—these are the subjects of Landon's poetry, from her earliest adolescent verses for *The Literary Gazette* to her mature novels and final poems.

Designed to appeal, as her first editor William Jerdan defined her audience, to those in whom "the love of poetry is not extinct—the young, the sensitive, the imaginative, the natural, the refined, the tasteful, the innocent, and the good,"[10] Landon's poems repetitively construct the narrative of female love as love rejected, love thwarted by fate and circumstances, love known only to be lost. Deriving her plots intertextually from medieval courtly love lyrics and Greek poetry (especially Sappho), rather than from her personal experiences (a disjunction frequently noted by her critics), Landon consciously created a poetry of beauty, a poetry of "baffled hopes and blighted affections," as her admiring biographer put it.[11] She employed the very voice that Burke had recommended: a voice of sweetness, softness, clarity and harmonious musicality, working quickly, improvisationally, often carelessly, but with what one critic called a "fatal felicity."[12] Successfully gauging the taste of the time, she earned enough from her numerous publications to support separate establishments for herself and her mother (she rented rooms in her former boarding school while her mother, whom she disliked, continued to live in the family house after her father's death in 1824) and to send her beloved brother to university and purchase him a clerical living; her editor William Jerdan estimated her income at a minimum of two hundred-fifty pounds per annum, and 2,585 pounds in all.[13]

Landon's poetry was designed to *be* feminine beauty, a beauty both of the body and of the heart. In her preface to her 1829 volume of poetry, *The Venetian Bracelet*, she defined the moral and aesthetic purpose of her writing:

> A highly-cultivated state of society must ever have for concomitant evils, that selfishness, the result of indolent indulgence; and that heartlessness attendant on refinement, which too often hardens while it polishes. Aware that to elevate I must first soften, and that if I wished to purify I must first touch, I have ever endeavoured to bring forward grief, disappointment, the fallen leaf, the faded flower, the broken heart, and the early grave. Surely we must be less worldly, less interested, from this sympathy with the sorrow in which our unselfish feelings alone can take part.[14]

Having aligned herself with Lord Shaftesbury's conception of sympathy or "disinterestedness" as the basis of morality, she defends her choice of Love

> as my source of song. I can only say, that for a woman, whose influence and whose sphere *must* be in the affections, what subject can be more fitting than one which it is her peculiar province to refine, spiritualise, and exalt? I have always sought to paint it self-denying, devoted, and making an almost religion of its truth; . . . [15]

Landon, despite her personal experiences, is here supporting an *essentialist* definition of the woman as the *one who loves*, insistently endorsing Byron's dictum that love is "woman's whole existence."

Once Landon accepted her culture's hegemonic definition of the female, she could only repeat the same story over and over. Her poetry obsessively details every nuance of female love, of female sympathy, of female imagination in the service of the affections, always arriving at the same narrative conclusion: such love is futile. Having taken her culture's limited construction of gender as ontological "truth," Landon could only map a terrain whose roads all converged on the same center, the same dead end; she thus *exhausted* Burke's category of the beautiful even as she inhabited it.

Let me pursue this argument in terms of the two themes to which Landon returns obsessively in all her poetry and which for her were indissolubly linked: Love and Poetry. Arbitrarily, I choose out of her enormous canon three discussions of love: *The Troubadour*, a long narrative derived from medieval courtly love ballads; *The Lost Pleiad*, a reworking of Greek myth; and a short poem located in her own time, *Love's Last Lesson*. *The Troubadour* (1825) begins with the noble knight Raymond pledging his love to the orphaned Eva, who reciprocates his love and gives him her token when he sets off on his heroic quest for honor and fame. On his travels, Raymond meets and falls passionately in love with Adeline, who "loved him not," and who thus becomes the *belle dame sans merci* of courtly love poetry, and who causes Raymond "burning pain."[16] In despair, Raymond goes on a Crusade against the Spanish Moors, rescues Eva's long-lost father, is captured, then aided to escape by a Moorish maid Leila who loves him deeply, but whom he abandons, vowing to go back to his first love Eva. Raymond however seeks out Adeline's castle instead, only to find it now in ruins and to hear the ballad of her downfall, "The Proud Ladye," the imbedded story of Adeline's rejection by the only man *she* ever loved. During these many years, misled by Adeline's assertion that Raymond has died in prison, Eva has been wasting away in grief.

The poem thus recounts not one but three versions of female love, all self-destroying: Eva faithful to her plighted love, yet upon whose lip and brow came "day by day/ Some other emblem of decay" (106); the lovely Leila, abandoned, dead of a broken heart, finally turned to stone, "So cold, so colourless, so lone—/ A statue nymph" (96); and Adeline, the chaste Diana who resisted all suitors, setting them the impossible task of riding horseback around the high narrow walls of her castle, only to fall hopelessly in love with a "stranger knight" who passed the test but then contemptuously rejected her hand, saying he rode but to gain fame and to avenge his dead brother, since "far more was to me his love,/ Than woman's love can be" (100). In each case, the woman who loves is rejected, abandoned, or merely forgotten by her cruel lover.

When Raymond finally does return to Eva, Landon's narrative abruptly ends, since

> . . . what has minstrel left to tell
> When love has not an obstacle?
> My lute is hush'd, and mute its chords,
> The heart and happiness have no words!
> (109)

Landon cannot write the story of successful, enduring love because that is not the category of love the language of Beauty has constructed; she can tell only the love of the beautiful woman, a love she—and Burke—defined as essentially "melancholy." She therefore concludes *The Troubadour*, not with the story she has been narrating of Raymond and Eva, not with the tale of a love "whose

truth was kept, come life, come death" (110)—a line that, paren-
thetically, forces the reader to ask, *whose* truth? Surely not Raymond's! Rather, she ends with a question—"Alas! has modern love
such faith?"—and a turn to the present, to the narrator's own love,
a love that is here constructed as the only possible "modern love," the love of a daughter for her father. But this father is,
inevitably, dead, and the "best feelings" of the author are therefore
in the grave: "Never, dear father, love can be,/ Like the dear love I
had for thee!" (112)

The Lost Pleiad rewrites the Greek myth of Endymion from the
perspective of the woman, just as the ballad of *The Proud Ladye*
refocused Keats's ballad of *La Belle Dame sans Merci* on the feelings
of the rejected "proud ladye" (Adeline, in despair, there "grew wan
and pale" and finally took refuge from the homosocial desire of
men in an all-female but still imprisoning community, "Saint Marie's cell"). *The Lost Pleiad*, Landon's answer to Keats's *Endymion*
or Percy Shelley's *Alastor*, tells the story of Cyris who, having
known all human glory and fame, seeks the perfect woman, the
ideal love. He finally falls in love with the youngest of the starry
Pleiades, the cold, fair, bright, proud Cyrene. And she returns his
love, begging and winning her father's permission to descend to
earth and join her beloved.

In a rhetorical move we can now recognize as constitutive of
Landon's construction of female beauty, the narrator refuses to tell
the story of happy love:

> —I cannot sing as I have sung;
> My heart is changed, my lute unstrung.
> Once said I that my early chords
> Were vow'd to love or sorrow's words:
> But love has like an odour past,
> Or echo, all too sweet to last;
> And sorrow now holds lonely sway
> O'er my young heart, and lute, and lay.
> Be it for those whose unwaked youth
> Believes that hope and love are sooth—
> The loved, the happy—let them dream
> This meeting by the forest stream.
>   (195)

The only narrative Landon can tell is one of female love rejected,
and this is the narrative we get.

Said I not, that young prince was one
Who wearied when the goal was won;
To whom the charm of change was all
That bound his heart in woman's thrall?
(196)

Prince Cyrus abandons his devoted star-bride, even though she gave up both immortality and "her glorious sphere" to die with him, to "share earthly tear, and earthly sigh"—but "What mattered that?—She now was here" (196). The Pleiad has entered into the category of the human female: "Thou hast but left those starry spheres/ For woman's destiny of tears" (196). And so Cyrus and Cyrene part, she

with her wrong'd and breaking heart;
But he, rejoicing he is free
Bounds like the captive from his chain,
And willfully believing she
Hath found her liberty again!

What both these narratives construct is the *cause* of female sorrow and despair: the reckless, unfeeling, even deliberate, cruelty of *men*. This anti-patriarchal argument is transferred to "modern" love in Landon's *Love's Last Lesson*, in which the modest young nineteenth-century woman, virginal and pure, who is "unconsciously" aroused to love—"you first call'd my woman's feelings forth,/ And taught me love ere I had dream'd love's name" (315)—and believing she is loved in return, "gave all I could" (315)—only to be told by the man that she must "forget" him, since he does not love her and does not desire her love. The sufferings of loving women may be caused by men, in Landon's verse, but women are portrayed as powerless to prevent such suffering; instead, they (masochistically) "submit."

Love's Last Lesson exposes a great deal more than women's voluntary or involuntary submission to the cruelty of men. Once the maiden cannot speak her love, she cannot speak *at all:*

. . . Why should she write?
What could she write? Her woman's pride forbade
To let him look upon her heart, and see
It was an utter ruin;—and cold words,
And scorn, and slight, that may repay his own,

Were as a foreign language, to whose sound
She might not frame her utterance.

(316)

Since woman's whole existence is love, she has no language but that of love. A man's language is "foreign," constituting a public realm women cannot enter. Landon here insists upon the absolute division of the male and female spheres, a division marked not only by feelings and values but by language. Her poetry can construct only the private realm of female affections.

The grounding figure of Landon's essentialist doctrine of sexual difference is, necessarily, Nature. Landon appropriates the traditional Western cultural identification of Nature as female, of the female as body rather than mind, as nature rather than culture, only to turn it in upon itself. In *Love's Last Lesson*, love's ending is troped as the "history of some fair southern clime," as geology and botany and biology. But instead of writing the female as Mother Earth, all-procreative, abundant and fertile, Landon writes the love of the "natural" female and female nature as a volcano erupting onto a paradisiacal landscape, laying "all waste before it," bringing not fertility but "pestilence" and "ashy waters" and "desert" barrenness (316). Thus "the tale that I would tell," "a common tale/ Of woman's wretchedness," can be only the tale of a female "heart, burnt and crush'd/ With passion's earthquake, scorch'd and wither'd up," for "this is love" (316).

If for Landon the essence of woman is love, a love that can exist only in the private sphere—and is therefore denied, rejected, devalued, destroyed whenever it depends on the fidelity of a man whose contrary essence commits him to "stern ambition's dream, to that fierce strife/ Which leads to life's high places" (317)—what happens in Landon's poetry when a woman moves into the public sphere? In two poems often read by her contemporaries as autobiographical, *Erinna* and *A History of the Lyre*, the woman of poetic genius gains public recognition and fame. *Erinna* reinscribes Mme. de Staël's *Corinne* (Landon translated the odes for Isabell Hill's English translation of *Corinne* in 1833) as the story of a woman whose very face bears the sign of contradiction: on the one hand, her "mouth" smiles "a woman's gentle feeling" while, on the other, her noble "brow" manifests the "melancholy pride of thought/ Conscious of power, and yet forced to know/ How little way such power as that can go" (214). Having organically created the music of nature in her solitary contemplations, "catching from green wood and lofty pine/ Language mysterious as musical," Erinna had known perfect happiness. But her songs had won her fame, and by drinking "the maddening cup of praise," she had entered the public realm. Once there, "I lived/ Only in others' breath; a word, a look,/ Were of all influence on my destiny" (218). Worse, she learned that the breath circulated like money in the public realm was but "hollowness": the "base exchange of flattery" and the blame, mockery and criticism of those "whose every thought falls foul/ Plague spot on beauty, which they cannot feel" (219).

Rejecting the "waste of feeling and of life" of public glory, Erinna tries to return to her natural paradise, only to find that "it is fallen from its first estate" (220). Knowledge of the social world, brought to her by "the gift of mind," has become "a barrier to so much that makes/ Our life endurable,—companionship,/ Mingling affection, calm and gentle peace" (221). Landon inscribes the gulf between the private and the public spheres as unbridgeable: once Erinna becomes a public persona, she loses her life's very breath, existing only parasitically on "others' breath." Landon further writes of this division as one between body and mind: it is Erinna's intellect that has betrayed her female nature, those "songs . . . Of woman's tenderness and women's tears," "the fittest for my maiden hand" (221). In returning to the body, to female nature, however, Erinna must reject the poem's opening suggestion that her face is the "fitting shrine" of a "divine" spirit; she can now know only the limits of mortality, of death: "O lute of mine, that I shall wake no more." Both her music and her body must die, since neither can survive in the masculine realm of "stern ambition" and "worldly cares" (222).

When she retells the narratives of both Corinne and Erinna as that of Eulalia in *The History of the Lyre*, Landon further identifies a woman's movement from the private to the public sphere with the progress of a disease, with pestilence and death. When the famous poet Eulalia, "she whose smile/ Should only make the loveliness of home," is drawn into the public realm by her desire not only for fame and social success but also for artistic immortality, "this triumph intellect has over death" (226), she feels she has taken a dangerous drug:

> praise is opium, and the lip
> Cannot resist the fascinating draught,
> Though knowing its excitement is a fraud,—
> Delirious,—a mockery of fame.
>
> (228)

Having entered the public sphere, Eulalia discovers within its "great outline" apparently so "noble and ennobling" only the "base alloy" of disappointment, envy, vanity, doubts and vain aspirings. But when Eulalia attempts to return to the private sphere, she cannot find the perfect love she has too idealistically constructed in her verse. Deprived of both love and ambition, her heart can know only "utter weariness"; within three years she is dead.

Landon's poetry is grounded on the ideological construction of the female as essentially beautiful, essentially loving. By equating the essence of woman with her body (the specular object of beauty), Landon defined the kind of knowledge women could possess. From within the body, women can know only physical sensations and the emotions they produce. Implicitly embracing David Hume's sceptical argument that the mind can know only the empirical sensations transmitted through the body, Landon restricted Hume's epistemology to the female sex, confining her heroines' consciousness to what they can experience through the body, *on earth*. Her heroines have no conviction of an afterlife; when love dies, they die.

Working from *within* an essentialist construction of the female as the beautiful and the loving, Landon's poetry uncovers the emptiness, the self-defeating consequences, of such a construction. The beauty of her heroines inevitably fades, leaving them "wan and pale," withered up, dying; even the air they breathe is taken away from them: "I lived/ Only in others' breath." Her heroines are faithful to the love that constitutes their whole existence, but that love is never reciprocated; hence their potential fertility is rendered barren. If they attempt to cross over the barrier between the private and the public, taking their ideology of love and beauty into the public realm, their lifeblood is infected by the fatal plague of ambition and vanity. By revealing the hollowness at the core of the Burkean category of the Beautiful, Landon undermined the very construction of femininity upon which her poetry was grounded; ideologically, her poetry implodes upon itself.

As did her life. Having reified not only her writing but her very self into a purchasable icon of female beauty, Landon was trapped in the social discourse of her day. Although she lived alone, among female teachers, students and friends, and remained a virgin until seven months before her death in 1839 at the age of 37, her life was the constant subject of public scrutiny and gossip. "Was she young? Was she beautiful? Was she rich?" Her subjectivity was produced as much by the print culture which commodified her as by her own behavior. Warm, outgoing, friendly, Landon showed to her friends a spontaneity that was often at odds with respectable codes of propriety in manner and speech, an eager wit and easy laughter, a persona of innocent enthusiasms at odds with the consistently melancholy tone of her poetry. Friends interpreted this disjunction differently: some insisted that she carried a "secret sorrow" buried deep within; others, probably more perceptively, argued that her poetry was a conscious fiction.[17] Either way, her life was regarded (as are the lives of famous literary and artistic figures today) as "public property"; indeed L. E. L. can be seen as among the first of a long line of media-created "stars" in the new print culture of the nineteenth century. Presenting herself to her public as virginal female beauty, she was constantly susceptible, as her autobiographical heroines Erinna and Eulalia lament, to praise, blame, mockery, censure, to "others' opinions." Landon commented revealingly in a letter to her friend Mrs. Antony Todd Thomson, "With regard to the immoral and improper tendency of my productions, I can only say it is not my fault if there are minds which, like negroes, cast a dark shadow on a mirror, however clear and pure in itself."[18] Landon here explicitly aligns herself with British colonial imperialism, demanding protection for its virginal white maidens against the threat of racial violence or miscegenation.

Despite her appeal to the racist prejudices of her hearers, Landon fell prey to the voices of rumor and scandal. Her innocent friendships with the painter Daniel Maclise and the Irish journalist William Maginn were maliciously read as sexual affairs, especially after Landon's effusive letters to Maginn, addressed to "My dearest William," were released to the press by his jealous wife.[19] The scandal, emanating from an unnamed source, became so powerful that it forced Landon to break off her engagement to the ten-year's-younger author John Forster in 1835; as she wrote to Forster,

> The more I think, the more I feel I ought not—I cannot—allow you—to unite yourself with one accused of—I cannot write it.[20]

Forster may already have expressed his desire to end the relationship; as his powerful older friend, the actor William Charles Macready, recorded in his diary on November 20, 1835,

> Called on Forster, and stayed some time listening to a tale of wretched abandonment to passion that surprised and depressed me. He told me that he had been on the point of marriage with Miss L———, but that rumours and stories pressed in such num-

ber and frightful quality upon him that he was forced to demand explanation from one of the reported narrators or circulators, Mr. A. A. Watts [Alaric Alexander Watts, 1797–1842, journalist, verse-writer and essayist]—that his denial was positive and circumstantial, but that it was arranged between themselves and their mutual friends that the marriage should be broken off. A short time after Forster discovered that Miss L——— made an abrupt and passionate declaration of love to Maclise, and on a subsequent occasion repeated it! It has lately come to light that she has been carrying on an intrigue with Dr. Maginn, a person whom I never saw, but whom all accounts unite in describing as a beastly biped; he is married and has four children. Two letters of hers and one of his were found by Mrs. Maginn in his portrait, filled with the most puerile and nauseating terms of endearment and declarations of attachment! I felt quite concerned that a woman of such splendid genius and such agreeable manners should be so depraved in taste and so lost to a sense of what was due to her high reputation. She is fallen![21]

Once the icon of female beauty has been rewritten in the public discourse as the fallen woman, she no longer has a viable life. Landon's problem, like that of Caroline Norton in her relationship with Lord Melborne, was that the public discourse of her day had no social or linguistic category for, no words to describe, a *non-erotic* male-female collegial friendship. Desperate to regain her reputation and literary marketability, at the age of thirty-five Landon eagerly accepted the only marriage proposal she received, from George Maclean, Governor of the British outpost at Cape Coast, West Africa. When Maclean also heard of the rumors concerning Landon and tried to break off the engagement, her clergyman brother Whittington informed Maclean that as a "man of honour" he had to remain true to his word. In marrying Maclean, Landon was forced to leave London for a desolate military garrison in Africa, where she would be deprived of all literary and even of female company. But she professed herself deeply in love with Maclean, inspired by his accounts of his heroic exploits in negotiating with the warlike Ashanti tribe, and eager to visit new and exotic landscapes. Maclean, a stern Scottish bachelor of thirty-six, although originally attracted by Landon's admiration and charm, responded to their wedding breakfast toasts with the sardonic comment, "If Mrs. McLean has as many friends as Mr. Hall says she has, I only wonder they allow her to leave them."[22]

Within seven months of her marriage, Landon was dead. The

cause of her death from an overdose of prussic acid remains a mystery: was it suicide? an accident? murder? or even, possibly, from natural causes? When the news of her death reached her friends in London, speculations and rumors were rife, giving rise to a formal King's Enquiry into the situation. Probably the most reliable account was given by Brodie Cruickshank, a young British naval officer attached to the Cape Coast garrison, who spent the evening prior to Landon's death at her house and who was summoned by Maclean to the house the next morning after her body was found in her bedroom. Cruickshank, insisting upon Landon's good spirits the evening before and carrying her last, happy letters with him back to England, argued that Landon, in a sudden attack of the condition previously diagnosed as "spasmodic affections," had accidentally taken more than the two prescribed drops of her medication, prussic acid.[23]

Landon's commodified life did not end with her death, however. For another century, culminating in D. E. Enfield's *L. E. L.-A Mystery of the Thirties* (London, 1928), her readers reconstructed her death—killed out of jealousy by Maclean's banished black mistress; or overcome by suicidal despair at the departure of Cruickshank, the only lettered man in the colony; or killed by Maclean himself in a rage at her poor housekeeping; or, as her family and friends insisted, killed by the "spasmodic affections" or hysterical nervous attacks to which she was prone even before she went to Africa.[24] By writing her self as female beauty, Landon effectively wrote herself out of existence: she became a fluid sign in the discourse that constructed her, a discourse that denied her authenticity and overwrote whatever individual voice she might have possessed. For a modern reader, both her life and her poetry finally demonstrate the literally fatal consequences for a woman in the Romantic period who wholly inscribed herself within Burke's aesthetic category of the beautiful.

Where Landon constructed her self and poetry as the icon of female beauty, Felicia Hemans constructed her self and poetry as the icon of female domesticity, the embodiment of the "cult of true womanhood." As she wrote to her good friend, Mary Russell Mitford, "there is *no* enjoyment to compare with the happiness of gladdening hearth and home for others—it is woman's own true sphere."[25] The most popular female poet in the Romantic period, indeed second only to Byron (who did not welcome the competition[26]), Hemans' nineteen volumes of poetry and two dramas sold thousands of copies; her tragedy, *The Vespers of Palermo*, was produced at Covent Garden in 1823 and in Edinburgh, with Sarah Siddons, the following year; and she regularly contributed to the annual gift-books of her day, earning enough to support five sons single-handedly.[27] Her poetry was especially well received in America, where she was offered an annual salary of $1,500 to accept the sinecure of the nominal editorship of a literary magazine.

As Landon did with the cult of beauty, Hemans situated her self and her poetry wholly within the category of feminine domesticity: her poetry celebrates the enduring value of the domestic affections, the glory and beauty of maternal love, and the lasting commitment of a woman to her chosen mate. In contrast to Landon, Hemans tried to reconcile her private and public personae, drawing on her personal experiences as subjects for her poetry. As a result, she provided a far more complex analysis of the ways in which her culture's construction of gender finally proved destructive to women. The problematic status of "woman's own true sphere" surfaces in the very same letter to Mary Mitford, as Hemans continues,

> I am not at all well just now; I believe it is the great fatigue I have had of late with my boys; and this time of the year makes one so long for the far away—do not you think so? If my sister were near me now, I should lay my head down upon her shoulder and cry "like a tired child." (Chorley I:183)

Hemans' poetry locates ultimate human value within the domestic sphere. At the same time it emphasizes just how precarious, how threatened, is that sphere—by the passage of time, by the betrayals of family members, by its opposition to the dominant ideology of the masculine public sphere, the domain of ambition, military glory and financial power. We need to read her lyrics not as single statements but as parts of a corpus that constantly reminds us of the fragility of the very domestic ideology it endorses.

Many poems insistently celebrate the emotional gratification produced by a loving home. In *The Two Homes*, she represents the home as an earthly paradise:

> See'st thou my home?—t'is where yon woods are waving . . .
> There am I loved—there prayed for—there my mother
> Sits by the hearth with meekly thoughtful eye;
> There my young sisters watch to greet their brother;
> Soon their glad footsteps down the path will fly.
>
> There, in sweet strains of kindred music blending,
> All the home-voices meet at day's decline;

One are those tones, as from one heart ascending,—
There laughs *my* home. . . .[28]

In *The Homes of England*, she further identifies the "merry" homes
of England with a natural permanence, with religious truth, with
a freedom that transcends class distinctions (the virtues of home
are experienced by those in both stately homes and humble cottages), and with British patriotism:

> The stately homes of England,
>   How beautiful they stand
> Amidst their tall ancestral trees,
>   O'er all the pleasant land!
> The deer across their greensward bound,
>   Through shade and sunny gleam;
> And the swan glides past them with the sound
>   Of some rejoicing stream.
>
> The merry homes of England!
>   Around their hearths by night,
> What gladsome looks of household love
>   Meet in the ruddy light!
> There woman's voice flows forth in song,
>   Or childhood's tale is told,
> Or lips move tunefully along
>   Some glorious page of old.
>
> The blessed homes of England!
>   How softly on their bowers
> Is laid the holy quietness
>   That breathes from Sabbath hours!
> Solemn, yet sweet, the church-bell's chime
>   Floats through their woods at morn;
> All other sounds, in that still time,
>   Of breeze and leaf are born.
>
> The cottage homes of England!
>   By thousands on her plains,
> They are smiling o'er the silvery brooks,
>   And round the hamlet fanes.
> Through glowing orchards forth they peep.
>   Each from its nook of leaves;
> And fearless there the lowly sleep,
>   As the bird beneath their eaves.
>
> The free fair homes of England!
>   Long, long, in hut and hall,

May hearts of native proof be reared
  To guard each hallowed wall!
And green for ever be the groves,
  And bright the flowery sod,
Where first the child's glad spirit loves
  Its country and its God!

This poem endorses as "natural" the maintenance of a hierarchical class system: the stately home is identified with its "ancestral trees," the cottage is indistinguishable from the orchard through which it peeks. Freedom is here equated with the preservation of one's allotted position in God's ordained social order, from stately manor down to humblest cottage. The homes of England, moreover, are explicitly patriarchal, as Hemans' reverent portrait in *A Father reading the Bible* makes clear. Hemans here endorses Burke's conservative political model of good government as the preservation of "our little platoon," of a nuclear English family controlled by the authority of "canonized forefathers." She consciously reinscribes an established social order: her lips, like those of the "merry" homes, "move tunefully along/ Some glorious page of old," speaking an already-written text. Although she begins by invoking a threat against these homes—"Where's the coward that would not dare/ To fight for such a land?" (an epigraph from Scott's *Marmion*)—the sources of danger are unnamed, leaving the reader to speculate that they may lie not only *outside* these homes (in the social unrest of crime, poverty, industrialization, foreign wars) but also *within*, inherent in the very hierarchy the poem celebrates.

Affirming the enduring value of the patriarchal family, Hemans enrolled the leading male poets of her time within this domestic ideology. In *To Wordsworth*, she described the poet of nature and solitary walks as the poet who fused the voices of hills, gardens, hearths and graveyards into a single "spring of living water," an enduring domesticity. As she wrote to her friend, Maria Jewsbury, after reading Wordsworth's *Miscellaneous Poems*, Wordsworth is "the true *Poet of Home*, and of all the lofty feelings which have their root in the soil of home affections" (Chorley I:141).

Again and again in Hemans' poetry, wandering narrators yearn for home, for the love they knew as children gathered round their mothers' knee. The Spaniard exiled to North America by Philip the Second in what Hemans considered her best work, *The Forest Sanctuary* (1825), begins with an agonized cry for "the voices of my home!—I hear them still." The wanderer in *The Two Homes* dreams of a home "Far o'er the deserts and the tombs away;/ T'is where *I*, too, am loved with love undying,/ And fond hearts wait my step. . . ." And the young female protagonist of *The Sicilian Captive* literally dies of a broken heart after singing a lay of her native land, a song that ends with her willed release: "I break my chain—I come/ To dwell a viewless thing, yet blest—in thy sweet air, my home!"

These three examples point to the darker countercurrent in Hemans' poetry, to what her contemporary admirers called her "tender melancholy." Dugald Stewart claimed that his admiration for Hemans' poetry "was mingled with regret that she so generally made choice of melancholy subjects" and once sent her a message expressing his wish

> that she would employ her fine talents in giving more consolatory views of the ways of Providence, thus infusing comfort and cheer into the bosoms of her readers, in a spirit of Christian philosophy, which, he thought, would be more consonant with the pious mind and loving heart displayed in every line she wrote, than dwelling on what was painful and depressing, however beautifully and touchingly such subjects might be treated of. (Rossetti 375n)

For even as Hemans consistently represents the home as an earthly paradise, she constructs this home as *absent*. *The Two Homes* immediately contrasts the present happy home to the forever-lost home. In her poetry, the idyllic homes of England are usually *far away*, as in *The Exile's Dirge*, or *abandoned* by their inhabitants, as in *The Deserted House*, or *rejected* by the protagonist, as in *Come Home*, or—most often—*annihilated by death*, as in *The Graves of a Household*.

This last poem, one of Hemans' best known works, was a direct response to the death of her younger brother, Claude Scott Browne, at Kingston, Upper Canada, in 1821.[29]

They grew in beauty side by side,
  They filled one home with glee;—
Their graves are scattered far and wide,
  By mount, and stream, and sea.

The same fond mother bent at night
  O'er each fair sleeping brow:
She had each folded flower in sight—
  Where are those dreamers now?

One, 'midst the forest of the West,
  By a dark stream is laid—
The Indian knows his place of rest,
  Far in the cedar shade.

The sea, the blue lone sea, hath one—
  He lies where pearls lie deep,
He was the loved of all, yet none
  O'er his low bed may weep.

One sleeps where southern vines are drest
  Above the noble slain:
He wrapt his colours round his breast
  On a blood-red field of Spain.

And one—o'er *her* the myrtle showers
  Its leaves, by soft winds fanned;
She faded 'midst Italian flowers—
  The last of that bright band.

And parted thus they rest, who played
  Beneath the same green tree;
Whose voices mingled as they prayed
  Around one parent knee!

They that with smiles lit up the hall,
  And cheered with song the hearth!—
Alas, for love! if *thou* wert all,
  And nought beyond, O Earth!

This poem stages the dispersal of the home, defining the disparate locations into which it has fragmented. Hemans thus exposes the fictiveness of the very category she valorizes—the home—by consigning it to the genre of the memorial. For if the poem creates the gleeful home only to memorialize it, to define it as always already lost, it effectively creates a fiction of the private sphere for the public domain. The final lines reveal the problematic status of Hemans' domestic ideology, the undermining possibility registered in the word "if." For if domestic love is all, as Hemans' poetry repeatedly insists, then the destruction of that love leaves life without purpose and meaning. The reference to an undefined something beyond earth is here voided into "nought." And if *thou* refers to earth itself, the message is even bleaker: if there is nothing beyond the physical universe, if we are nought but material, earthly bodies, then love *must* die. Like Landon, Hemans questions the relevance of a Christian afterlife to a woman whose love must be expressed through the body. This doubt is underscored by the poem that concluded this volume, *Fairy Favours*, in which the narrator explicitly renounces the gift of immortality: "No gift be mine that aside would turn/ The human love for whose founts I yearn."

The precarious status of the domestic sphere is troped visually as well as discursively in Hemans' poetry. She frequently employed the image of the circle as the constitutive figure for the desired home. The cottage homes of England smile *round* the hamlet fanes; parents and children gather "*Around* their hearths by night"; the children's voices mingle "as they prayed/ *Around* one parent knee" (my emphases). Ideally, the home—the family circle—is "filled," as at the beginning of *The Graves of a Household*, and specifically "filled with glee." But more often, the circles in Hemans' poetry are empty, a "nought," a zero.

Time and space inevitably intervene between the earthly paradise of home and the position of the narrator articulated both in Hemans' poetry and in her private letters: home becomes a paradise lost that can never be regained, a place which cries out to the prodigal, as in *The Voice of Home to the Prodigal*, but to which the prodigal never returns. Hemans' letters and manuscript notes frequently comment on the breaking up of her own home. Her sister's marriage in 1828 caused Felicia Hemans to cry out to Joanna Baillie, "O how many deaths there are in the world for the affections!" (Chorley I:122). Her mother's death on January 11, 1827, was a blow from which Felicia Hemans never fully recovered; her health declined steadily from that point until her death seven years later. Calling herself an "orphan" to whom fame can mean nothing (Chorley I:191), in spite of the devotion of her five sons, at the age of 35 Felicia Hemans defined herself to Mary Mitford as

> a drooping creature, for months ill, and suffering much from the dispersion of a little band of brothers and sisters, among whom I had lived, and who are now all scattered, and strange as it may seem to say, I am now for the first time in my life holding the *reins of government*, independent, managing a household myself; and I never liked any thing less than "*ce triste empire de soi-même.*" (Chorley I:190)

Summing up her vision of home in her journal, Hemans connected the word with "all that it breathes of tenderness and sadness" (Chorley II:64):

> Our home!—what images are brought before us by that one word! The meeting of cordial smiles, and the gathering round the evening hearth, and the interchange of thoughts in kindly words, and the glance of eyes to which our hearts lie open as the day;— there is the true "City of Refuge";—where are we to turn when it is shut from us or changed? Who ever thought his home could change? And yet those calm and deep, and still delights, over which the world seems to have no breath of power, they too are like the beautiful summer clouds, tranquil as if fixed to sleep for ever in the pure azure of the skies, yet all the while melting from us, though imperceptibly "passing away!" (Hughes I:112)

Hemans' affirmation of domestic felicity is constantly posed against a melancholic emphasis upon its temporal mutability. Even more destructive forces than the passage of time threaten the stability of the domestic sphere in Hemans' poetry. The success of a domestic ideology depends upon a historically lived experience of family loyalty, of mutual parental, filial and sibling affection and support. Numerous poems in Hemans' canon, especially those published in *Songs of the Affections* in 1830, assert the existence of such familial bonds. Here are recorded a son's love for his father (in *The Return* and *Bernardo del Carpio*), a brother's love for his brother (in *The King of Arragon's Lament for his Brother* and *The Message to the Dead*), a sister's love for a sister (in *The Sisters of Scio*), and above all, a mother's love for her child (in *The Tomb of Madame Langhans* and *The Dreaming Child*). Sometimes these bonds are cemented only in death, as in *The Meeting of the Brothers* where two brothers, long separated into opposing military camps, embrace each other as they lie dying side by side on the battlefield.

Yet equally many of Hemans' poems implicitly or explicitly acknowledge that sons do not always love their fathers, nor brothers their siblings, nor even mothers their daughters. The speaker of *Kindred Hearts* begins by warning the reader, "ask not, hope thou not too much/ Of sympathy below," recognizing that "It may be that thy brother's eye/ Sees not as thine," and concludes that "Never to mortals given" are

> . . . those bonds all perfect made
> Wherein bright spirits blend
> Like sister flowers of one sweet shade,
> With the same breeze that bend.

And *The Forsaken Heart* records that

Alas! the brother knows not now when falls the sister's tears!
One haply revels at the feast, while one may droop alone:
For broken is the household chain, the bright fire quenched and
　gone!

Most destructive of the ideology Hemans espoused is the possibility that a mother could abandon her daughter, as does *The Lady of
the Castle* when she elopes with her lover. Here, the mother eventually returns in shame to her daughter, only to die of guilt at their
meeting. Written shortly after her mother's death (Chorley I:106),
this poem reflects Hemans' desperate desire to recuperate her ideology of maternal love and the domestic affections, even in the face
of her intellectual recognition of its possible fictiveness. It is Hemans' knowledge of the human capacity to betray the domestic affections that produces the overriding tone of loss and grief in her
poetry of domesticity, her tendency to dwell, as her first biographer
put it, "a little too exclusively upon the farewells and regrets of
life—upon the finer natures broken in pieces by contact with a
mercenary and scornful world" (Chorley I:36). Commenting on her
own poem, *Fairy Favours*, Hemans remarked more perceptively,

It is, indeed, filled with my own true and ever yearning feeling;
that longing for more affection, more confidence, more entire interchange of thought, than I am ever likely to meet with. (Hughes
I:134–5)

The complex dialogue between ideology and historical experience that characterizes Hemans' best poetry appears again in the
representations of the nature and roles of women put forth in her
Records of Woman (1828), the work by which she was "most univer-
sally known" (Chorley I:103). Here again, Hemans idealizes the
woman who is committed above all to an enduring love, either for
an adored man or for her family. Such female devotion is depicted
as far more valuable than either fame or artistic achievement. In
Joan of Arc in Rheims, Joan cares little for her fame or military success, eagerly turning away from the throngs of her admirers to embrace her father and brothers. Properzia Rossi, a Bolognese sculp-
tor and poet, insists that her artistic gifts and fame are "worthless,"
entirely without value, in comparison to a requited love; she will
therefore die, a "forsaken Ariadne," since her love for a Roman
knight is not returned. Throughout her *Records of Woman*, Hemans
insists that a woman's love is greater than a man's love can ever be.
When both father and brother have forgotten the young warrior

Aymer, still the peasant girl of the Rhone continues to deck his grave with flowers, until she dies of a broken heart. Many poems passionately celebrate the enduring love of a mother for her child, most powerfully in *Madeline* and *The Memorial Pillar*. But even a mother's love for her children finally takes second place to a woman's fierce commitment to a beloved husband, as in *The Indian Woman's Death-Song*, in which an abandoned wife rows both herself and the infant at her breast over a fatal waterfall.

Even as she celebrates female love, devotion and self-sacrifice, Hemans acknowledges the futility of these feminine commitments. In *Records of Woman*, almost all of Hemans' heroines are either *separated from* those they love, or express a love that is *unrequited*. Arabella Stuart is in prison and can never rejoin her husband William Seymour; the groom of the Bride of the Greek Isle has been killed by pirates; Gertrude's husband is tortured to death before her eyes; Imelda's lover is assassinated by her brothers; Edith's husband has been killed by American Indians; Maimuna's son is murdered in *The Indian City;* both Pauline and the daughter she tried to save are burned to death; and the memorial pillar records the final parting of Ann, Countess Dowager of Pembroke, and her mother. For Hemans, all female love finally becomes nought but a memorial, the sign of something lost, of something that no longer exists.

If not separated forever from their beloved, these women love men who do not love them. Properzia's love for the Roman Knight is unrequited, as are Constanzia's and the peasant girl's; while the husbands of both the Indian Woman and Juana, wife of Philip the Handsome, have abandoned or neglected them. For all these women, their love, as Hemans concludes *The Peasant Girl of the Rhone*, is "love in death." At the narrative level in Hemans' poetry, domestic and passionate love cannot be kept separate from death. Even in *Madeline—A Domestic Tale*, the survival of what Hemans calls the "true and perfect love" between Madeline and her mother is possible only because the husband who carried Madeline away from her childhood home has died, permitting Madeline to return to her mother's arms.

Madeline, which is arguably the most autobiographical poem in this self-revealing volume,[30] alerts us to the tension between ideology and history in Hemans' construction of her self as the icon of domesticity. Although Hemans consistently celebrated, and explicitly advocated, the enduring love of a wife for her husband, she was not able to live such a love. When Fèlicia Dorothea Browne was eighteen, in the summer of 1812, she married the man she had loved for three years, Captain Alfred Hemans of the 4th or King's Own Regiment, a survivor of the Peninsular Campaign who had served at Corunna and in the Walcheren expedition and a man "by no means destitute of advantages, either of person or education" (Hughes I:11). Within the next six years she bore him five sons. Shortly before the birth of his last son, Captain Hemans set sail for Italy where he lived for the rest of his life. He never returned to England and Felicia never visited him in Italy (although his two eldest sons did so). They corresponded concerning the education of their sons, but when Felicia offered to join him in Italy after the death of her mother, he rejected her offer.[31] Felicia Hemans never saw her husband again.

The reasons for this abrupt and final separation are obscure. Captain Hemans publically claimed that his health made it necessary for him to live in a warmer climate; her sister's *Memoir* mysteriously acknowledged that "such were not the only reasons which led to this divided course," a rupture that placed Felicia Hemans in "a position so painful, as must ever be that of a woman for whom the most sacred of ties is thus virtually broken" (Hughes I:29). Felicia Hemans herself, although she never publically complained of her husband,[32] always considered this event a tragedy, confessing to Dugald Stewart that "a cloud hung over her life which she could not always rise above" (Rossetti 375n). She frequently quoted Madame L'Espinasse when confronted with the vexations of daily life, "*Un grand chagrin tue toute le reste*" (Hughes I:263).

As with Landon, later editors and critics have speculated about the cause of this marital separation. William Michael Rossetti suggested that something may have been lacking in "the marital deportment of the Captain" (Rossetti xv), causing his continuously pregnant wife a chagrin more of shame than sorrow. Rossetti also noted that Felicia Hemans seems to have preferred her mother's company to that of her husband:

> it may perhaps be inferred, in a general way, that the family affections of daughter and mother were more dominant and vivid in Mrs. Hemans than conjugal love: her intense feeling of the sacredness of home, which it would be both idle and perverse to contest, may have set before her, as more binding and imperative, the duties of service to her own mother, and of guidance to her own children, than the more equal, passionate, and in some sense self-indulgent relation between wife and husband. (Rossetti xv)

Peter Trinder posits a more general lack of compatibility between Felicia Hemans and her husband, citing her friend Mary Howitt's Journal entry for July 18, 1827, in which Mrs. Howitt notes, "I have just received a letter from Mrs Hemans. She congratulates me, I can fancy, with a mournful reference to herself, in possessing in a husband a kindred spirit and a friend."[33] Rose Lawrence, a close friend of Felicia Hemans during her three years in Wavertree, Liverpool, also attributed the separation to an "utter incompatibility of habits and feelings."[34]

Whatever the cause of the failure of her marriage, Hemans' continuing poetic endorsement of a woman's primary love for and enduring devotion to her husband stood in stark contrast to her own domestic experience.[35] Her anguished sense of this unresolvable contradiction may explain her obsession, in her final years, with a particular German legend as the subject of a long poem, a subject she was forced to abandon, her biographer tells us, "in consequence of the injurious influence its contemplation exercised upon a frame so fragile as hers" (Chorley II:4). This legend, he explains,

> was the tale of an enchantress, who, to win and secure the love of a mortal, sacrifices one of her supernatural gifts of power after another:—her wand, first, then her magic girdle, then the talismanic diadem she wears,—last of all, her immortality. She is repaid by satiety—neglect—desertion. (Chorley II:4)

Here again, the image of the empty circle resurfaces: the talismanic diadem, meant to be filled by a woman's head and mind and even supernatural power, is emptied, even of life itself.

In public, Hemans reconciled the tension between her poetic commitment to the domestic realm and the failure of her marriage by adopting the congenial position of the patiently suffering, neglected wife. As William Wordsworth commented after her death,

> I remember her . . . above all, for her delicate and irreproachable conduct during her long separation from an unfeeling husband, whom she had been led to marry from the romantic notions of inexperienced youth. Upon this husband I never heard her cast the least reproach, nor did I ever hear her even name him, though she did not wholly forbear to touch upon her domestic position; but never so as that any fault could be found with her manner of adverting to it.[36]

Accepting her public self-construction, her first biographer, Henry Chorley, refused to discuss the details of her private life, "purposely refraining from touching upon any such details of the delicate circumstances of her domestic life, as were not necessary to the illustrations of her literary career" (Chorley, vii). Thus Hemans, like Landon, was prevented from uttering her own private voice: "delicate circumstances" prevented her, just as Chorley's title, *Memorials of Mrs. Hemans,* denied her the authoritative self accorded by the genre of biography, instead obscuring her self by confining it within the elegiac, and consciously fictive, mode of the "memorial."

If William Michael Rossetti was right—and I think he was—that for Felicia Hemans, mother-daughter love was more intense, enduring, and rewarding than heterosexual love,[37] we must look more closely at what happens to maternal love in her poetry. Specifically, we must consider her most intensely felt, her most thickly textured, and hence her finest literary work,[38] her verse drama *The Siege of Valencia* (1823). For it is here that Hemans stages her most powerful dialogue between the public and the private spheres, testing her domestic ideology against the social realm of history.

Set in the sixteenth century, *The Siege of Valencia* pits Hemans' ideology of the domestic affections directly against a second set of values which she had embraced as a child and which continued to inspire her poetry, a masculine code of military glory and individual heroism. Although less deeply felt than her commitment to the home, medieval concepts of knightly honor and heroic virtue had stimulated Hemans' imagination ever since she had avidly read the *Song of the Cid* as a girl and had followed her brother's and Captain Hemans' exploits in the Peninsular Campaign. Many of her poems commemorate the chivalric deeds of famous warriors: *The Troubadour and Richard Coeur de Lion, The Death of Conradin, Songs of the Cid,* and her tragic drama, *The Vespers of Palermo,* to name only the most important. All these poems endorse the doctrine of the separate spheres, representing women as purifying and sustaining the private realm while men seek glory and noble conquest in the public realm.

In *The Siege of Valencia,* Hemans deliberately collapses the boundaries between the private and the public spheres. As her first biographer recognized, the story of *The Siege of Valencia*—"a thrilling conflict between maternal love and the inflexible spirit of chivalrous honor—afforded to [Hemans] an admirable opportunity of giving utterance to the two master interests of her mind" (Chorley I:90). When the private and the public come into direct conflict in Hemans' drama, when maternal love fights against a heroic commitment to a religious and nationalist cause, the domestic ideol-

ogy on which Hemans' poetry is grounded both triumphs and collapses.

Under siege by Muslim Moors, the Christian city of Valencia is
on the verge of defeat, despite the endurance and valor of its governor, Gonzalez. Significantly, Hemans sets her play within a
bounded circle, in a space where the public and the private spheres
are overlaid: a walled city under siege, where the soldier and the
mother must occupy the same enclosed terrain. The play opens
with the announcement that Abdullah, the leader of the Moorish
army, has captured the two still-living sons of Gonzalez, whom he
is holding as ransom for the city; they will be executed the following morning unless the city is surrendered. Invoking Abraham's
sacrifice of Isaac, Gonzalez, loyal to his King and his God, will not
submit and courageously prepares to witness the murder of his
young sons from the walls of Valencia, saying "We have but/ To bow
the head in silence, when Heaven's voice/ Calls back the things we
love" (481).

Gonzalez' wife Elmina cannot bear to see her beloved children
die, and in a searing outcry, fiercely tries to persuade Gonzalez to
save his sons. Articulating Hemans' own passionate devotion to her
five sons, Elmina insists that Gonzalez can know nothing of genuine love:

> . . . There is none,
> In all this cold and hollow world, no fount
> Of deep, strong, deathless love, save that within
> A mother's heart.—It is but pride, wherewith
> To his fair son the father's eye doth turn,
> Watching his growth. Ay, on the boy he looks,
> The bright glad creature springing in his path,
> But as the heir of his great name, the young
> And stately tree, whose rising strength ere long
> Shall bear his trophies well.—And this is love!
> This is *man's* love!
>
> (481)

The play proceeds as a contest between mother and father for the
loyalty of their children, a contest that represents the fundamental
conflict between a domestic ideology and a public code that valorizes reputation and fame above all. Remembering her devoted care
of her sons, articulating an ethic of care in the face of Gonzalez'
stern ethic of justice, Elmina insists that if her husband sacrifices
his sons, he will be left with nothing but "shadows—dim phantoms

from ancestral tombs" and an "utter desolation" that will be peopled only by "immortal *fame!*/ Fame to the sick of heart!" (482). Significantly, this counter-narrative to the story of Abraham and Isaac invoked by Gonzalez, this narrative of maternal love, can be heard in the public realm only as a kind of madness:—"my brain grows wild" (479), cries Elmina.

What is at stake here is the control of language itself. Gonzalez writes the sacrifice of his sons as honor, heroism and "steadfastness" (477); his daughter Ximena becomes his "heroic child" when she refuses to kneel beside her mother in a plea for her brothers' lives. Ximena thus dons the "breastplate" of masculinity, "Courage and faith and generous constancy" (480), assuming the role allotted to women in *Le Cid,* that of devotion to the male cause of honor and glory. But Elmina writes this sacrifice as cruelty, as meaningless destruction. Gonzalez has destroyed the very meaning of the word Father, she insists:

> . . . he beneath whose eye their childhood grew,
> And in whose paths they sported, and whose ear
> From their first lisping accents caught the sound
> Of that word—*Father*—once a name of love—
> Is—Men shall call him *steadfast.*
>
>   (498)

Elmina here refuses the masculine construction of her domestic affections as "betrayal," asserting instead the universal validity of love.

Gonzalez refuses to yield and in her desperate agony, Elmina seeks help elsewhere. The play proceeds as a powerful critique of the patriarchal code of heroism. Gonzalez is portrayed as inflexible and unfeeling. The priest Father Hernandez to whom Elmina turns is even more adamant that a Christian city cannot be sacrificed to a heathen faith. While a Christian audience might sympathize with Hernandez' position, it is undercut by his excessively harsh response to Elmina's agony:

> And who are *thou*, that, in the littleness
> Of thine own selfish purpose, wouldst set bounds
> To the free current of all noble thought
> And generous action, bidding its bright waves
> Be stayed, and flow no further? . . .

Thy children too shall perish, and I say
It shall be well.

(487, 488)

Hernandez' righteous indignation is further undercut by the revelation that he, a former soldier and a father, actually killed his only
son in a battle in which they fought on opposite sides. Hernandez
thus stakes out the opposite construction of "home" within the
play: for Hernandez, home is not the soil where domestic affections
flourish but the site of betrayal and bitterness, the place where
sons reject fathers, "the home of my despair" (491). Hernandez here
articulates a "masculine" contempt for domesticity, but the dramatic validity of his position is undermined when we learn that his
son left him because he loved a woman, a Moorish maid, even more
than his father. His son died "because" he was loyal to the domestic
affections, killed by the father who denied them.

This masculine code is further called into question by the fact
that everyone to whom Elmina speaks acknowledges that the city
will fall within a few days in any case, so widespread is disease and
so desperately short are food and water. She persuasively argues
that to yield the city will save not only the lives of her two sons but
also those of her daughter and the few remaining citizens.

Through the first half of the play, our sympathies are entirely
with Elmina, who is motivated by a selfless devotion to her children. Risking her life, she dares to venture into the enemy camp, to
plead with Abdullah to spare her sons in the name of a mother's
love she constructs as universal:

. . . In your own land
Doth no fond mother, from the tents beneath
Your native palms, look o'er the deserts out,
To greet your homeward step? You have not yet
Forgot so utterly her patient love;—
For is not woman's in all climes the same?

(498)

Abdullah, of course, like Gonzalez, stands resolute in his commitment to military victory, regarding the lives of children as of no
greater value than the leaves of a tree, broken off in passing. Having
drawn the contrast between the public and the private realms as
starkly as possible, having aligned domesticity with nature itself,
Hemans now shows that the doctrine of the separate spheres can-

not survive in a nature divided against itself. The two spheres here not only intersect but cancel each other out. In the Moorish camp Elmina is confronted by her fifteen-year-old son Alphonse who begs her not to shame his name and honor by accepting Abdullah's treacherous terms, even as her youngest son rushes to his mother in tears, crying to her to save him. Loyal above all to her children, Elmina in despair finally agrees to open the gates of Valencia to Abdullah that night. Significantly, this triumph of the domestic affections over masculine honor cannot be staged in public; Elmina's commitment to Abdullah takes place offstage, in a private domestic space that in this play now becomes increasingly invisible.

After her betrayal of the city, the play shifts its focus to the public realm, calling into question Elmina's maternal devotion. Divided by her conflicting love for her sons and for her husband, Elmina finally confesses to Gonzalez, and the gate is secured. Her daughter Ximena rejects her mother and instead unites with her father's cause, raising the banner of the Cid, rousing the exhausted citizens to one last attack on the Moorish army to rescue her brothers, only to die, heartbroken, when her lover is killed in the ensuing battle. The death of Ximena suggests that women survive no better in the public than in the private realm: the female warrior not killed in battle will be killed by her own divided heart, a heart broken by the very division between the public and the private that the play is staging.

Gonzalez, after witnessing the execution of Alphonse, leads the Spanish charge against Abdullah in a vain attempt to save his youngest son, who dies during the charge in which Gonzalez receives his death-wound. In Hemans' rewriting of Judaeo-Christian theology, God does not prevent the sacrifice of Isaac; the Christian cross and the Moorish crescent are equally the emblem of human blood, of sacrifice. Nonetheless, on his deathbed, Gonzalez is rewarded with a *deus ex machina*, the last-minute arrival of reinforcements led by the King of Castile and the rout of the Moorish army. The play ends as Elmina, the only one of her family left alive, accompanies the noble funerals of her husband and daughter:

> . . . I follow thee
> With an unfaltering and a lofty step,
> To that last home of glory. She that wears
> In her deep heart the memory of thy love,
> Shall thence draw strength for all things, till the God
> Whose hand around her hath unpeopled earth,

Looking upon her still and chastened soul,
Call it once more to thine!

(530)

At the generic level, this verse drama has enacted a wrenching reinscription of domestic tragedy within heroic tragedy: the sacrifices of Gonzalez and Ximinez are eulogized, the deaths of Alphonse and his brother Carlos deemed necessary to save this Christian city from heathen. Individual heroism, military glory, and fame are the values overtly celebrated at the end of the play.

But this seeming resolution of the conflict between masculine heroism and feminine maternal love is called into question by the fact that, at the end of the play, only Elmina remains alive. William Michael Rossetti read her survival as a punishment:

> death would in fact have been mercy to Elmina, and would have left her undistinguished from the others, and untouched by any retribution: survival, mourning, and self-discipline are the only chastisement in which a poetic justice, in its higher conception, could be expressed. (Rossetti xix)

But Rossetti ignores what Elmina finally says, that she follows a God who, like his priest Hernandez, has "unpeopled earth" and that in the face of such universal annihilation, she is sustained only by "the memory" of love. Elmina thus reminds us that what the public realm, the state, finally displays, what we actually see on the stage, are but corpses.

Moreover, there is a final irony in what survives: Elmina remains as the voice of "memorialization," the voice of the grave. And what she recalls is not fame but love—the love of Gonzalez for his wife and hers for him, the love of Elmina for her children and theirs for her—this alone can sustain her life. The ending of the play visually represents what Elmina has predicted all along: "the desolate space of rooted-up affections" (478), "immortal . . . fame to the sick of heart," and "a gorgeous robe,/ A crown of victory, unto him that dies/ In the burning waste" (482)—another emptied circle.

We can thus read Elmina's survival as an ironic affirmation of Hemans' domestic ideology, the triumph of maternal love over a futile heroism. For the noble name which Gonzalez has fought to preserve unsullied has died with him. Elmina is the true heroine, the noble and self-sacrificing woman who has struggled only to save those she most intensely loves: the play is finally the story of *her* suffering, *her* tragedy—the tragedy of a woman whose "feminine" love and virtue has been rejected by a patriarchal state and religion.

Hemans' drama thus exposes the emptiness at the core of her domestic ideology. As Elmina bitterly cried out upon hearing of her sons' capture,

> . . . Men! Men! too much is yours
> Of vantage; ye that with a sound, a breath,
> A shadow, thus can fill the desolate space
> Of rooted-up affections, o'er whose void
> Our yearning hearts must wither!—So it is,
> Dominion must be won!
>
> (478)

When the heroic masculine code of the public sphere demands the sacrifice of the private domestic affections, the female is powerless to prevent it. But man's "dominion" is finally over an empty circle, a "cold void" (482), to which he can give no new life. When the public sphere takes control of the private, both realms are destroyed.

Equally, when the domestic affections attempt to govern the actions of the public realm, they prove futile and self-destructive, as Hemans suggested in her most famous poem, *Casabianca:*

> The boy stood on the burning deck
>   Whence all but he had fled;
> The flame that lit the battle's wreck
>   Shone round him o'er the dead.
>
> Yet beautiful and bright he stood,
>   As born to rule the storm—
> A creature of heroic blood,
>   A proud, though child-like form.
>
> The flames rolled on—he would not go.
>   Without his father's word;
> That father, faint in death below,
>   His voice no longer heard.
>
> (373)

The poem presents an attempt to fuse the values of the domestic and the heroic: Giacomo Casabianca, a noble ten-year-old boy, remains fiercely loyal simultaneously to his father and to his assigned military post. But his father, Louis de Casabianca, the Admiral of the French flagship *Orient*, lies unconscious, unable to hear the boy's plea to be released from his "lone post of death," unable to sustain through war the bonds of the domestic affections. And in an act of futile and meaningless heroism, the boy remains upon the burning deck long after his ship has been abandoned in the Battle of the Nile of 1798, until the exploding gunpowder kills him. Here the attempt to sustain filial fidelity in the midst of warfare is not only futile, but counterproductive: the boy would have lived had he not obeyed his father. "The noblest thing which perished there" was perhaps not Casabianca's "young faithful heart" so much as the domestic values to which that heart foolishly adhered, values rendered nugatory in the public realm.

Everywhere Hemans' celebration of home is complicated by her recognition that domestic felicity may be merely a fiction: lost in the past, or destroyed in the present by the refusal of individual family members to sustain its affectional bonds, or relentlessly sacrificed to a more powerful masculine code of individual ambition and personal fame. Having accepted her culture's hegemonic inscription of the woman within the domestic sphere, Hemans' poetry subtly and painfully explored the ways in which that construction of gender finally collapses upon itself, bringing nothing but suffering, and the void of nothingness, to both women and men. Hemans' poetry thus exhausts—both in the sense of thoroughly investigating, finding the limits of, and in the sense of using up, emptying out—the very domestic ideology it espouses.

Perhaps this explains Hemans' enormous popularity with her peers. We should not assume that the ideological collapse I have been describing was invisible to her contemporaries. They too emphasized her pervasive melancholy, her elegiac tone, her obsession with suffering and death. Some critics attempted to locate this collapse wholly within a construction of sexual difference. They defined her consciousness of loss, of a lack of emotional fulfillment on this earth, as a peculiarly *feminine* attribute. As Rossetti concluded, Hemans' poetry is:

> not only "feminine" poetry ... but also "female" poetry: besides exhibiting the fineness and charm of womanhood, it has the monotone of mere sex. Mrs. Hemans has that love of good and horror of evil which characterize a scrupulous female mind; and which we may most rightly praise without concluding that they favour poetical robustness, or even perfection in literary form. (Rossetti xxvii)[39]

Setting aside Rossetti's gender politics (his implicit claim that masculine "poetical robustness" is superior to "feminine" scrupulosity), I would suggest that Hemans' popularity rested on a broader social recognition of the general truth of her vision. Perhaps both men and women in large numbers read her work, perhaps schoolchildren were asked to memorize her poems, just because this audience also mourned—or feared—the loss of the home as a haven of domestic happiness. Perhaps they too felt that the hegemonic domestic ideology Hemans espoused—her commitments to hearth and home, to the familial affections, above all to maternal love—was an ideology now in danger of permanent collapse under the double pressure of an increasingly industrialized, materialistic, competitive society and the redefinition of gender roles explicit in the texts of feminine Romanticism. Perhaps it was this very sense of loss—real or impending—that produced the violent Victorian cultural effort to separate the public from the private sphere and to inscribe the woman solely as the "angel in the house."

7

Writing the Self/Self Writing: William Wordsworth's Prelude/ *Dorothy Wordsworth's* Journals

Central to the construction of both masculine and feminine Romanticism is the conception and linguistic representation of the self. Dorothy Wordsworth's Alfoxden and Grasmere Journals are exceptionally revealing autobiographical self-writing. And yet several recent readers of these Journals have described Dorothy as a person without a self or identity. Margaret Homans insists that her "poetic identity" was silenced by her adherence to her brother's equation of unspeaking nature with the female; James Holt Mc-Gavran, Jr., claims that in her relations with her brother she paid the "terrible price" of "the loss of any firm sense of personal identity"; and even Susan Levin's far more insightful and complex rendering of Dorothy Wordsworth's subjectivity finally describes her "self" as precarious, vulnerable, ambivalent, as a "negative center" whose writing is primarily characterized by gestures of "refusal."[1] Why has Dorothy Wordsworth's self so often been read as either repressed or inadequate, her writing defined as the failure to achieve narrative representation of a distinct subjectivity? Is this the only, or even the most appropriate, way to read her *Journals?* To answer these questions, we must consider both the way in which the self was constructed in the Romantic period, and the role played by autobiography in culturally reinforcing this particular Romantic self.

Writing the Self

Masculine Romanticism has traditionally been identified with the assertion of a self that is unified, unique, enduring, capable of initiating activity, and above all aware of itself as a self. The construction of such self-consciousness was the project of one of the most influential literary autobiographies ever written, William Wordsworth's *The Prelude*. Responding to Locke's sceptical insistence that since human consciousness is mutable, constantly receiving new sensations and ideas, so also must human identity be discontinuous, Wordsworth attempted to represent a unitary self that is maintained over time by the activity of memory, and to show that this self or "soul" is defined, not by the body and its sensory experience, but by the human mind, by the growth of consciousness. In the last decade, however, deconstructive critics, most notably Paul de Man and those influenced by his work, have rightly argued that Wordsworth's project was undercut by his own recognition that language can never be more than an alienating "garment," can never be "the air we breathe." They have tracked the way images of an achieved unitary self give way in *The Prelude* to figures of effacement and defacement, to images of a lost boy, a self "bewildered and engulfed," and the "broken windings" of the poet's path.[2]

However fragile and tenuous the self linguistically constructed in *The Prelude*, the poem's overt rhetorical argument and structure locate it, as Meyer Abrams argued, within the genre of "crisis autobiography," a secularization of seventeenth- and eighteenth-century religious autobiographies grounded in a narrative of confession and conversion, of retrospection and introspection, based on the literary model of St. Augustine's *Confessions*.[3] It tells the story of Wordsworth's fall and possible (but never certain) redemption. Or more precisely, as Herbert Lindenberger argued,[4] Wordsworth constructs his past as a series of moments in which he experienced a separation from all that he felt to be most sacred and from which he was restored, however momentarily, to a sense of wholeness and well-being. The most traumatic episodes for Wordsworth are stealing the boat on Lake Ullswater, which left him, he claimed, with a sense of a power in Nature outside of his own mind, of "huge and mighty forms that do not live/ Like living men" (I:424–5);[5] his residence at Cambridge University, during which his "imagination slept" and he was reduced to an aimless wanderer, a "floating island, an amphibious thing,/ Unsound, of spungy texture" (III:340–1); and his political commitment to the French Revolution, to an abstract theory of social justice that was denied by historical events. This last produced in Wordsworth what he portrayed as the crisis of the true believer, a radical disillusionment that resulted in an allegiance to pure reason, mathematics, and an aesthetic theory which deadened both his feelings and his ability to perceive imaginatively. But Wordsworth's falls, couched in tropes borrowed from Milton's *Paradise Lost*, are represented as potentially fortunate. As he asserts in moments of high rhetorical confidence, they have led him to an ever subtler understanding and more profound conviction of his poetic vocation, of the "one life" that flows between his mind and nature, and of the enduring coherence of his self, the tenuous bridge strung by memory over the abyss between his past existence and his present writing self, over that

> vacancy between me and those days
> Which yet have such self-presence in my mind
> That sometimes when I think of them I seem
> Two consciousnesses—conscious of myself,
> And of some other being.
>   (II:29–33)

Wordsworth bases the construction of his self or poetic identity upon a genetic, teleological model, one that establishes three developmental stages of consciousness, beginning with the unselfconsciousness of the child who experiences the external world and his own being as one ("I communed with all that I saw as something not apart from, but inherent in, my own immaterial nature"), progressing through the growing self-consciousness of the schoolboy ("more like a man/ Flying from something that he dreads, than one/ Who sought the thing he loved"), and arriving finally at the realization of the power of consciousness as such, at the achievement of that "philosophic mind" which is the "counterpart" of Nature's own creative power (XIII:88). The self thus empowered is imaged positively in many ways during the poem: as a river or stream, now visible, now hidden, that gathers force as it flows (XIII:166–80); as a circuitous path or journey that leaves home only to return, spiralling upward, at a higher level of knowledge;

as a wanderer or tourist exploring the "cabinet or wide museum" of nature and society (III:653); and as an organic growth ("Fair seed-time had my soul," I:305). Each of these tropes, of course, has negative implications that are also figured in the poem: the stream can be turned aside or dry up, the circuitous path can return only pointlessly to its own beginning, the tourist-wanderer can remain an alien, organic growth can produce mutations and monstrous abnormalities. These attempts to stage the growth of the self, and the role played by language in the construction of this subjectivity, have been fully described by numerous Wordsworth scholars, most notably Geoffrey Hartman,[6] and I need not dwell upon them longer here.

What I wish to emphasize is the way in which the self or consciousness linguistically constructed by William Wordsworth, as both the subject and the author of *The Prelude,* is not the "higher"— and potentially universal—self he dreamed of, but rather a specifically *masculine* self. This self is represented as the struggling hero of an epic autobiography in which Wordsworth asserts without irony that the growth of the poet's mind can represent the growth of the common *man.* Marlon Ross has identified the tropes of heroic quest and conquest that structure the poet's efforts in *The Prelude,* and Alan Liu has tracked the subtle discourses in which Wordsworth rhetorically envelops Napoleon's achievements within his own.[7] The goal of Wordsworth's epic quest, his "heroic argument and genuine prowess" (III:183–4), is nothing less than the triumph of the maker of the social contract, the construction of the individual who owns his own body, his own mind, his own labor, and who is free to use that body and labor as he chooses, the achievement of "Man free, man working for himself, with choice/ Of time and place, and object" (VIII:152–3). As Wordsworth enthuses, "Now I am free, enfranchis'd and at large,/ May fix my habitation where I will" (I:9–10).

Moving from the level of the rhetorical to the psychological, we can recognize with Richard Onorato the Oedipal pattern of exclusively masculine childhood development and regression that is embedded in *The Prelude.*[8] Wordsworth conceives the development of the poet's self as dependent first upon a definitive separation from the mother, imaged both as a pre-Oedipal source of primal sympathy or "first-born affinities" for the "blessed babe" and, after his own mother's death by which "I was left alone" (II:292) and "destitute" (V:259), as the "ministry of beauty and of fear" provided by a female Nature to whose "care" he was "entrusted" (V:451).

This childhood separation produces in Wordsworth a never-satisfiable desire for reunion with that originating mother. His desire, Marlon Ross has argued, is contoured by its rivalry with other males, be they powerful father figures (troped in Wordsworth's poem as either the divine creative power and authority of "God" or as numerous isolated male figures of resolution and independence—the old soldier, the blind beggar, the good shepherd) or as challenging peers (especially Coleridge, to whom *The Prelude* is anxiously addressed). This Oedipal model operates at both a psychological and a discursive level, as what Harold Bloom has called an "anxiety of influence" that produces strong misreadings of earlier prophet-poets, of Spenser, Milton and the Bible.[9] The result, announced by Wordsworth in *The Prelude* in a moment of surpassing confidence, is the construction of an autonomous poetic self that can stand alone, "remote from human life" (III:543), face to face with Nature and the poet-prophets of the past, "as I stand now,/ A sensitive, and a *creative* soul" (XI: 255–6).

This egotistical sublime, as Keats named Wordsworth's portrait of his heroic masculine self, depends upon the conventions of classical Western literary narrative: it has a beginning, a middle, and an end; it is the "story of my life" (I:667). To achieve coherence and endurance, this self or subjectivity must transcend the body and become pure mind, become a consciousness that exists only in language. It is the imagination that climactically reveals to Wordsworth not only the "glory" of his own soul, but the conviction that the "destiny" of *every* soul, its "nature" and its "home," is "with infinitude" (VI:538–9). Whether or not we as readers can accept Wordsworth's appropriation of the general or royal we in *The Prelude*, it is crucial to see that the soul or self he constructs is bodiless. Despite Wordsworth's myriad sensory interactions with nature as child and man, his minute and detailed recollections of what he saw and heard and felt, his self remains curiously disembodied—we never hear whether he is hot or cold, whether he washes himself or defecates, whether he has sexual desires or intercourse.[10] Only rarely does he mention that he eats or sleeps—and when he does, these quotidian details are either heightened into Shakespearean allusion, as when the "noise of waters" outside his hotel near Lugarno makes "innocent sleep/ Lie melancholy among weary bones" (VI:579–80), or they function to demonstrate Nature's "sterner character," that admonitory power which serves to rouse the poet's heroic efforts, as when, on the banks of Lake Como, "the stings of insects" remind the poet that

Not prostrate, overborne—as if the mind
Itself were nothing, a mean pensioner
On outward forms—did we in presence stand
Of that magnificent region.

(VI: 642–3, 666–9)

The Wordsworthian self thus becomes a Kantian transcendental ego, pure mind or reason, standing as the *spectator ab extra*, the detached observer both of Nature—that scene spread before his feet at the top of Mount Snowdon that becomes "the perfect image of a mighty Mind"—and of his own life.

. . . Anon I rose
As if on wings, and saw beneath me stretched
Vast prospect of the world which I had been,
And was; and hence this song, which like a lark
I have protracted, in the unwearied heavens
Singing. . . .

(XIII:377–82)

Deliberately denying his material physicality, even his mortality, Wordsworth represents his poetic self as pure ego, as "the mind of man," which thereby

. . . becomes
A thousand times more beautiful than the earth
On which he dwells, above this frame of things
(Which, 'mid all revolutions in the hopes
And fears of men, doth still remain unchanged)
In beauty exalted, as it is itself
Of substance and of fabric more divine.

(XIII:446–52)

Precarious indeed is this unique, unitary, transcendental subjectivity, for Wordsworth's sublime self-assurance is rendered possible, as many critics have observed,[11] only by the arduous repression of the Other in all its forms: of the mother, of Dorothy, of other people, of history, of nature, of "unknown modes of being," of that very gap or "vacancy" which divides his present from his past identity. To sustain such a divine intellect, unspeaking female earth must be first silenced, then spiritually raped (as in *Nutting*), colonized, and finally completely possessed. By the end of *The Prelude*, female Nature is not only a thousand times less beautiful than the mind of man but has even lost her gendered Otherness.

But Wordsworth's masculine control of the female remains as problematic as his possession of an enduring self. The representation of gender in *The Prelude* is more complex than I could detail in the broad overview sketched in my earlier discussion in chapter one. Wordsworth consistently genders Nature and "the earth" as female; he also assigns the feminine gender to the moon and to flowers. He specifically identifies the small or hidden aspects of Nature with Dorothy:

> thou didst plant its [my soul's] crevices with flowers,
> Hang it with shrubs that twinkle in the breeze,
> And teach the little birds to build their nests
> And warble in its chambers.
> (XIII:233–6).[12]

On the other hand, he assigns the masculine gender to the river Derwent, to the sea (I:596), and to the sun (II:175); and he appropriates the sterner dimensions of nature to his masculine self:

> My soul, too reckless of mild grace, had been
> Far longer what by Nature it was framed—
> Longer retained its countenance severe—
> A rock with torrents roaring, with the clouds
> Familiar, and a favorite of the stars. . . .
> (XIII:228–32)

The immaterial soul or mind of man thus exists in tension with material Nature. Wordsworth initially genders the mind as feminine, taught by a female Sovereign Intellect that manifests herself through the "bodily image" of earth and heaven (V:10–17). But as the poem progresses, the mind or soul is increasingly identified with an imagination gendered as neuter, a *sui generis* or "unfathered" power (VI:525–42). As the mind moves ever further away from, or above, nature, it finally becomes simultaneously masculine and feminine: "the mind/ Is *lord* and *master,* and that outward sense/ Is but the obedient servant of *her* will" (XI:270–2, italics mine).

Gender is thus rhetorically implicated in Wordsworth's philosophical and psychological struggle to establish a stable linguistic relationship between the mind and nature, to construct a masculine identity distinct from that of the mother. In the climactic ascent of Mount Snowdon, Wordsworth finally wrestles gender to the ground—only to have the repressed rise up again. Having defined

poetic genius as definitively male in Book XII, existing in productive interchange with female Nature (XII:6–14), he confidently
climbs Mount Snowdon, representing the scene before his feet and
the mighty mind of which it is an image as a neutral "it." But what
gender is creative power? When Nature exerts a domination upon
the outward face of things, that domination is gendered as feminine. But when the higher mind of the poet exercises that same
power, it is first neutered—"in the fullness of *its* strength/Made visible"(my italics)—and then, remarkably, regenerated as specifically masculine. Even Nature's power becomes masculine, the
"Brother" of the poet's imagination (XIII:89). At this moment, Nature is effectively both repressed and cannibalized by the male
poet, who now defines himself as a "sovereign" power "from the
Deity" (XIII:114, 105). "Oh, who is *he* that hath *his* whole life long/
Preserved, enlarged, this freedom in *himself?*" (XIII:120–1, my
italics). When Nature reemerges in the poem as a sexual other, she
is but "A handmaid to a nobler than herself" (XIII:240), subservient
to the masculine poetic genius.

But Wordsworth recognizes that his hold on male supremacy is
as insecure as his hold on his autonomous self. At the very end of
this poem dedicated to a revelation of the male poet's possession of
a godlike imagination "in all the might of its endowments"
(VI:528), Wordsworth acknowledges that this very imagination,
"the main essential power" which throughout *The Prelude* he has
tracked "up her way sublime" (XIII:290), is resistantly female.
Wordsworth thus reveals the stubborn Otherness of all that he has
labored so long and hard to absorb into his own identity: the ori-
ginary power of the female, of the mother, of Nature.

Wordsworth's attempt to represent an autonomous self with
clearly defined, firm ego boundaries, a self that stands alone, "un-
propped" (III:230), entirely self-sufficient and self-generating, both
unmothered and unfathered, is undercut by Wordsworth's own
slippery pronouns as a heuristic fiction, a "story." Hence the horta-
tory mode of the following:

> Here must thou be, O man,
> Strength to thyself—no helper hast thou here—
> Here keepest thou thy individual state:
> No other can divide with thee this work,
> No secondary hand can intervene
> To fashion this ability
>
> (XIII:188–93)

Although Wordsworth himself acknowledged its fictive nature, the existence of the autonomous individual self Wordsworth once so boldly claimed—"Behold me then/ Once more in Nature's presence, thus restored" (XI:392–3)—has become one of the enduring myths of modern Western culture.[13]

Wordsworth's *Prelude* rhetorically depended upon, and has been read by Meyer Abrams and many others as giving additional authority to, the historical emergence of the individual (male) self of social contract theory and economic capitalism, that "every Man" who, in Locke's famous formulation, "has a *Property* in his own *Person.*"[14] More important, Abrams' influential way of reading *The Prelude* through the 1960s and '70s helped to shape the genre of literary autobiography, to determine the linguistic conventions by which the viable self has been represented in contemporary critical discourse. Although studies of autobiography as a genre have tended to focus on works in prose, taking as seminal texts Augustine's *Confessions,* Rousseau's *Confessions* and Goethe's *Dichtung und Wahrheit, The Prelude* has been hailed as the first work to present the writing of a single man's life within the conventions of the classical epic, thus elevating the genre of autobiography to the highest aesthetic status.

Contemporary theorists of autobiography have wrestled with the very problems that Wordsworth foregrounded in his poem, the uncertain relation between the self-as-lived and the self-as-imagined, between the referential and the written self, the gap or vacancy between "two consciousnesses." If the writing self can remember how it felt but what it felt remember not, to what degree can it claim referential authority for its memories? To what degree is the written self always already a metaphor, in James Olney's phrase?[15]

Even as they debate whether an autobiography can claim a special truth status, or whether it is only a literary fiction,[16] too many of the leading theorists of autobiography have assumed that the self constructed either by memory or by figurative language is finally unified, coherent, and capable of agency. Georges Gusdorf argued that autobiography arose in the eighteenth century out of a combined Christian and Romantic belief in the value and uniqueness of the individual life. Structurally, he asserted, autobiography "requires a man to take a distance with regard to himself in order to reconstitute himself in the focus of his special unity and identity across time" and is thus "a second reading of experience," one that "is truer than the first because it adds to experience itself consciousness of it."[17] Explicit in Gusdorf's influential formulation of the genre is the assumption that the self so reconstituted will express "a complete and coherent" image of "inmost being," what Gusdorf calls "my destiny"; implicit in his formulation is a capitalist ideology that defines value in terms of material possession—"In narrating my life," Gusdorf claims, "I give witness of myself even from beyond my death and so can preserve this *precious capital* that ought not disappear" (my italics).[18]

Philippe Lejeune and Elizabeth Bruss, in their highly regarded efforts to codify the conventions or literary rules of autobiography, also assumed that the subject revealed in autobiography is unified. Lejeune famously defined autobiography as a "retrospective prose narrative written by a real person concerning his own existence, where the focus is his individual life, in particular the story of his personality,"[19] a definition that implies that the self has a structure and chronological development that can be narrated, that coherence exists between the present and the past (a "retrospective" of "his own existence"), and that the ontological presence of this self (this "real" person) is not in doubt. Elizabeth Bruss also assumed that a written autobiography requires a "unity of subjectivity and subject matter—the implied identity of author, narrator, and protagonist,"[20] the identity marked by what Lejeune has called the "autobiographical pact," the identity of the signature on the title page with that of the subject of the narrative.[21] Despite poststructuralist and deconstructive critiques of the existence of a referential self or an author outside of the linguistic text, Bruss continued to regard the autobiographical self as "an arbitrary cultural fact but *not* a delusion."[22] Drawing on speech-act theory, she defined the "fundamental identification (or conflation) of two subjects—the speaking subject and the subject of the sentence" as "crucial to the autobiographical project, to the unity of observer and observed, the purported continuity of past and present, life and writing."[23]

Wordsworth's *Prelude*, for the most part read too simplistically by theorists of autobiography, nonetheless helped to establish the generic conventions of autobiography, conventions that predicate the existence of a subjectivity that is coherent over time, that can be represented linguistically as a bounded image, a completed "soul," and that can exist beyond the confines of the physical body, beyond death. This is the self which in several canonical masculine Romantic texts was glorified as the creator of reality, as the "human form divine":

So was it with me in my solitude;
So often among multitudes of men.

Unknown, unthought of, yet I was most rich,
I had a world about me; 'twas my own,
I made it; for it only liv'd to me,
And to the God who look'd into my mind.
                    (*The Prelude*, 1805, III:139–44)

Self Writing

What if there are other ways of constructing the self than that attempted by William Wordsworth? As both post-modernist and feminist theorists have argued, the unified, agential, coherent self sought by the author of *The Prelude* and assumed in most social contract and rational choice theories may not exist. Deconstructionists, following Nietzsche's trenchant insistence that the subject is "not something given" but "something added and invented and projected behind what there is,"[24] have insisted with Derrida and Lacan that the self can only be a subject position in language, therefore fluid, mutable, non-essential—what Kristeva called the "questionable subject-in-process."[25]

Most feminists have been unwilling to follow *Roland Barthes par Roland Barthes* and embrace the reduction of the subject to a purely textual and rhetorical production because they have not wished to relinquish the authority and the referentiality of the self as an agent of political change and social justice. Nonetheless, they have contested the masculine concept of the self proposed in the canonical autobiographical texts from Augustine's *Confessions* to *The Autobiography of Malcolm X*. They have suggested alternate models of the self, grounded in the specific historical and political experiences of both women and men, and produced by the social construction of both sexuality and gender in a particular culture and time.[26]

Reading Dorothy Wordsworth's Alfoxden and Grasmere Journals, we find a very different concept of self from the egotistical sublime proposed in her brother's poetry. We need to be able both to recognize this alternative model of subjectivity and to grant it equal status with her brother's if we are accurately to describe the range of "Romantic self-consciousness." First let us look at the poem that, critics agree, most succinctly captures this other mode of identity, Dorothy's *Floating Island at Hawkeshead, An Incident in the schemes of Nature.*

Harmonious Powers with Nature work
On sky, earth, river, lake, and sea:
Sunshine and storm, whirlwind and breeze
All in one duteous task agree.

Once did I see a slip of earth,
By throbbing waves long undermined,
Loosed from its hold;—*how* no one knew
But all might see it float, obedient to the wind.

Might see it, from the verdant shore
Dissevered float upon the Lake,
Float, with its crest of trees adorned
On which the warbling birds their pastime take.

Food, shelter, safety there they find
There berries ripen, flowerets bloom;
There insects live their lives—and die:
A peopled *world* it is;—in size a tiny room.

And thus through many seasons' space
This little Island may survive
But Nature, though we mark her not,
Will take away—may cease to give.

Perchance when you are wandering forth
Upon some vacant sunny day
Without an object, hope, or fear,
Thither your eyes may turn—the Isle is passed away.

Buried beneath the glittering Lake!
Its place no longer to be found,
Yet the lost fragments shall remain,
To fertilize some other ground.[27]

Having assumed "one duteous task" in which all "harmonious powers," including human life, "agree" with Nature, the poem presents
a floating island loosed from its hold, passively moved by the wind.
And yet this fluid, constantly shifting, circumscribed island is a
"peopled *world*" where birds, insects, flowers all find food, shelter,
safety, then death. A domesticated world—"in size a tiny room"—
the island survives till Nature takes it away, till it is "buried." Yet
even then its "fragments" remain "to fertilize some other ground."

Composed shortly before her madness and often repeated during
it, this poem constitutes Dorothy's most mature response to her

brother's concept of the self.[28] Recall that William had denounced his youthful life at Cambridge in these terms:

> Rotted as by a charm, my life became
> A floating island, an amphibious thing,
> Unsound, of spungy texture, yet withal,
> Not wanting a fair face of water-weeds
> And pleasant flowers.
>   (*Prelude* III:339–344).

In contrast, Dorothy's poem affirms a floating island life or self that is interactive, absorptive, constantly changing, and domestic—it can be contained within a tiny room. It is a self that produces and supports other lives—warbling birds, blooming flowers, a "crest of trees"—a self that provides food, shelter, safety for others. It is a self that is sometimes visible, sometimes not, a self that can appear and disappear in a moment, a self that is constructed in part—but only in part—by the gaze of others. "*I* see" it but some day "you" may not. It is a self that is profoundly connected to its environment, to those "harmonious powers" of sunshine and storm, of nature and human society, that surround it, direct it, even consume it. Margaret Homans reads this "diffuse" self negatively as a figure of dissolution, even annihilation,[29] but Susan Wolfson is surely right in seeing the movement from "I" to "you" to "all" as an "expansion of individual subjectivity into visionary community."[30] Above all, this is a self that is *embodied*, that is composed of organic fragments that literally fertilize the ground. Significantly, it is a self that *does not name itself as a self;* the metaphor of the floating island as a life or self is one that has to be intertextually transferred from her brother's poem.

Susan Levin has noted the degree to which Dorothy Wordsworth's floating island self conforms to one model (among several possible models) of feminine identity, that proposed by the contemporary Self-in-Relation school of psychology derived from British object-relations theory by Nancy Chodorow, Jean Baker Miller and Carol Gilligan.[31] Dorothy's sense of self is fluid, relational, exhibiting the permeable ego boundaries Chodorow attributed to the social construction of the feminine gender in those Western cultures in which females are assigned the role of primary infant caregiver, of mother. Like many female autobiographers who preceded her—like Margaret Cavendish, Margery Kempe, Julian of Norwich, and Anne Bradstreet—Dorothy Wordsworth constructed her identity "by way of alterity,"[32] in relation to a significant other, whether a man, a woman, God, nature, or the community.

Dorothy's *Journals* linguistically represent a self that is not only relational, formed in connection with the needs, moods and actions of other human beings, but also physically embodied—not a "mighty mind" but an organic body that feels heat and cold and hunger, that sees and hears and smells, that defecates and "washes her head," that suffers both psychosomatic and physical disease. Such physical bodies have been for the most part absent from the canonical male autobiographies which have attempted to construct a permanent, even transcendental, ego that endures beyond the limits of matter, time and space. Shirley Neuman, pointing to "this near-effacement of bodies in autobiography," has suggested the main reasons for it—a Platonic and Christian tradition that identifies the self with the soul and hence the spiritual as opposed to the sensual, together with an Enlightenment definition of "man" as the Cartesian ego which has only to think in order to be.[33] Perhaps equally determining, the canonical male-authored autobiographies have been for the most part the production of a leisured, bourgeois, racially dominant class, of men who are at least temporarily free from the physical deprivations of hunger, cold and poverty, and thus have the luxury of constructing a mind detached from a body. In contrast, Dorothy's *Journals* join much African-American, working-class, and female autobiographical writing in an inscription of the body as a determining condition of subjectivity.

Most important, when reading Dorothy's *Journals*, we must resist the generic contracts imposed by contemporary theorists of autobiography, Philippe Lejeune's demand for a linear, coherent, "retrospective narrative in prose" or James Olney's defining trope for the self, metaphor. Instead, we must expand the generic range of "autobiography" to include *all* writing that inscribes subjectivity, to diaries, journals, memoirs and letters. As readers, we must open ourselves to other ways of conceptualizing identity, to other verbal structures, other rhetorical figures. Dorothy's *Journals*, like most diaries, by men or by women, are discontinuous, episodic, fragmentary, responsive to the randomness and arbitrariness of events. As Felicity Nussbaum has forcefully argued, many eighteenth- and nineteenth-century diaries represent a self that is not unified, rational or intentional, and thus register an ideological contestation with the dominant belief in a unitary self promoted in the religious, philosophical, political and economic tracts of the time.[34]

For examples of male-authored diaries in the Romantic period that represent such a discontinuous subjectivity, we might go to Coleridge's *Journals* and *Biographia Literaria*, to Byron's *Letters and Journals*, to Keats' *Letters*, or to Godwin's unpublished *Diary*. Yet when we do, as I hope to show in detail in my reading of Keats' letters in the next chapter, we find that gender still makes a difference in the construction of subjectivity. To take a brief example here, consider the following passages from Byron's letters to his fiancée, Annabella Milbanke:

> The great object of life is Sensation—to feel that we exist—even though in pain—it is this "craving void" which drives us to Gaming—to Battle—to Travel—to intemperate but keenly felt pursuits of every description whose principal attraction is the agitation inseparable from their accomplishment.—I am but an awkward dissembler—as my friend you will bear with my faults—I shall have the less constraint in what I say to you—firstly because I may derive some benefit from your observations—& next because I am very sure *you* can never be perverted by any paradoxes of mine.   (September 6, 1814)

> You don't like my "restless" doctrines—I should be very sorry if *you* did—but *I* can't *stagnate* nevertheless—if I must sail let it be on the ocean no matter how stormy—anything but a dull cruise on a level lake without ever losing sight of the same insipid shores by which it is surrounded.   (September 26, 1813)[35]

Byron like Dorothy Wordsworth takes the randomness and fluidity of life as a given (I have elsewhere described this as Byron's endorsement of the ontology of Romantic irony). But for Byron, such mutability produces a subjectivity defined not as a "peopled world" but rather as a "craving void." The absence of a defined and controlling self produces in Byron a desperate desire for just such a bounded ego, one that leads him tendentiously to assert a stable self he does not in fact possess: "*I* can't *stagnate*." Byron's insistence on his independent selfhood here produces not a relationship of sympathetic exchange with his fiancée, but rather one of contested opposition—"*you* can never be perverted by any paradoxes of mine," "You don't like . . . I should be very sorry if *you* did." Where a feminine subjectivity like Dorothy's enthusiastically embraces a relational, fluid self, a masculine subjectivity like Byron's anxiously resists it.

Structurally, diaries and journals both satisfy and frustrate the reader's desire for linear narrative, telling embedded stories but abruptly concluding or interrupting them to record whatever else happened. Their governing trope is not metaphor but *metonymy*, both in the sense proposed by Roman Jakobson—in which the governing structural principle is contiguity, either temporal or spatial, a contiguity Jakobson associated with stylistic realism[36]—and in the traditional rhetorical sense of synecdoche, in which a part stands for a whole, a single individual for the community of which it is a member.[37] But even as we embrace metonymy as a destructuring principle occasioned by random contiguity, by happenstance, we must also recognize the counterforce at work in structuring all diaries, and Dorothy's *Journals* in particular: the principle of repetition, a repetition that creates the illusion of continuity, of connections sustained through time and space.

The opening entries of Dorothy Wordsworth's Alfoxden Journal, written in 1798 as an *aide-mémoire* upon learning that she and her brother must soon quit the first house they had rented together, illustrate her characteristic linguistic construction of subjectivity:

ALFOXDEN, 20th January 1798. The green paths down the hillsides are channels for streams. The young wheat is streaked by silver lines of water running between the ridges, the sheep are gathered together on the slopes. After the wet dark days, the country seems more populous. It peoples itself in the sunbeams. The garden, mimic of spring, is gay with flowers. The purple-starred hepatica spreads itself in the sun, and the clustering snow-drops put forth their white heads, at first upright, ribbed with green, and like a rosebud; when completely opened, hanging their heads downwards, but slowly lengthening their slender stems. The slanting woods of an unvarying brown, showing the light through the thin net-work of their upper boughs. Upon the highest ridge of that round hill covered with planted oaks, the shafts of the trees show in the light like the columns of a ruin.

    21st. Walked on the hill-tops—a warm day. Sate under the firs in the park. The tops of the beeches of a brown-red, or crimson. Those oaks, fanned by the sea breeze, thick with feathery sea-green moss, as a grove not stripped of its leaves. Moss cups more proper than acorns for fairy goblets.[38]

Significantly, there is no "I," only an observing eye, an empathic consciousness that exuberantly reaches out to the natural environment, noting colors (green paths, silver lines of water), forms (sheep gathered together, paths become water channels, slanting woods, shafts of trees), and especially movement (oaks fanned by the sea breeze). Typically, she catalogues minute particulars: purple-starred hepatica, early and then more mature snow-drops, brown-red or crimson beech-tops. And yet this disparate, random catalogue finds connection: nature is not an alien other but a humanized community: the country "peoples itself in the sunbeams." Rhetorically constructing this interconnection, Dorothy relies on simile ("like a rosebud," "like the columns of a ruin," "as a grove not stripped of its leaves"), metaphor (the upper boughs are a "thin network," significantly a metaphor drawn from the realm of female domestic production), allegory ("moss cups" for "fairy goblets"), and centrally, metonymy ("the garden, mimic of spring"). Dorothy's is a subjectivity-in-process, an eye hungry for change—always responsive to the constant movement in nature ("after the wet dark days")—and invoking endings when they are not immediately present (the tree shafts become the "columns of a *ruin*"). Above all, Dorothy's is an embodied consciousness, one that walks and sits, one that feels the warmth of the day.

When the "I" enters this discourse, as it does for the first time on 3 February, it functions as a point of reference and not as a controlling subject:

> I never saw such a union of earth, sky, and sea. The clouds beneath our feet spread themselves to the water, and the clouds of the sky almost joined them. Gathered sticks in the woods; a perfect stillness. (4–5).

"I never saw"—Dorothy's "I" serves to emphasize the uniqueness of this event in her experience; at the same time, it assumes the existence of a potential harmony in nature, one that reconciles motion and stillness, her self and the other ("our feet"). Dorothy's subjectivity is one that *shares* its consciousness—this vision "with Coleridge," this journal entry with William, this work ("gathered sticks") with the entire household that will be warmed by her firewood.

Dorothy reaches out to her natural surroundings as a source of unfailing pleasure and nourishment: nature is constructed as both bountiful and vast, so encompassing that her own subjectivity can be entirely absorbed into it.

> February 26. . . . Walked to the top of a high hill to see a fortifica-
> tion. Again sat down to feed upon the prospect; a magnificent
> scene, *curiously* spread out for even minute inspection, though so
> extensive that the mind is afraid to calculate its bounds. (8)

Dorothy can "feed upon" this expanse of nature without the terror
of the Burkean sublime: only a mind detached from the body fears
self-annihilation, a fear that her embodied subjectivity does not
share.

As Dorothy feeds upon nature, so she provides food for others.
She feeds not only the body—going to Coombe for eggs, to the bak-
ers for bread and pies, to the woods for fir-apples—but also the
imagination. Literally, as many have noted, she fed William's and
Coleridge's poetry, providing images and tropes for William's *A
Night-Piece* ("the moon . . . in the centre of a black-blue vault"), *The
Ruined Cottage* ("the sheep, that leave locks of wool, and the red
marks with which they are spotted, upon the wood"), and most famously, the daffodils for *I wandered lonely as a cloud.* For *Christabel,*
she supplied "The night cloudy but not dark" and "One only leaf
upon the top of a tree—the sole remaining leaf—danced round and
round like a rag blown by the wind"—but note that Coleridge
transformed Dorothy's image of quotidian domesticity into one of
alienation—"The one red leaf, the last of its clan." Dorothy's *Journals* thus nourish the work of those she most loves, William and
Coleridge.

Dorothy's subjectivity is most complexly constructed in her
Grasmere Journals, written between 1800 and 1803, so that "I will
not quarrel with myself" and to "give Wm pleasure" (15). She thus
defines the dual purpose of her writing: to give form to her conviction of relatedness at those moments when it is threatened, when
she is alone, and to share her subjectivity with others. It is this
need to embody her relationships, in writing and in the material
world, that produces the kind of comment some readers have found
ludicrous or excessive:

> Now for my walk. I *will* be busy, I *will* look well and be well when
> he comes back to me. O the Darling! Here is one of his bitten
> apples! I can hardly find in my heart to throw it into the fire. I
> must wash myself, then off. . . . (97)

For Dorothy, William's absence must be written over by his continuing presence—in her thoughts, in her writing, and especially
in the material evidence of his presence, the half eaten apple. For

her, relationships exist in and through the body, bodies that must be exercised and washed in the effort to look well and be well, bodies that document their existence by eating apples.

These *Journals* thus construct, not so much that narrative of loss proposed by Susan Levin, a narrative of William's courtship of Mary Hutchinson and Dorothy's emotional devastation at her brother's marriage,[39] as a substantiated record of *relatedness*, of loving and being loved, and of the constant physical and emotional effort required to achieve and sustain that condition of "blessedness."

> 24 May 1800. Walked in the morning to Ambleside. I found a letter from Wm and from Mary Hutchinson and Douglass. Returned on the other side of the lakes—wrote to William after dinner, nailed up the beds, worked in the garden, sate in the evening under the trees. I went to bed soon with a bad head-ache. A fine day. (20)
>
> 24 July 1800. W. went to Ambleside. John walked out. I made tarts etc. Mr. B. Simpson called and asked us to tea. I went to the view of Rydale to meet William. John went to him—I returned. W. and I drank tea at Mr. Simpson's. Brought down Lemon Thyme, greens etc. The old woman was very happy to see us and we were so in the pleasure we gave. She was an affecting picture of patient disappointment, suffering under no particular affliction. (30)

These two entries, selected at random, communicate the texture of an ongoing life, one grounded in physical necessities (baking, gardening, making beds), in social communication (drinking tea with neighbors), in meaningful work.

Dorothy Wordsworth's ambition was not to become a poet—"I should detest the idea of setting myself up as an Author," she told her friend Catherine Clarkson[40]—but to create a home. Orphaned at seven when her mother died and her father sent her away, never to see her again before his death five years later, Dorothy lived happily with her "Aunt" Elizabeth Threlkeld until she was fifteen. But then she was abruptly removed to her maternal grandparents' house where she felt ignored, unloved, oppressed. She eagerly accepted her uncle William Cookson's offer to live with him and his new wife, but soon found that she was expected to do an enormous amount of childcare and housework; in effect, she functioned in the Cookson household as an unpaid *au pair* for five years.[41] Although she was fond of the Cooksons and their rapidly growing family, she soon began to crave her own home, one that in her fantasy life was always connected with the ties of blood, with her brothers, and, increasingly, with William and John. Dorothy's deepest need and desire—to be loved and needed, as well as to love—was fully gratified by William's growing tenderness toward her and by his obvious need for the service she could provide, the making of a comfortable home on a very small income.

The Grasmere Journals document Dorothy's successful achievement of her heart's desire, the creation of a domestic community where she could speak and act freely and where she knew that she was wanted and secure.[42] Modern feminists may well be appalled by the exhausting burden of physical labor that Dorothy performed: as the *Journals* amply record, at Dove Cottage Dorothy did the vegetable and flower gardening (sowing, weeding, harvesting, preserving), baking, laundry (washing, bleaching, drying, starching, ironing, folding), clothes-making and mending, shoemaking, housecleaning, wallpapering, whitewashing and wall painting, carpet binding, mattress making, carpentering and window glazing. In addition, she copied and recopied William's poems. But Dorothy did this work with vigor and pride; her subjectivity was grounded on the conviction that she was of as much use to others as they were to her.

Dorothy's Grasmere Journals are extraordinarily rich and compelling autobiographical self-writing. In episodic, irregular entries, Dorothy linguistically recreates the texture of a particular woman's life, a life lived in great part outdoors, in a natural environment she found constantly stimulating and delightful, a life lived in a body that felt the cold and the heat, that suffered headaches and toothaches and bowel disfunctions, a life of relentless physical labor but also of intellectual stimulation and, most important, of almost constant affectionate companionship.

Dorothy Wordsworth could articulate what she saw perhaps as vividly as any writer of English prose; only John Ruskin can equal her ability to teach us *how to see*. As *readers*, we treasure her autobiographical journals for enabling us to see as she did, to see a birch tree:

> It was yielding to the gusty wind with all its tender twigs, the sun shone upon it and it glanced in the wind like a flying sunshiny shower. It was a tree in shape with stem and branches but it was like a Spirit of water. (61)

or daffodils:

they grew among the mossy stones about and about them, some rested their heads upon these stones as on a pillow for weariness and the rest tossed and reeled and danced and seemed as if they verily laughed with the wind that blew upon them over the lake, they looked so gay ever glancing ever changing. (109)

For Dorothy, however, such observations are valuable not so much for their inherent beauty, as because they document an ongoing interaction with what is for her "a blessed place" (118), a place where God and trees and daffodils and the "busy highway" of human life all fuse. The birch, for instance, is a "favorite" which she and her brother seek out in all seasons; six months later it "is all over green in *small* leaf more light and elegant than when it is full out. It bent to the breezes as if for the love of its own delightful motions" (122). Not only does Dorothy return to the same spots month after month—the black quarter of the wood, Churnmilk Force, Rydale—but she also *names* those spots that she particularly associates with people she loves—"John's Grove," "Sara's Gate." Thus Dorothy, like Susan Ferrier and Sydney Owenson Morgan, systematically *domesticates* the sublime.[43]

The blessedness of Grasmere, for Dorothy, is constituted both by the abundant and ever varying beauty of the lake country and by her daily participation in a human community. More prominently than her observations of nature, her *Journals* record her interactions with other people. We see her involvement with the numerous beggars which the particularly severe winters and economic "hard times" of the war years (1800–1803) produced, beggars she never failed to succor to the best of her limited abilities; with her neighbors, and especially those in dire circumstances, Peggy Ashburner and the Fishers; with her friends, both those of childhood (Jane Pollard, Mary and Sara Hutchinson) and of adulthood (Catherine Clarkson), with whom she kept up an almost daily correspondence; and with all those who were welcome visitors to the meagre accommodations of Dove Cottage (in addition to the Hutchinsons, the Coleridges, the Lloyds, de Quincey, Basil Montagu, the Lambs, the Pooles, the Simpsons and many more). Dorothy's sense of being grounded *in a community* is articulated in its most linear form, as Susan Wolfson has shown, in the *Narrative of George and Sarah Green* she wrote in 1808, her account of what she and her neighbors did to relieve the distress of the eight suddenly orphaned children of the impoverished Greens.[44] But this sense of *belonging* radiates through the Grasmere Journals: "May 31, 1802. . . . My tooth broke today. They will soon be gone. Let that pass I shall be beloved—I want no more" (129).

Dorothy's empathic involvement in her friends' emotions was so intense that it often made her physically ill. Again and again, after receiving a letter or visit from Coleridge during his agonies of opium withdrawal, unrequited love for Sara Hutchinson and domestic incompatibility, she recorded her reactions: "I was melancholy and could not talk, but at last I eased my heart by weeping—nervous blubbering says William. It is not so. O how many, many reasons have I to be anxious for him" (57). Her participation in their joy could be equally overwhelming. On the day of her best friend's marriage to her brother, 4 October 1802, an event that secured Dorothy's place forever in the Wordsworth household, she was physically prostrated by the power of her feelings:

> William had parted from me upstairs. I gave him the wedding ring—with how deep a blessing! I took it from the forefinger where I had worn it the whole of the night before—he slipped it again onto my finger and blessed me fervently. When they were absent my dear little Sara prepared the breakfast. I kept myself as quiet as I could, but when I saw the two men running up the walk, coming to tell us it was over, I could stand it no longer and threw myself on the bed where I lay in stillness, neither hearing or seeing any thing, till Sara came upstairs to me and said "They are coming." This forced me from the bed where I lay and I moved I knew not how straight forward, faster than my strength could carry me till I met my beloved William and fell upon his bosom. He and John Hutchinson led me to the house and there I stayed to welcome my dear Mary. (154).

Some commentators, seeking to emphasize Dorothy's vulnerability and deep-seated anxieties concerning her brother's marriage, have read this passage as a form of "psychic suicide," the unconscious revelation of her powerfully repressed anger at William for his betrayal of their primary relationship.[45] A legitimate self-concern certainly underlies this passage. As William later wrote to the wife he so passionately loved and desired, he felt "the blessed bond that binds husband & wife so much closer than the bond of Brotherhood—however dear."[46] Nonetheless, returning to the Hutchinson's house on the arm of her brother, Mary following behind; accompanying them—seated in the middle—on their honeymoon coach journey home to Grasmere; then walking in John's Grove—"the first walk that I had taken with my Sister" (161)—

Dorothy became convinced that she was still beloved and at home. Her Journal ends four months later, on an intensely cold winter day, with Dorothy's account of yet another moment of tactful communal charity, buying gingerbread she didn't need but which had been baked for her by the blind Matthew Newton and his wife. As Kurt Heinzelmann so perceptively commented, this is "bad home economics but right neighborly action," specifically directed toward a family that "had the good sense to leave a special place for 'the sister' to read to them beside the fire."[47]

The self that is written in Dorothy Wordsworth's *Journals* is one embodied in a routine of physical labor, of the daily production of food and clothing and shelter. It is a subjectivity embedded in the communal life of a village in the English Lake District in the early nineteenth century, a time of severe hardship for both Dorothy and her neighbors. It is a self that derives its sense of well-being from its continuing connections with those significant others she herself carved, in an ideogram of relatedness, both in her Journal (126) and on stone: her brother William above all, but also her sister-friend Mary Hutchinson, Coleridge, Sara Hutchinson, and John Wordsworth. It is a self built, as were many other nineteenth-century women's selves, on a model of affiliation rather than a model of individual achievement.[48] The life-writing of her Journals linguistically constructs a subjectivity that in its detail, physical embodiment, energetic activity, and *enacted consciousness*—Dorothy Wordsworth *is* what she sees and does and eats and feels and speaks and writes—is one of the most convincingly recorded subjectivities of the Romantic era.

A self grounded, as Dorothy Wordsworth's was, in relationship, in connection, always runs the risk, as contemporary feminists have reminded us, of masochistic self-sacrifice, even of annihilation. Indeed, many readers of her *Journals* have concluded that Dorothy's self was arrested in its development, overwhelmed by her brother's egotism, crippled and even finally entombed in her brother's household.[49] For such readers, the temptation to interpret Dorothy's madness, at the age of 64, as an unconscious rebellion against a life of "persistent, almost obsessional self-sacrifice" in which she insistently fulfilled "the role of nurse, housekeeper, secretary, and slave to any household in sickness or trouble"[50] will probably prove irresistible. And indeed there is a "crazy logic of reversal"[51] in Dorothy's dementia. After years of walking, she will not move, but demands the support of not one but two attendants; after years of doing the family laundry with the help only of old

Molly Fisher, she becomes incontinent, requiring a maid *"entirely* devoted to her" because her laundry must be done every day; after years of eagerly welcoming guests, she refuses to see anyone; after years of hanging on William's every word, she no longer cares if he is present; after years of providing verbal inspiration to poets, she now speaks in an obscene or entirely private language; after years of letter-writing, she now refuses either to write or to read them, because she is "too busy with her own feelings"; after years of patiently enduring cold (sleeping in rooms without a fire, her insides sometimes so "sore with cold" that she could not sleep at all), she demanded a bright fire in her room at all times: " 'Stir the fire' is her first salutation," wrote Mary, "and that must either be done or a hubbub ensues."[52]

But those of us who have observed the impact of Alzheimer's disease or senile dementia[53] on relatives or friends we know well may be loath to read Dorothy's behavior as revenge. We might equally validly construe her twenty-year madness as a triumph of the relational self. For in her sickness she received from Mary Hutchinson Wordsworth nursing so attentive, efficient, patient and loving that she survived long beyond the usual five to eight years prognosis common for nineteenth-century sufferers of senile dementia. Dorothy Wordsworth gave help for as long as she could, even voluntarily renouncing her comfortable home at Rydal Mount when she was sixty to move to grim, dirty, cold lodgings at Whitwick to keep house for her nephew John, a move that led to her physical collapse. And when she in turn needed help, she received it, to the last day of her eighty-four years, enjoying moments of lucidity in which she articulated a continuing sense of connection with those around her—as in her last written words, a postscript to Mary:

> Mrs. Pearson is very poorly and the Doctors say she cannot live. We have got a cow and very good milk she gives. I only wish you were here to have some of it. Thomas Flick is a little better and we are all quite fit. Mary Fisher's Sister is just dead.[54]

If the linguistic representation of subjectivity is the ultimate goal and achievement of autobiography, of self-life-writing, then diaries and journals construct a subjectivity or kind of self as effectively as do linear prose or poetic narratives. The self they present is of course different, different in each diary, different in its continuities and discontinuities, in its coherences and incoherences. By excluding such journals and diaries as Dorothy Wordsworth's from the canon of English autobiography, students of the genre have notably impoverished our understanding of the complexity and range of human subjectivity, of the role of gender in constructing subjectivity (both masculine and feminine), and of the bodily or somatic dimension of identity.

In the context of academic English Romanticism, the traditional tendency to view Dorothy Wordsworth's *Journals* primarily as sourcebooks for Coleridge's and William's life and poems—a practice vigorously contested in recent years—has led to a more serious misunderstanding. By taking her brother's proposed model of subjectivity as *the* Romantic self, cultural historians have failed to see the continuity between Dorothy Wordsworth's floating island self and the subjectivities embodied in earlier and later texts by both women and men. The self that authors and is represented in the writings, both in prose fiction and in poetry, of the women writers of the Romantic period, is by and large (but certainly not always) the self constructed in Dorothy Wordsworth's *Journals*—a relational, fluid, embodied self. Let me underline this point. I am not suggesting that male Romantic writers constructed one kind of self and female Romantic writers another. Rather, I am arguing against Foucault that there is no such thing as "*the* Romantic self" or "*the* Modern self," but only differing modes of subjectivity which can be shared by males and females alike, and even by the same person in the course of a long and variegated life. A male writer, as I shall discuss in the next chapter, can produce a feminine subjectivity and vice versa. I have been calling Dorothy Wordsworth's relational self a "feminine Romantic self" only because I wish to contrast it to the ideologically dominant construction of subjectivity in this age, that "masculine Romantic self" too often assumed by literary critics and psychologists to be the only authentic, or at least the most viable, self.

A final point on the relation of genre to the construction of subjectivity. To the objection that I have been comparing generic apples and oranges, an epic poem and a journal never intended for publication, I would respond that I could have grounded my argument concerning William Wordsworth's desire to construct a self that is bounded, unitary and agential upon a literary genre as confined as Dorothy's quatrains in *Floating Island at Hawkeshead*, the sonnet. A glance at William's sonnet, *With ships the sea was sprinkled,* may illustrate this point. Confronted with fluidity and randomness (a sea covered with ships "veering up and down, one knew not why"), the poet immediately attempts to impose a teleological order upon both the universe and his own experience by selecting one ship to serve as master of the whole: "A goodly Vessel did I then espy/ Come like a giant from a haven broad." Gendering this ship as a sexually available female ("lustily along the bay she strode"), the poet immediately desires to possess her ("I pursued her with a Lover's look"). The ship becomes the object of desire: as such it is immediately equated with political and economic power—"where she comes the winds must stir." Troped as a "rich" and highly apparelled ship, the self or way of being in the world that the poet desires is one that can rule the elements, control its own destiny, "brook no tarrying." That Wordsworth here genders this self as female only underlines my argument that he conceives of the unitary, independent, agential self as universal, available to men and women alike.[55]

PART III

IDEOLOGICAL CROSS-DRESSING

John Keats/Emily Brontë

John Keats

The two Romanticisms that I have been distinguishing as masculine and feminine should not be identified with biological sexuality. Some romantic writers were "ideological cross-dressers." It was possible for a male Romantic writer to embrace all or parts of feminine Romanticism, just as it was possible for a female to embrace aspects of masculine Romanticism. But these are complicated crossovers and need to be described with care. There are some senses in which a male could not enter a feminine ideology, nor could a female fully identify with a masculine ideology. To adapt our current vocabulary, certain Romantic writers might have been ideological transvestites but they were not transsexuals. To explore these complications in greater detail than hitherto, I would like to take as representative that male Romantic poet who has most often been characterised as "effeminate"[1]—John Keats— and that female Romantic writer who has been characterised as "crude" and "virile"[2]—Emily Brontë.

Keats subtly complicates the issue of gender and ideology, as others have remarked, either by occupying the position of the woman in life or in discourse, or by blurring the distinction between genders, between masculinity and femininity.[3] Let us focus first on a few aspects of Keats' life and death, which has been so fully described by Walter Jackson Bate and others.[4] Orphaned at the age of fourteen, the second son in a family of four children, Keats immediately took on the role of mother to his younger siblings. He corresponded faithfully with his sister Fanny, comforting and advising her. When his brother Tom fell sick of the family disease, tuberculosis, he became Tom's nurse, tending Tom until his death. Keats' first choice of a profession, that of apothecary or, in modern terminology, a combination of pharmacist and lower-level general practitioner, may also be significant. While the male medical profession has long sought to cure disease, nursing the sick and the dying has traditionally been an occupation associated with women, and Keats' desire—to help others to bear their pain and suffering—might be construed as feminine.

Small in stature (Keats was only five foot two inches tall) and fine-boned, Keats considered his appearance to be "girlish." This "effeminacy" was emphasized—or constructed—in the portrait of a wan, delicate Keats on his deathbed, painted by Joseph Severn and widely copied ever since. As Susan Wolfson has shown, Victorian critics intensified the "feminization" of Keats by endorsing the apocryphal legend of his death propounded in Shelley's *Adonais*, the legend of a sensitive poet driven to despair by hostile reviews, "snuff'd out," as Byron famously put it in *Don Juan*, "by an article."[5]

Keats was more subtly feminized by being characterized as a lower-class writer. When John Gibson Lockhart, in *Blackwood's Edinburgh Magazine* in 1818, assigned Keats to the "Cockney School of Poetry,"[6] he was engaging in a politics of both class and gender. To recognize this, as Marjorie Levinson and others have reminded us,[7] we need only look at the *Oxford English Dictionary* entries under "Cockney":

COCKNEY—egg: lit. "cocks' egg"
1. hen's egg, or perh. one of the small or misshapen eggs occasionally laid by fowls, still popularly called in some parts "cocks' eggs".

2. "A child that sucketh long," "a nestle-cock," . . .hence a squeamish or *effeminate* fellow, "a milk-sop" . . .sometimes applied to a squeamish, over-nice, wanton, or affected *woman*.

3. A derisive appellation for a townsman, as the type of *effeminacy*, in contrast to the hardier inhabitants of the country.

4. One born in the city of London; . . . Always more or less contemptuous or bantering, and particularly used to connote the

characteristics in which the born Londoner is supposed to be inferior to other Englishmen. (my italics)

Byron's vitriolic attacks on Keats' *Lamia, Isabella, The Eve of St. Agnes, and Other Poems* (1820) focused on the same class and gender ambiguity that troubled Lockhart. Assigning Keats to the transitional class of the "shabby genteel" (those members of the working class who asserted a false claim to the "finery" of respectability), Byron also called Keats' masculinity into question by defining his work as "*p–ss a bed* poetry," "a sort of mental masturbation" produced by "f[ri]gg[in]g his *Imagination*."[8] In describing Keats' poetry as the erotic fantasies of an adolescent masturbator, Byron implicitly equated Keats not only with the puerile and unmanly ("the drivelling idiotism of the Mankin"[9]) and the lower classes but also with the female.

In Byron's day, since "proper" ladies were forbidden to have sexual intercourse before marriage, adolescent girls channelled their erotic desires into passionate friendships with other females. While the "romantic friendships" of upper- and middle-class women were assumed to be platonic, sophisticated men and women knew very well that female masturbation and other lesbian acts occurred within them, although they usually categorized such practices as the "dirty little vice" of boarding-school girls, female servants, and actresses. Mrs. Piozzi freely discussed the lesbianism of actresses in her diary, and *The Lady's Dispensatory; or Every Woman her Own Physician* (1740) explicitly warned mothers against allowing their daughters to be corrupted by masturbation, with the clear suggestion that such corruption originated in the lower classes.[10] Since female masturbation did not seem to threaten male patriarchal control over sexual reproduction, it was tolerated, although this "dirty" activity was never spoken of in polite society and was thus consigned to the realm of the "vulgar." In the discourse of the Romantic period, the definition of Keats as a masturbatory poet aligned him both with the lower classes and with adolescent girls.

In an even more direct way, the description of Keats as an adolescent masturbator identified him as feminine. Contemporary medical theory concerning the consequences of masturbation relied heavily on Tissot's notorious and hugely popular *An Essay on Onanism, or a Treatise upon the Disorders produced by Masturbation: or the Dangerous Effects of Secret and Excessive Venery* (1758), written in Latin but by 1800 translated into French, English, Dutch, Italian and German. Tissot argued that the masturbator, by turning his or her erotic energies solely inward, would not only be disinclined to marry but would "degenerate" into self-absorption and an abnormal reversal of conventional sex roles: if male, he would decline into "effeminacy," if female, she would manifest a perverse virility. Tissot also attributed to masturbation the following consequences: melancholy, idleness, inactivity, the weakening of all the bodily senses and the faculties of the soul, the loss of imagination and memory, even imbecility. As Ludmilla Jordanova concludes, Tissot defined physical and mental "health in terms of a particular kind of self, one that is not self-indulgent and hence has that degree of self-control which allows it to function in society." [11] Here, it is most important to see that masturbation in men, in Tissot's account, leads to excessive feminization of the body and mind, to "lying too long a-bed, over soft beds," passivity, the "unnatural acts" of homosexuality, and a loss of both individual and class identity. In the medical discourse of the Romantic era, then, the absence of an autonomous or agential self in men became a symptom both of gender-crossing and of disease, which is why both Hazlitt and Byron attacked Keats' effeminacy so strongly.

Keats' poetic theory is self-consciously positioned within the realm of the feminine gender. Keats' famous definitions of the "poetical character" and of "negative capability," as Barbara Gelpi and Adrienne Rich recently reminded us, presuppose an antimasculine conception of identity.[12] If we take the examples of William and Dorothy Wordsworth as representative of a wider construction of gendered subjectivity in the nineteenth century, the masculine self was thought to have a strong sense of its own ego boundaries, the feminine self was not. In his descriptions both of his own sense of identity and of the appropriate consciousness of the true poet, Keats reversed these gender stereotypes:

> As to the poetical Character itself (I mean that sort of which, if I am any thing, I am a Member; that sort distinguished from the wordsworthian or egotistical sublime; which is a thing per se and stands alone) it is not itself—it has no self—it is every thing and nothing—It has no character—it enjoys light and shade; it lives in gusto, be it foul or fair, high or low, rich or poor, mean or elevated—It has as much delight in conceiving an Iago as an Imogen. What shocks the virtuous Philosopher delights the camelion Poet.[13]

Keats here resists a masculinist construction of the self as bounded, unitary, complete, and instrumental—the consciousness of self-as-agent which he (perhaps unfairly) assigned to the William Wordsworth of *The Prelude.*

In its place Keats promotes a very different concept of self, one similar to Dorothy Wordsworth's floating island self. Like the contemporary Self-in-Relation school of psychology or the French psychoanalytic school inspired by Lacan and Kristeva,[14] Keats images the self as unbounded, fluid, decentered, inconsistent—not "a" self at all. Keats—like the Poet he describes—"has no Identity—he is continually in for[ming] and filling some other Body."[15]

A self that continually overflows itself, that melts into the Other, that *becomes* the Other, is conventionally associated with the female, and especially with the pregnant woman who experiences herself and her child as one. Such a self erases the difference between one and two, and by denying the validity of logical, Aristotelian distinctions, has seemed to many rationalists to embrace irrationality and confusion. Keats advocates such "confusion" (and appropriates such a self for the male sex) when he insists that the quality which forms "a Man of Achievement especially in Literature and which Shakespeare possessed so enormously" is "*Negative Capability,* that is, when man is capable of being in uncertainties, Mysteries, doubts, without any irritable reaching after fact and reason."[16] Above all, Keats defines the true poet as empathic, a quality everywhere identified with femininity in the eighteenth century. The literature of sensibility, even as it developed the new image of "the man of feeling," appropriated to that man qualities traditionally defined as feminine: tears, heightened emotions, excessive passion or love, extreme irrationality, wasting diseases, suicidal impulses and madness.[17]

Not only does Keats define the true poet as one who possesses a self with permeable ego boundaries that exists *only* in its relations with others, but he also locates poetic creation in the realm of the feminine, identifying it with pregnancy or, in another metaphor borrowed from the realm of female production, as weaving or spinning. To take Keats' more humorous examples first, here he observes his friend Charles Brown:

Brown has been walking up and down the room a breeding—now at this moment he is being delivered of a couplet—and I dare say will be as well as can be expected—Gracious—he has twins![18]

Or, in a more extended, even grotesque, depiction of poetic creation as maternal birth:

> If you do not see me soon it will be from the humour of writing, which I have had for three days, continuing. I must say to the Muses what the maid says to the Man—"take me while the fit is on me." Would you like a true Story "there was a Man and his Wife who being to go a long journey on foot, in the course of their travels came to a River which rolled knee deep over the pebbles—In these cases the Man generally pulls off his shoes and stockings and carries the woman over on his Back. This Man did so; and his Wife being pregnant and troubled, as in such cases is very common, with strange longings, took the strangest that ever was heard of. Seeing her Husband's foot, a handsome on[e] enough, look very clean and tempting in the clear water, on their arrival at the other bank she earnestly demanded a bit of it; he being an affectionate fellow and fearing for the comeliness of his child gave her a bit which he cut off with his Clasp Knife—Not satisfied she asked another morsel—supposing there might be twins he gave her a slice more. Not yet contented she craved another Piece. 'You Wretch cries the Man, would you wish me to kill myself? take that!' Upon which he stabb'd her with the knife, cut her open and found three Children in her Belly two of them very comfortable with their mouths shut, the third with its eyes and mouth stark staring open. "Who would have thought it" cried the Widower, and pursued his Journey. . . ."[19]

Both these passages emphasize the extraordinary degree to which Keats identified the process of poetic creation with the process of female pregnancy and giving birth. Keats almost seems to feel that before one can become a poet, one must occupy the position of a woman and a mother.[20]

Keats' identification of poetic creation with the act of giving life receives its most extended articulation in his famous Vale of Soul-making letter. Here Keats draws an explicit analogy between the process of creating a myth which will give meaning to one's life—constructing "a system of Salvation which does not affront our reason and humanity"—and the process of making a Soul or "*Intelligence destined to possess the sense of Identity.*"[21] The human heart, the human capacity for empathy and relationship, becomes in this letter both the source of knowledge and "the *teat* from which the Mind or intelligence sucks its identity" (my italics). The heart is thus female, a nursing mother, and Keats' "system of Spirit-creation" or personal and poetic self-development grows out of this

primary mother-infant bond. For Keats, the mother is the source
of life, and poetic mythmaking can only represent at the level of
metaphoric discourse the primal dependence of the child and
adult upon its female origin.

Keats' identification of both poetic creation and the acquisition
of knowledge with feminine work is revealed in the letter to Reynolds in which he compares the gaining of wisdom to the weaving of
a spider's web.[22] Beginning with a justification of "delicious diligent Indolence," Keats locates himself in the sphere of feminine
passivity rather than heroic masculine endeavor, and then argues:

> it appears to me that almost any Man may like the spider spin
> from his own inwards his own airy Citadel—the points of leaves
> and twigs on which the spider begins *her* work are few, and *she*
> fills the air with a beautiful circuiting. (my emphasis)

By gendering the spider as female, Keats has aligned himself not
with the busy bee of a masculine, Protestant work ethic or the neo-
classical, rationalist aesthetics of Swift's *Battle of the Books*, but
with the traditionally feminine occupations of spinning, weaving,
and tale-telling.[23] Keats' web of spiritual and practical knowledge
empathically connects the disparate: "minds would leave each
other in contrary directions, traverse each other in numberless
points, and at last greet each other at the journey's end." And the
insights and information gained by such traversings—"An old Man
and a child would talk together and the old Man be led on his path
and the child left thinking"—would not be proclaimed, argued or
disputed but rather "whisper[ed]. . .to his neighbor." Keats here invokes the village gossip, whispering stories to her friends and
neighbors, as his image of shared wisdom. The result of such empathically gained and shared experience is, suggests Keats in a
move from the epistemological to the political, an egalitarian community: "Humanity instead of being a wide heath of Furze and
Briars with here and there a remote Oak or Pine, would become a
grand democracy of Forest Trees!"

That Keats identifies the gaining of wisdom and the construction
of a genuine community with the work of women is underlined by
the reversed courtship ritual that immediately follows, in which
Keats initially embraces the role of the female:

> it seems to me that we should rather be the flower than the Bee—
> for it is a false notion that more is gained by receiving than giv-
> ing—no, the receiver and the giver are equal in their benefits. The

flower, I doubt not, receives a fair guerdon from the Bee—its leaves blush deeper in the next spring—and who shall say between Man and Woman which is the most delighted? Now it is more noble to sit like Jove tha[n] to fly like Mercury—let us not therefore go hurrying about and collecting honey-bee like, buzzing here and there impatiently from a knowledge of what is to be arrived at: but let us open our leaves like a flower and be passive and receptive—budding patiently under the eye of Apollo and taking hints from every noble insect that favours us with a visit— sap will be given us for meat and dew for drink.

In this remarkable letter, to which I shall return, Keats has anticipated the categories of what modern feminist philosophers have called "women's ways of knowing."[24] Keats' "hints" and "whispers" and "delicious diligent Indolence" all point to modes of rational knowing, distinct from those produced by a scientific or analytic method that presupposes both a neutral observer and an objective body of facts that can be known. Feminist philosophers have accurately located the biases and unwarranted assumptions inherent in such rationalist—and masculinist—epistemologies: most notably, the impossibility of a genuinely impartial observer, and the failure to recognize that "a fact is a contestable component of a theoretically constituted order of things."[25] Instead, Keats, like Wordsworth and Coleridge before him, suggests that knowledge can be gained from many different kinds of activities: intuiting, imagining, giving, suggesting, receiving.

Keats extends this alternative concept of rational knowledge in his letter on the nature of reality written to his friend Benjamin Bailey:

As Tradesman say everything is worth what it will fetch, so probably every mental pursuit takes its reality and worth from the ardour of the pursuer—being in itself a nothing—Etherial things may at least be thus real, divided under three heads—Things real—things semireal—and no things. Things real—such as existences of Sun Moon & Stars and passages of Shakespeare. Things semi-real such as Love, the Clouds &c which require a greeting of the Spirit to make them wholly exist—and Nothings which are made Great and dignified by an ardent pursuit. . . .[26]

For Keats, truth or reality cannot exist apart from the perceiving and constructing mind: if "passages of Shakespeare" are among those things which are undeniably "real," then reality is a human production. And while Keats acknowledges the capacity of the

mind to hallucinate and distort, to produce "nothings" which exist
only as the product of human desire, he nonetheless insists that the
only knowledge to which the human mind can lay claim is that
produced by "a greeting of the spirit," a reaching out of the empathic imagination toward a perceived other. Keats' realm of the
"semi-real," which is for Keats the realm of value and wisdom, is a
realm of "connected knowledge," of what we know as a result of
having established a relationship between our minds and the
Other, be it other minds, other objects, other social constructions.
Keats' cognition-by-sympathy here draws on Coleridge's interrogations of the shifting boundaries between the object and the subject in his *Biographia Literaria* and elsewhere, as well as on Wordsworth's argument, in his 1802 Preface to the *Lyrical Ballads*, that
knowledge is produced by the pleasure that comes from love.[27]
Keats also anticipates what Mary Hawkesworth has recently defined as the foundation of a critical epistemology: "the conception
of cognition as a human practice" that includes the full

> complexity of the interaction between traditional assumptions,
> social norms, theoretical conceptions, disciplinary strictures, lin-
> guistic possibilities, emotional dispositions, and creative impo-
> sitions in every act of cognition.[28]

This complexity is richly present in Keats' letters and consciously
included in that "greeting of the Spirit" which makes things hitherto semi-real "wholly exist."

Occupying the position of a woman in the poetic discourse of the
early nineteenth-century was however a source of anxiety for
Keats. During the early 1800s in England, the production of the
less prestigious forms of poetry—of sonnets, odes and romances—
was dominated by women, by such popular poets as Felicia Hemans, Charlotte Smith, Mary 'Perdita' Robinson, Anna Seward,
Joanna Baillie, Anna Laetitia Barbauld, Hannah Cowley, Hannah
More, Mary 'Psyche' Tighe, and Helen Maria Williams. Of course,
there were many men who wrote sonnets, odes and romances—one
remembers the youthful Wordsworth and Coleridge, Scott, Bowles,
Campbell, Moore, Southey, and a host of others. But male poets
tended to regard these particular poetic forms as less important
than the more "elevated" forms of the epic, heroic tragedy, or even
satire. Recall Wordsworth defining the sonnet, in *Nuns fret not*, as
a "scanty plot of ground" that provides but "brief solace." In choos-
ing to begin his poetic career by writing only in these "lesser"

genres, Keats professionally aligned himself with these women poets.

That Keats was not entirely comfortable playing the role of a "female" poet, participating in the ideological cross-dressing that I have been describing, surfaces even in the letter quoted earlier on the value of assuming the position of the female flower. Here, as Margaret Homans has acutely observed, Keats finally forces both the flower and the woman into an identification with Jove, the most powerful of the male gods, thus anxiously reclaiming a masculine identity that can resist the seductiveness of the feminine.[29] Keats' discomfort with being aligned with the feminine erupts more violently in his bitter attacks upon the leading women poets of his day:

> The world, and especially our England, has, within the last thirty years been vexed and teazed by a set of Devils, whom I detest so much that I almost hunger after an acherontic promotion to a Torturer, purposely for their accommodation. These Devils are a set of Women, who having taken a snack or Luncheon of Literary scraps, set themselves up for towers of Babel in Languages Sapphos in Poetry—Euclids in Geometry—and everything in nothing. Among such the name of [Elizabeth] Montague has been preeminent. The thing has made a very uncomfortable impression on me.—I had longed for some real feminine Modesty in these things, and was therefore gladdened in the extreme on opening the other day one of Bayley's books—a Book of Poetry written by one beautiful Mrs. Philips, a friend of Jeremy Taylor's, and called "the matchless Orinda."[30]

Keats then writes out for John Hamilton Reynolds the entire text of Katherine Philips' *Ode to Mrs. M. A. at Parting,* a poem that celebrates the delights and glory of an immortal female friendship: "Thus our twin Souls in one shall grow,/ And teach the world new Love." Perhaps Keats applauds this celebration of passionate female friendship because it is a world from which he is necessarily excluded, a world that cannot seduce or unman him. Moreover, "the matchless Orinda" was widely revered for her commitment to the concept of the female as spiritual, chaste, loving, self-sacrificing, nonrational. In contrast, Elizabeth Montagu, "the Queen of the Blues," advocated a more assertive, intellectual, and critical role for women, writing a widely acclaimed *Essay on the Writings and Genius of Shakespeare* (1769) and hosting a famous literary salon where Frances Burney described her as reigning forth, "brilliant in diamonds, solid in judgment, and critical in talk."[31] Nor did Keats' hostility to female intellectuals or blue-stockings diminish as he grew older. In 1818 he wrote to his brother and sister-in-law,

> Mrs. Tighe and Beattie once delighted me—now I see through them and can find nothing in them—or weakness—and yet how many they still delight! Perhaps a superior being may look upon Shakespeare in the same light—is it possible? No—This same inadequacy is discovered (forgive me little Georg[ianna] you know I don't mean to put you in the mess) in Women with few exceptions—the Dress Maker, the blue Stocking and the most charming sentimentalist differ but in a Slight degree, and are equally smokeable.[32]

Keats later asserted that one of his literary goals was the conquest of the women writers in his chosen genres:

> One of my Ambitions is to make as great a revolution in modern dramatic writing as Kean has done in acting—another to upset the drawling of the blue stocking literary world.[33]

Keats' ambivalent attitude toward gender infiltrates his poetry as well as his letters. On the one hand, Keats repeatedly assigns to the feminine gender the possession of beauty, power and knowledge, everything that the male poet yearns to possess. On the other hand, he anxiously tries to establish a space between the male poet and the female object of desire, a space where the poet can preserve a recognizable masculinity. In the *Ode to Psyche*, Keats explicitly engenders his own imagination, his soul or psyche, as feminine, following a classical convention that represents both the soul and the muse as female. At the same time, he defines his possession of that imagination or soul as a kind of rape: his "tuneless numbers" are "By sweet enforcement" wrung and his inspired chorus song will "make a moan/ Upon the midnight hours." The poems Keats will write as a result of this ravishment of, or by, his own imagination—the poem calculatedly obscures who is ravishing whom—are figured as "the wreath'd trellis of a working brain." The visual image of the spatially radiating, interwoven trellis resembles that of the spiderweb, the trope of feminine production. And the poem ends with an affirmation of female sexuality, of a vaginal "casement ope at night/ To let the warm Love in!" In this ode, Keats triumphantly and climactically occupies the positions

of *both* the male and the female lover: he has made love to, penetrated, received, and possessed his own Fancy, his own "shadowy
thought."

Such cross-gendering is presented far more anxiously in Keats'
Ode on Indolence, a poem whose transgression of both ecphrastic
and sexual boundaries has been compellingly analysed by Grant
Scott.[34] Keats first situates himself in the traditionally feminine
pose of passivity, indolence, waiting. In contrast, the female figures
on the urn actively turn before his eyes (the pun on "spin" in Keats'
epigram associates their energetic movement with the work of
both spinsters and spiders). But rather than comfortably accepting
his location within this female-dominated realm (Love and Poesy
are clearly female in the poem, and even Ambition wears "skirts,"
although these could refer to a Greek man's tunic), Keats tries to
open a gap between the sentimental odes of such women writers as
Mary Tighe and Mary Robinson—"Upon your skirts had fallen no
tears of mine"—and his own more virile version of indolence—"I
would not be dieted with praise,/ A pet-lamb in a sentimental
farce!" But his insistent adieus to the three Ghosts suggest less a
confident turn to an alternative kind of poetry—"I yet have visions
for the night,/ And for the day faint visions there is store"—than a
remarkable anxiety concerning the excessive hold of feminine poetic subjects and practices upon his imagination. For if Keats de-
risively dismisses both heroic masculine Ambition, which with
pale cheek and "fatigued eye" here "springs / From a man's little
heart's short fever-fit," and also his favorite poetic subjects of love
and creativity, here identified with a bluestocking "maiden most
unmeek," where can he turn? The poem ends in an aporia, a void:
"Vanish, ye phantoms, from my idle spright, /Into the clouds, and
never more return!" Keats has separated himself both from virile
masculine action and from feminine production, leaving him simultaneously without a gender identity and without a subject: unlike the lilies of the field, that in Keats' epigraph from Matthew,
"toil not, neither do they spin," Keats cannot do the work of poetic
creation organically, unself-consciously.

Nor could he write those genres of poetic production that he
himself defined as masculine: the Miltonic epic, the classical tragedy, the Shakespearean comedy. He remained attracted to those
genres and subjects associated by his contemporaries with
women:[35] the ode and the romance; the affections, nature and art.
His odes focus obsessively on female power—on the "still unrav-
ish'd bride of quietness," on the "light-winged Dryad of the trees,"

on "Veil'd Melancholy" and "her sovran shrine," on Autumn, which in Keats' originating letter had been gendered as female: "chaste weather—Dian skies."[36] In each of the great odes, a male poet seeks to penetrate and possess the power of the female object—whether the imaginative capacity of Psyche, the beauty and truth of the Grecian Urn, the perfect and unself-conscious happiness of the nightingale, the consciousness of mutability which intensifies our appreciation of both joy and beauty that Keats calls melancholy, or the acceptance of death, with the understanding that ripeness is all, that Keats personifies as Autumn. In each case, the male poet attempts to establish a perfect fusion with the female symbol, only to acknowledge his inability to achieve such total union. Elsewhere I have described this formal and thematic strategy as Keats' romantic irony,[37] but here I wish to emphasize the way gender complicates these strategies. Having defined the female Other as the object of desire, the male poet is finally forced to recognize the distance that separates the male from the female. In the terms I used earlier, Keats here succeeds in "cross-dressing," in occupying the subject position of the female, but he is not a "transsexual": he cannot *become* the female.

All but one of the long poems in Keats' famous 1820 volume are written in that genre Keats himself identified with female authorship, the romance:

> I shall send you the Pot of Basil, St. Agnes Eve, and if I should have finished it a little thing call'd the "eve of St. Mark" you see what fine mother Radcliff names I have—it is not my fault—I did not search for them.[38]

Keats' anxiety concerning his predilection for romance-writing surfaces in the defensive "it is not my fault" as well as in his earlier attempt to parody Ann Radcliffe's sublime landscapes in his letter from Devonshire to Reynolds:

> I am going among Scenery whence I intend to tip you the Damosel Radcliffe—I'll cavern you, and grotto you, and waterfall you, and wood you, and water you, and immense-rock you, and tremendous-sound you, and solitude you.[39]

Despite Radcliffe's precedent and the preeminence of women in this genre, Keats wrote romances, serious poems which complexly explore the ways in which the greeting of the spirit is enabled by love or disabled by scepticism and which have long enjoyed immense critical success. But Keats remained anxious about his participation in a genre dominated by women writers, at first refusing to publish *Isabella, or The Pot of Basil*, because

> it is too smokeable. . . .There is too much inexperience of life, and simplicity of knowledge in it. . . .I intend to use more finesse with the Public. . . .There is no objection of this kind to Lamia—A good deal to St. Agnes Eve—only not so glaring. . . . [40]

Anxiously trying to develop what might be recognizable as a less "smokeable" or more virile romance, in *La Belle Dame sans Merci*, as Karen Swann has shown, Keats finally allied himself with the male against the female. [41] If we assume that the *belle dame* is a mortal woman and that she has, however ambivalently and ambiguously, offered the knight or wretched wight the opportunity to experience a reciprocated love, then we must ask why he has lost or refused this love. And if the explanation lies in his dream—"Pale warriors, death-pale were they all; / They cried—'La belle dame sans merci/ Hath thee in thrall!' "—then we must ask what both the knight and the warriors of his dream have to gain by defining the *belle dame* as cold, cruel, lacking in compassion—in modern parlance, a "bitch." What the men gain is clear. Even though the knight is left "Alone and palely loitering" in a wasteland where the "sedge has wither'd" and "no birds sing," even though his harsh dream has become his reality and he remains unloved, unloving, even dying, nonetheless *he gets to tell the story.* The male voice both appropriates and silences the female—we never hear what the *belle dame* thought or felt. This poem thus becomes, in Swann's memorable phrase, a case of "harrassing the muse," an unwarranted sexual and verbal assault upon a female whose response is neither listened to nor recorded. This short romance calls our attention to the extreme anxiety Keats felt toward his feminine subject matter, even as he could not turn away from it.

For Keats, the process of poetic creation was inextricably associated with female biology and feminine production. More than other male Romantic writers, he reverently acknowledged the creative power of women. Recognizing that this awareness threatened his own masculinity and poetic endeavors, he strenuously tried to establish a space in which his male ego could assert its difference from the female. Yet when he turned to the heroic, masculine Miltonic epic, in *Hyperion* and *The Fall of Hyperion*, he continued to assign to the female the possession of tragic beauty and Athenaic wisdom.[42] At the same time he granted to the vigorously struggling male poet the final capacity to translate that feminine historic and graphic consciousness into an adequate poetic language. Here the visual (the face of Moneta) and the verbal (the discourse of the male poet) finally fuse, in Keats' emblematic description of Moneta's "bright-blanch'd" face, "deathwards progressing / To no death." The male poet thus achieves an enduring relationship of equality *and* difference with the female divinity. Having approached the goddess like a child to his mother, reaching only to her "broad marble knees" (I:214) and hearing her "immortal's sphered words" softened "to a mother's" (I:250), having gazed upon her sublime face, the poet-narrator "ached to see what things the hollow brain/ Behind enwombed" (I:287). The pregnant tragic consciousness of Moneta becomes the poet's power "of enormous ken/ To see as a God sees, and take the depth/Of things" (I:303–4), translated into a language that Keats defines as "humanize[d]" (II:2). The words of Moneta and the discourse of the poet finally fuse, as Keats modestly implies at the end of Canto I:

> . . . And she spake on,
> As ye may read who can unwearied pass
> Onward from the antichamber of this dream,
> Where even at the open doors awhile
> I must delay, and glean my memory
> Of her high praise: perhaps no further dare.
>   (I:463–8)

Through "daring" and the courage to suffer "without stay or prop. . .The load of this eternal quietude" (I:388–90), the male poet discovers what is ultimately for Keats the appropriate relationship between female and male in poetic discourse: that of goddess/ mother/muse to human/son/poet, a relationship that sustains the role of humble submission and dependency Keats has everywhere adopted in relation to feminine creative power. But this obedience enables the poet to speak for the next generation, for posterity. For Keats, female reproductive biology takes precedence over male poetic creation, but poetic language sustains that reproductive process both by acknowledging its sacred priority and by articulating its cultural meaning, the meaning of life itself. Keats' poetics is finally not the women-excluding "male preserve" Homans describes, so much as the reverent description of a sublime power here located in the mother, another mode of what I have called the domesticated sublime.

Because I want to contest the traditional academic assumption that poetry and fiction are superior genres of literary discourse, more deserving of analysis and propagation than other kinds of writing such as journals and letters, I have focused in this discussion of Keats' gender ideology as much on his letters as on his poetry. Keats' letters have long been recognized by scholars and critics to be exceptionally complex, thickly textured and profound meditations on issues that obsess us: love, friendship, death, the nature and function of language and poetry, the purpose of suffering.[43] Perhaps these letters are ideological and cultural artifacts of even greater significance than his more famous odes. If the ultimate function of language is to construct and represent ourselves and our relations with other objects and selves both living and dead, then the "self-life-writing" of Keats' letters, like Dorothy Wordsworth's Journals, Byron's letters and journals, Frances Burney's letters, and Mary Robinson's Memoirs, "self-life-writing" that I have associated with the fluid subjectivity of feminine Romanticism, are as successful an achievement of such discourse as we are likely to find.

Emily Brontë

To find a female writer whose personal history and ideological investments more closely approximate masculine Romanticism than feminine, I have moved beyond the historical confines of the Romantic period (1780–1830) into the mid-nineteenth century. Emily Brontë's poetry and fiction have long been viewed as triumphs of "Romanticism"; Walter Pater in 1889 significantly called *Wuthering Heights* "a more really characteristic fruit" of "the spirit of romanticism" than the writings of Walter Scott.[44] (Pater's comment underlines the very gender distinction in Romanticism to which I have been drawing attention, since many of the writings of Walter Scott, in their commitment to the equality of women, clan loyalties, and the primacy of the domestic affections, as in, for instance, *The Heart of Midlothian*, might be described as examples of feminine Romanticism.) Here I wish to explore the ways in which Brontë's works conform to a specifically masculine Romanticism, as well as the ways in which they also come to resist it. Like Keats, as we shall see, Brontë was a literary cross-dresser but not a transsexual.

Nicknamed "The Major" by the curate William Weightman for

her vigilant protection of her sisters from his flirtatious advances (a nickname that struck the family as so appropriate that Charlotte incorporated it into her portrait of her sister as Captain Keeldar in *Shirley*), Emily Brontë in many ways occupied the position of a man in the Brontë household. The tallest (at five foot seven inches), strongest and healthiest of the four surviving Brontë children, she was also the most self-reliant and self-sufficient. As a young girl, she boldly roamed the moors in all weathers, mischievously "leading Charlotte where she would not dare to go of her own free-will" and tormenting her with tales of the nearby presence of frightening animals, "laughing at her horror with great amusement."[45] Ellen Nussey recalled a revealing moment with Emily, when they visited the stream they called "The Meeting of the Waters":

> Emily, half reclining on a slab of stone, played like a young child with the tadpoles in the water, making them swim about, and then fell to moralizing on the strong and the weak, the brave and the cowardly, as she chased them with her hand.[46]

As C. Day Lewis revealingly observed, these values—the strong and the weak, the brave and the cowardly—"are a boy's values, rather than a girl's."[47] Emily's childhood identification with the masculine gender is further suggested by the alacrity with which she seized upon Branwell's toy soldiers, immediately selecting as her own the most grim-visaged and naming him Parry after the arctic explorer Captain Edward Parry, a name that later became one of her own pseudonyms.

As a young woman, Emily's acts of physical courage became legendary among the villagers of Haworth: she plunged into the midst of a savage dogfight with a can of pepper to separate her beloved Keeper from a wolfhound; when she encountered a possibly rabid dog that bit her, she calmly walked into the kitchen, thrust a poker into the fire, and cauterized the wound without a sound; when Branwell accidentally set his bed and himself on fire, she alone had the presence of mind to fetch water and douse him. All her life, her chief delight was to roam the Yorkshire moors in her characteristically long, lanky gait, wearing unfashionably loose skirts, accompanied only by her faithful Keeper, "to whom she would whistle in masculine fashion."[48] When her father became too ill to protect the house from possible invasion, he taught Emily to shoot his pistols, a sport she took up avidly, with pleasure and skill. When Branwell returned to live at the parsonage, in despair at the failure of all his professional aspirations and hopelessly in love with the married Mary Robinson, broken in body and spirit, a drunkard, gambler and opium addict, it was Emily who defied the decorum of the proper lady to fetch him home from the pub, carry him up to bed, and calmly, even compassionately, endure his violent curses and physical abuse.

Emily's refusal to conform to the conventions of nineteenth-century femininity was acknowledged, with both admiration and incomprehension, by her sister Charlotte in her *Biographical Notice of Ellis and Acton Bell:*

> Stronger than a man, simpler than a child, her nature stood alone. . . .
> In Emily's nature the extremes of vigour and simplicity seemed to meet. Under an unsophisticated culture, inartificial tastes, and an unpretending outside, lay a secret power and fire that might have informed the brain and kindled the veins *of a hero;* but she had no worldly wisdom; her powers were unadapted to the practical business of life; . . . Her will was not very flexible, and it generally opposed her interest. Her temper was magnanimous, but warm and sudden; her spirit altogether unbending.[49] (my italics)

Emily's most perceptive teacher also testified to her masculine character: as Monsieur Heger told Elizabeth Gaskell after Emily's eighteen months residence at his wife's school in Brussels,

> She should have been a man—a great navigator. Her powerful reason would have deduced new spheres of discovery from the knowledge of the old; and her strong imperious will would never have been daunted by opposition or difficulty; never have given way but with life.[50]

Heroic, reserved, unbending, intensely private, Emily Brontë could not conceive of a life for herself outside the freedom provided by her own household and the surrounding moors. She became psychosomatically ill whenever she left Haworth, lasting only six months at Law Hill School and returning from Brussels as soon as she could. She never married, never had a lover, never bore a child. Her most passionate relationships were with nature, her own dog Keeper, and her family—in that order, a priority scrupulously preserved by her father when he insisted on the following procession for Emily's funeral cortege:

behind the coffin walked Mr. Brontë with Keeper, who at Mr. Brontë's wish stayed at the head of the little procession and entered the family box-pew with them, where he remained throughout the service. After them walked Charlotte and Anne, and behind them Tabby.[51]

Keeper returned Emily's love: he answered only to her voice, always lay with his head in her lap, and howled outside her bedroom door after her death, not for days, but for many weeks.[52]

In her writings as well as her life, Emily Brontë refused to be confined to the position of a woman. Her earliest Gondal poems reveal the ease with which she inhabited the positions of both men and women, speaking in the voices both of her aggressive heroine Augusta Geraldine Almeda and of AGA's rejected and accepted lovers, Ferdinand de Samara, Julius Brenzaida and Lord Alfred. Her 1845 "birthday letter" to Anne Brontë described her delight in what Margaret Homans called her "mobile adoption of fictive roles,"[53] roles that fluidly deny gender boundaries:

> Anne and I went [on] our first long journey by ourselves together. . . during our excursion we were, Ronald Macalgin, Henry Angora, Juliet Augusteena, Rosabella Esmaldan, Ella and Julian Egremont, Catharine Navarre, and Cordelia Fitzaphnold, escaping from the palaces of instruction to join the Royalists who are hard driven at present by the victorious Republicans. The Gondals still flourish bright as ever. . . .[54]

Emily's identification with her multiple creations is complete: "we were," not "we played." Her refusal to confine herself to the subject position of the woman in literary discourse not only produced the masculine Romantic ideology of *Wuthering Heights*, to which we shall turn in a moment, but also her insistence on the "authority" and use of her androgynous pseudonym, Ellis Bell, a commitment that was not shared by her sisters. When Charlotte inadvertently revealed to *her* publisher, Smith & Elder, that the Bells "are three sisters," Emily never forgave her. Critics have tended to read Emily's anger as caused by an invasion of her fiercely guarded privacy, but I would suggest that it also resulted from Charlotte's unwitting denial of Emily's conviction that she *was* Ellis Bell, a name her readers would assume belonged to a man, and that her fiction could only have been produced by a socially constructed man. In literary matters, Ellis Bell refused to deal with a publisher who perceived her as a woman, and therefore offered her not-yet-written second novel to her original publisher Thomas Newby, over Charlotte's strong opposition, and despite Newby's shady business practices and dishonest advertising of *Wuthering Heights.*

The earliest reviewers of *Wuthering Heights* not merely assumed, but insisted upon, its masculine authorship, even though "Ellis" had androgynous connotations (it is the assumed name of Frances Burney's heroine in *The Wanderer*) and many women writers used male pseudonyms. "No *woman* could write *Wuthering Heights,*" proclaimed the anonymous reviewer for the *Union Magazine of Literature and Art* in June 1848.[55] "It is a compound of vulgar depravity and unnatural horrors, such as we might suppose a person, inspired by a mixture of brandy and gun-powder, might write for the edification of fifth-rate blackguards. Were Mr. Quilp alive we should be inclined to believe that the work had been dictated by him to Lawyer Brass," grumbled *Graham's Magazine.*[56] The direct opposite of "the affectation and effeminate frippery which is but too frequent in the modern novel," *Wuthering Heights* nonetheless exposes too much of the "coarse and loathsome" in human life, complained the *Examiner*, although the *Literary World* admired the novel for its "rough, shaggy, uncouth power."[57] And George Washington Peck cautioned young ladies against the coarseness, rudeness and excessive profanity of the book, even as he acknowledged its imaginative power and extreme originality.[58] I cite these several reviews because they demonstrate that within the literary discourse of Brontë's day, her novel was unambiguously positioned within the masculine gender. Its coarse and vulgar language, its display of fierce passion and physical violence, could only have been constructed by a man, thought her readers, and a lower-class man at that—one "not accustomed to the society of gentlemen," as Peck put it.[59]

Even after Emily Brontë's authorship of *Wuthering Heights* was established with the publication of the second edition of the novel in 1850, critics continued to insist that it had been written by a man. Seeking a likely candidate, they invariably fixed on Branwell Brontë. The rumor, promoted by Branwell's surviving friends William Deardon and Francis Grundy, long after both Branwell and Emily were dead, that Branwell had written *Wuthering Heights*[60]— despite the adamant and informed denials of both Charlotte and the Rev. Patrick Brontë[61]—was resurrected and vigorously defended by the Victorian critic Francis Leyland in 1886.[62] Urbane, scholarly English gentlemen, heavily embedded in the ideology of the separate spheres and Victorian constructions of femininity, found it impossible to conceive that a clergyman's virginal daughter could write such a book; the cautious and highly regarded biographer, Sir Thomas Wemyss Reid, explained it in part by Emily's constant exposure to the opium-driven, lunatic ravings of her love-obsessed brother, an opinion still credited by some informed critics.[63]

If we situate *Wuthering Heights* within its literary, as well as its biographical, context, we can see it as the heir of a masculine Romanticism which Brontë had absorbed from her enthusiastic reading of Percy Shelley, Byron, and William Wordsworth. The identification of nature as the locus of a sublime, even transcendent, experience; the valorization of passionate love as the achievement of a wholeness of being available nowhere else; the celebration of the imagination as the entryway into a sacred vision of heaven on earth; the affirmation of radical social change to achieve this new Jerusalem (with the recognition, in the aftermath of the French Revolution, of the failure of political, as opposed to aesthetic, solutions); the identification of the autonomous individual as the maker of the social contract; the power of poetic metaphor to create orphic worlds together with the ironic recognition of the limits of language itself; and the criticism of Enlightenment rationality as intellectually divisive and opposed to the fulfillment of individual desire—these are the ideological investments Emily Brontë found in the romantic poetry she treasured, and the ones she upheld in *Wuthering Heights.*

Critics who have insightfully read *Wuthering Heights* as "disjunctive" in its apparent effort to straddle the unbridgeable gap between the genres of Romance and Realism have overlooked the gender issues at stake in this generic classification. Emily Brontë, by casting her lot, as Nancy Armstrong put it, "with artists of an earlier age,"[64] was identifying more with a masculine code of values than with the feminine Romantic ideology promoted in the Gothic novels of Ann Radcliffe, an ideology that by the Victorian period had been vanquished by patriarchal bourgeois domesticity and the doctrine of the separate spheres. Perhaps it is this ideological cross-dressing that has produced the critical confusion surrounding Brontë's text. As J. Hillis Miller noted several years ago, the published critical accounts of *Wuthering Heights* are mutually "exclusive" and hence "incoherent," a phenomenon he wished, incorrectly I believe, to attribute to "the unresolvable heterogeneity of the narration."[65]

Wuthering Heights, like many canonical Romantic poems, is

structurally grounded on a principle of polarity, the inevitable conflict of opposites, what Blake called the "Contraries" and Coleridge the irresolvable tension between "the FREE LIFE" and "the confining FORM." Brontë's text records the fierce battle between erotic desire and civilization, between nature and culture, between imagination and reason. In this struggle to the death, Emily Brontë—and her novel—are finally on the side of nature, of primal energy, of uninhibited desire.[66] In preferring the strong to the weak, the brave to the cowardly, she allied herself to the realm of the masculine; in preferring passion to reason, she joined Blake, Byron and Percy Shelley against the feminine Romantic exponents of rational love and self-control.

Primal passion is embodied in Catherine Earnshaw and in Heathcliff, that male muse who has no other name, that eponymous personification of nature itself, that being without origin. "Where did he come from, that little dark thing, harboured by a good man to his bane?" mutters Nelly Dean,[67] articulating our sense that Heathcliff is beyond explanation, what Kant would call the noumenal thing-in-itself, an elemental chaos. But this dark thing is always already interpreted, by Christian theologians and readers as evil and by Charlotte Brontë as "a demon life—a Ghoul—an Afreet" (322). Produced by Mr. Earnshaw as Frankenstein produces his creature, in a masculine appropriation of female childbirth and swaddling, "opening his great coat, which he held bundled up in his arms" (28),[68] Heathcliff is at once assigned to the position of the racial other: "as dark almost as if it came from the devil" (28). Speaking "gibberish that nobody could understand" (29), he remains liminal, occupying "the landing of the stairs" (29), on the margins of the household and society.[69] He is the "dirty"—"I shall be as dirty as I please, and I like to be dirty, and I will be dirty" (42)—the polluted, what Mary Douglas in *Purity and Danger* has defined as the threat of disorder to a precariously organized system.[70] And he remains on this border between the human and the nonhuman: "Is Mr. Heathcliff a man?" asks the appalled Isabella. "If so, is he mad? And if not, is he a devil?" (105) It is on the margin that Catherine Earnshaw joins Heathcliff, fuses with him, *becomes* him—"Nelly, I *am* Heathcliff"—uniting with him against society itself, whether the political tyranny of patriarchy (Hindley) or the social oppression of the church (Joseph), finding with him a paradise on earth—"no parson in the world ever pictured heaven so beautifully as they did, in their innocent talk" (34).

Catherine Earnshaw and Heathcliff represent a Blakean Innocence, the Wordsworthian child as "best Philosopher" and "Seer blest," the transcendental experience of a fullness of being beyond cultural construction, even beyond gender. No sex differences divide their youth; androgynous, they share the same bed, and grow up as ungendered children of nature, "half savage, and hardy, and free; and laughing at injuries" (97). Consistently identified with animals—Heathcliff is a "dog" (124), his biography a "cuckoo's story" (27), while Catherine recognizes the birds' feathers as though they were her own (95)—they know only the laws of nature, the predatory survival of the fittest. In *Wuthering Heights* as in the French essay on the butterfly Brontë wrote ten years earlier, nature is both prolific and devouring: "La nature . . . existe sur un principe de destruction; il faut que tout être soit l'instrument infatigable de mort aux autres, ou qu'il cesse de vivre lui-même . . . ."[71] Before Heathcliff's arrival, Catherine, eager to assert her will through physical domination, asks for a whip; in Heathcliff, she receives the embodiment of nature's amoral will to power and destruction.

Catherine and Heathcliff *are* nature, that nature of titanic force that Emily Brontë knew on the bleak Yorkshire moors. It is a nature that transcends gender. Never in *Wuthering Heights* is nature assigned a sex, although Emily Brontë elsewhere engendered both nature and the north wind as female, in her French essay and in her drawing of Lady Charlotte Harley as "The North Wind."[72] Charlotte Brontë also assigned the female gender to her sister's vision of nature in *Shirley:* there Shirley Keeldar proclaims, "Nature is now at her evening prayers; she is kneeling before those red hills . . . a woman-Titan" (ch. 18). But in *Wuthering Heights* nature is antithetical to culture, and hence to all social constructions, even those of sex and gender.

On the edge, where nature confronts culture, stands Wuthering Heights, the representation of what Levi-Strauss would call the *raw:*[73] the family sitting room, here referred to as "the house" itself (4), is uncarpeted, undecorated—save for a vast oak dresser whose shelves are filled with raw meat (legs of beef, mutton and ham) and whose lower depths house a bitch pointer with her squealing puppies. The distinction between the wild and the tamed is blurred; guns and horse pistols hang on the walls, sheepdogs haunt the interior recesses, and "cattle are the only hedge-cutters" (3). Significantly, the kitchen has been banished: "I observed no signs of roasting, boiling or baking about the huge fire-place; nor any glitter of copper saucepans and tin cullenders on the walls" (4). Defining the conflict between the raw and the cooked, Zillah's frying pan imposes a modicum of order when savage violence erupts in the "house."

In this house and on the moors beyond this house, Catherine Earnshaw and Heathcliff share a primal *oneness*, with nature and each other, that absence of a consciousness of self that Wordsworth in "Tintern Abbey" identified with the experience of wholeness on earth: "nature then/ . . . To me was all in all." But this oneness does not, cannot, endure. Separated by Hindley at puberty, Catherine and Heathcliff are further divided by the institutions of civilization, by Catherine's exposure to Thrushcross Grange and her consequent transformation into a proper lady, with the accompanying consciousness that it would "degrade" her to marry Heathcliff. The division of Heathcliff from Catherine is explicitly sexual, encoded in her decision to marry Edgar Linton, who is but frost to her fire. When Heathcliff returns after three years, now a presentable "gentleman," Catherine's frustrated sexual desire—vividly represented in the kitchen scene in chapter 11 where Catherine hurls the key into the fire and Heathcliff thrusts through the inner door with a red-hot poker, after which Catherine pulls so hard on the bell-rope that she breaks it[74]—is so overwhelming that she literally dies of it.

Here Emily Brontë, as Robert Polhemus has movingly reminded us,[75] is rewriting the age-old tale of Eros, the story told by Plato in *The Symposium*, retold by medieval chroniclers as *Tristan and Isolde*, and again by Shakespeare as *Romeo and Juliet* and *Antony and Cleopatra*. Eros, that primal desire for fusion with one's missing half, that desire to *be* the other, as we know all too well, can never be consummated in life but only in death.[76] For only with the annihilation of self-consciousness, the annihilation of the consciousness of one's body as a boundary, can such fusion be achieved. Therefore Catherine *must* separate her self from Heathcliff, as Tristan laid his sharpened sword between himself and Isolde, as Antony left Cleopatra to marry Octavia. Convinced that "it would degrade me to marry Heathcliff," Catherine cracks her self in two, splitting her very soul, as Heathcliff bitterly insists:

> Because misery, and degradation, and death, and nothing that God or Satan could inflict would have parted us, *you*, of your own will, did it. I have not broken your heart—*you* have broken it— and in breaking it, you have broken mine. (125)

Eros can be consummated only if bodily difference is eliminated. That is why Heathcliff flings himself upon the dying Catherine with "cannibal teeth" (136), gnashing and foaming like a mad dog, gathering "her to him with greedy jealousy" (124): if he can *eat* her, her body will become his body. But civilization thwarts this mad, passionate desire, and Catherine dies, leaving Heathcliff alive, with his "soul in the grave" (125).

Emily Brontë has retold the tale of Eros with the particular twist given to it by the male Romantic poets. For Byron and Percy Shelley, romantic love is narcissistic: the beloved is a mirror image, in a finer tone, of the lover, what Shelley in his "Essay on Love" called the anti-type.[77] The lover worships an idealised version of himself, incestuously projected as his sister. "I loved her, and destroy'd her," moans Manfred of his beloved sister Astarte, at the same time emphasizing that they were the same person:

> She was like me in lineaments—her eyes,
> Her hair, her features, all, to the very tone
> Even of her voice, they said were like to mine;
> But soften'd all, and temper'd into beauty.
> *(Manfred,* II:ii, 106–109)

Percy Shelley in *Epipsychidion* hails his beloved Emilia as "Spouse! Sister! Angel!," begging that they become

> One hope within two wills, one will beneath
> Two overshaodowing minds, one life, one death,
> One Heaven, one Hell, one immortality,
> And one annihilation.

Catherine Earnshaw and Heathcliff are raised as sister and brother; Heathcliff literally replaces her dead brother, taking his name from that of an Earnshaw "son who died in childhood" (29); and as Eric Solomon first suggested, they may even be half brother and sister, if Heathcliff can be construed as Earnshaw's bastard, a possibility supported by Earnshaw's preference for him over his other children.[78] Catherine's passionate absorption of Heathcliff into her own being—"he's more myself than I am" (62)—thus consummates the incestuous, narcissistic desire of romantic love.

After Catherine's death, Heathcliff desperately seeks to regain the wholeness he has lost. At first he thinks he can rejoin Catherine through consciousness: he demands that she "haunt" him; he insists that her spirit is a "presence" beside him; he systematically first possesses and then destroys everything that has separated them (Hindley, the Lintons, Thrushcross Grange, civilization itself). But he finally recognizes that he can unite with Catherine only *through the body*, through death; his attack on social institutions (property, lineage) has only been a misdirection of his natural energy away from Catherine. He then seeks out the coffin-bed they shared as children and, like Catherine before him, wills his death, having first assured that their two bodies will mingle though the opened walls of their adjacent coffins. His death, as Nelly realizes, is a triumph—the "frightful, life-like gaze of exultation" cannot be shut out of his eyes (254), for with a wrist gashed on the broken glass of the lattice window, Heathcliff has become the body of Catherine visioned in Lockwood's dream, the twenty-year wailing child now let in/out.[79] That Heathcliff's death is the consummation he so devoutly wished is signified in the text by the insistence of the villagers, of the innocent boy and even of Joseph, that Catherine and Heathcliff *walk*, in Catherine's words, "incomparably above and beyond you all" (125)—on the moors, in the churchyard, within Wuthering Heights itself (255).

Thus Emily Brontë's novel registers her overriding sense of a primal life that rages through nature, through the human body, through the soul, a life so free and infinitely expanding that all the institutions of civilization become to it but prisons of mind-forged manacles. As she affirmed in the last lines she ever wrote, "*No coward soul is mine*," "Life—. . . THOU art Being and Breath,/ And what THOU art may never be destroyed."[80] That Brontë's authorial sympathy is with Eros, with this passionate, primeval life-force/ death-force, is embedded in the grounding figures of her discourse. As Mark Schorer observed, albeit to a different purpose, Emily Brontë consistently tropes human events as natural events.[81] The rhythms of nature—weather, seasons, the passage from storm to calm—determine the rhythms of human events. Catherine, for instance, "had seasons" of gloom and sunshine (71). Human faces becomes landscapes ("a cloud of meditation" hangs over Nelly Dean's "ruddy countenance"); human activities become natural events (Jabes Branderham "poured forth his zeal in a shower"). Absorbing all of the human into itself, nature too is human. A tree bleeds—"I observed several splashes of blood about the bark of the tree" (129), comments Nelly. Thus Emily Brontë writes the human *back into* nature, grounding life itself on the primal elements of fire and water, earth and air.

Brontë sided with Blake and Percy Shelley in their hostility to the mind-forged manacles of existing social and political institutions, to the repressive abstractions of Enlightenment rationality, and to a language of thought divorced from feeling. But Brontë's opposition to the constructions of culture was more radical even than that of her male Romantic forebears—for it included a hostility to language itself. While she celebrated the power of the imagination to create new forms and to apprehend a transcendent truth, dedicating herself to her own "God of Visions," "My slave, my comrade, and my King,"[82] she finally located this truth not in language or art, but rather in physical nature, in that primal chthonic or dionysiac power which lies beyond all linguistic systems.

Wuthering Heights represents the constructions of civilization only to demonstrate their feebleness in the face of primitive nature. The "advantages" of culture are embodied in Thrushcross Grange, a house where, as Sandra Gilbert and Susan Gubar observed, everything is "cooked," decorated, clean; where the boundaries are sharply marked between the wild and the tame, the agrarian and the domestic, outside and inside. Here animals are clearly "pets" and human beings are either servants or ladies and gentlemen. This is the realm of law, of the Lacanian symbolic—Edgar Linton, like his father before him, is a magistrate. Here Catherine Earnshaw, violently seized by a bulldog at the age of twelve, at puberty, is transformed from a savage into a proper lady. She is washed, her hair combed, given fine clothes, taught to speak a refined language, provided with a "respectable" husband.[83]

Emily Brontë makes it clear that Catherine's transformation into a lady is a fall, a crippling, a self-division. Her new shoes—whether the "enormous slippers" or the "burnished shoes" (40–41) provided by the Lintons—are too large or too fragile to run in. Nor can she move easily in her "grand plaid silk frock," a "long cloth habit which she was obliged to hold up with both hands" in order to walk or mount stairs (40). More important, Catherine's primitive linguistic constructions—in which she said what she meant and uttered her desire as forthrightly as possible—have been complicated into a sophisticated linguistic irony or "doubleness." She adopts "a double character, without exactly intending to deceive anyone" (52), using one speech and behavior at Wuthering Heights, another at Thrushcross Grange. Whether one reads this linguistic splitting as the move from the Lacanian imaginary into the symbolic, as has Margaret Homans,[84] or in terms closer to Brontë's own conception, from a "natural" speech "commencing in strong feeling" into the duplicities of "artificial" speech, "the affected, wordy way that a schoolboy might use to a fancied, incorporeal sweet-heart" (172), one recognizes Catherine's entrance into linguistic imprisonment.

Such linguistic and psychological "doubleness" is aligned in this text with disease: Catherine is "laid up" for five weeks on the Lintons' sofa with the (castrating) wound to her ankle; she falls into a delirious fever after spending the night in the cold rain lamenting Heathcliff's departure (the departure she caused by her newly gained class consciousness that it would "degrade" her to marry him), a fever powerful enough to kill both Linton parents (69); and she finally dies of the recognition that she has split her own soul by marrying Edgar, that she can never possess both Edgar and Heathcliff. Her self-division is so acute that, dying, she cannot even recognize her mirror image (96). Separated from Heathcliff, from nature, from her own spirit/soul, Catherine cannot live. For her, the movement from nature to culture is the movement from life to death.

Emily Brontë is writing more than the story of Eros. She is inscribing civilization itself as a parasite upon and perversion of nature. In Thrushcross Grange, Catherine and Heathcliff's aggressive energy and passionate love is corrupted into spoiled selfishness: we first see Edgar and Isabella quarreling over a pet dog which "they had nearly pulled in two between them" (37), and Edgar's attraction to Catherine is sado-masochistic. Aroused to fever pitch when she boxes his ears, his desire for her is that of a cat to "a mouse half killed, or a bird half eaten" (56). In this brutal image Brontë insists that civilization is as predatory upon a weakened nature as nature is upon itself.

Her point is driven home throughout the novel by the career of the "gentleman," Heathcliff. Using entirely legal means, through calculated risk-taking and entrepreneurship, Heathcliff gains uncontested possession of both Wuthering Heights (by holding the mortgage Hindley has taken to pay his gambling debts) and Thrushcross Grange (by marrying Isabella who inherits the estate after her brother's death and by becoming the inheritor of his son's and his son's wife's personal property and lands). By documenting so exactly the system of arranged marriages, mortgage foreclosures, and wills, both entailed and otherwise, which enable Heathcliff to "rise" in the world, Emily Brontë suggests that bourgeois capitalism is but a more sophisticated version of the law of the jungle, of the survival of the fittest, of what would later be called Social Darwinism. Significantly, as Nancy Armstrong remarked,[85]

Brontë refuses to tell us *how* Heathcliff got the capital to initiate his rise; instead Lockwood fills this gap with all the possible ways in which a beggar can become a gentleman: "Did he finish his education on the Continent, and come back a gentleman? or did he get a sizer's place at college? or escape to America, and earn honours by drawing blood from his foster country? or make a fortune more promptly, on the English highways?" (70–71) Brontë's point is that the beginning—whether honorable or dishonorable, whether through education or menial labor or military service or theft—doesn't matter, because the result is the same.

Her argument is political as well as economic. She explicitly identifies Heathcliff with the course of the French Revolution. Heathcliff and Catherine announce that they "are going to rebel," as the first American reviewer of the novel noted, in 1776, the year of the Declaration of Independence.[86] Heathcliff later compares himself to Hercules, the figure chosen by the French National Convention for their seal and intended to represent, as transparently as possible, the strength, courage, labors and unity of the common man (or *sans-culottes*) as he destroyed the many-headed Hydra of monarchical, aristocratic and clerical tyranny[87]—"I get levers and mattocks to demolish the two houses, and train myself to be capable of working like Hercules" (244). In 1801, when the novel begins, Heathcliff has adopted the pose of Napoleon: "his fingers sheltered themselves, with a jealous resolution, still further in his waistcoat" (3).

Heathcliff's career embodies the course of political revolution, both in America and, closer to Emily Brontë's imagination, given her Gondal battles modelled on the careers of Wellington and Napoleon, in France. By 1801, Napoleon had become Consul; by May 1802, when Heathcliff dies, the decision to make him Consul for Life had been taken (though not voted through until August 1802). Heathcliff's rise and death thus parallel the origin and perversion of the desire for liberty in France. Like Blake's Orc, Heathcliff begins with a fierce sexual passion and love of freedom, but finally distorts that energy into a reign of terror at Wuthering Heights, oppressing and literally imprisoning his wife, son, daughter-in-law and former master's son.[88] As in Blake's Orc cycle, the will to freedom becomes the will to power. Brontë shares with Blake, Wordsworth, Coleridge and Percy Shelley an initial enthusiasm for and then disillusionment with the French Revolution. But Brontë's vision is more radical: unlike these male Romantic poets, she does not believe that creative energy or a revolutionary aesthetics *can* produce a New Jerusalem; in her view, all energy is finally a desire to possess, control or destroy the other. When directed to the beloved, this erotic desire can be consummated through the body, through sexual passion or death; when directed outward, to social and political institutions, this desire produces only masters and tyrants, Carlyle's heroes and Nietzsche's supermen.

The most seductive form that culture takes in this novel is the written word. Recent rhetorical and deconstructive analyses of *Wuthering Heights,* most notably by J. Hillis Miller, Margaret Homans and Carol Jacobs, have rightly stressed the degree to which the novel opens a gap between literal and figurative language and calls into question both the ontological status of the referent and the significance of the "good book." [89] But Brontë's sceptical undercutting of both the written word and of language itself is more radical than even these insightful critics have recognized.

Throughout the novel, books are associated with a *displacement* or weakening of emotional energy.[90] In his dream Lockwood piles up books to keep Catherine out; Edgar, "the cipher" (159), finds "consolation" for the absence of Catherine in his library (94, 99); Lockwood, "frequently very dull" at Thrushcross Grange, would be "desperate" without books (228); Isabella falls in love with Heathcliff, not because she knows him but because she has read sentimental romances in which a "hero" of his description carries off the heroine; while the totally selfish, peevish Linton Heathcliff can be entertained only with books. In this novel books are a barrier between the mind and passionate experience, a sublimation of feeling and worse, a way to prevent the joy and agony of intense emotions.

Moreover, as Carol Jacobs has shrewdly observed, the specific books and passages mentioned in the novel—Jabes Branderham's sermon on Matthew 18: 21–35, *Seventy Times Seven, and the First of the Seventy-First,* and Joseph's theological tracts, *The Helmet of Salvation* and *The Broad Way to Destruction*—are books which promise punishment rather than love and forgiveness.[91] The servant who fails to forgive, not seven times but seventy times seven, is cruelly tortured, both in the Bible ("And his lord was wroth, and delivered him to the tormentors, till he should pay all that was due unto him." Matthew 18:34) and in Lockwood's dream, where he is beaten by the whole chapel. And what Heathcliff has learned from the Bible is the Old Testament ethic of revenge: an eye for an eye, a tooth for a tooth; as he rightly tells Nelly, "I've done no injustice" (252).

If "a good book" only weakens passion or preaches revenge, then it can be thrown aside, which is exactly what Catherine and Heathcliff do. As Lockwood discovers, Catherine does not read; instead she writes *over* what is written, filling the margins of her Bible with her names, drawings, her diary. Writing thus becomes an act of rebellion, requiring more passion and energy than reading; but even the act of writing, in this novel, is finally parasitical upon desire. As Margaret Homans has perceptively observed, a gap occurs in Catherine's diary at the very moment when she and Heathcliff defy Joseph's instructions to read and run out instead for a ramble on the wet, windy moors.[92] That gap is the moment when, in Julia Kristeva's terms, the text moves from the symbolic (the law of the father invested in Joseph) into the semiotic (the rhythmic writing and drawing of Catherine's diary) and then beyond language altogether, into the realm that cannot be troped, noumenal nature, the thing-in-itself. And it is here that Heathcliff and Catherine find freedom, joy, completeness. Their rambles on the moors are never—cannot be—described as they happen, but only recollected in tranquillity, as mediated and literary "spots of time."

Thus Brontë, like Percy Shelley, reminds us that every linguistic construction is but "a fading coal" of the initiatory inspiration or experience or feeling. For her, language is always a fall away from that heaven that is nature, a nature which, as Lockwood discovers, is "unmappable." The failure of the signified to motivate the signifier, the gap between the sign and the referent, between language and nature, is brilliantly represented by Brontë at the moment when Lockwood, the city man of book-learning, tries to find his way home in the snow:

the whole hill-back was one billowy, white ocean, the swells and falls not indicating corresponding rises and depressions in the ground: many pits, at least, were filled to a level; and entire ranges of mounds, the refuse of the quarries, blotted from the chart which my yesterday's walk left pictured in my mind.

I had remarked on one side of the road, at intervals of six or seven yards, a line of upright stones, continued through the whole length of the barren: these were erected, and daubed with lime, on purpose to serve as guides in the dark, and also, when a fall, like the present, confounded the deep swamps on either hand with the firmer path: but, *excepting a dirty dot pointing up here and there*, all traces of their existence had vanished; and my companion found it necessary to warn me frequently to steer to the

right or left, when I imagined I was following, correctly, the
windings of the road. (25, my emphasis).

The attempt of language to chart or define elemental nature is as
useless as the imaginary map in Lockwood's mind, where the
"dirty dots" of his sentence periods create only a false sense of order or meaning.[93] Since word and thing are here disjunctive, the
signifiers in Brontë's discourse are deliberately slippery and fluid:
Branderham's "loud taps" on the pulpit become "merely" the
branch of a fir tree rattling its cones against the windowpane,
which becomes the importunate, ice-cold hand of a wailing child
knocking on the window (19–20), a sequence in which the literal—
the rattling cones—is both bracketed and finally subsumed into
the greater discursive authority of the figural—the enduring passion and presence of Catherine Earnshaw.

Brontë not only endorses the male Romantic poets' ironic recognition of the limits and self-referentiality of language; [94] she also
shares their more general suspicion of Enlightenment rationality,
that scepticism expressed in Blake's hostility to Aristotle's Analyt-
ics and the human abstract, in Wordsworth's fear that "we murder
to dissect," in Keats' reluctance to "unweave the rainbow." The rage
for order, for rational coherence, is structurally represented in the
novel's two narrators, both of whom impose a signifying form upon
the events they overhear or witness.

Educated rationality is figured in Lockwood, the urban sophisti-
cate who cannot live without books and who seeks both to "chart"
(25) and to "devastate" (231) nature. But Lockwood, we soon realize, is a parasite who feeds off the life of strangers, able to find emotional sustenance only by vicariously experiencing the histories of
the Earnshaws, Lintons and Heathcliff.[95] As his name indicates,
Lockwood "would lock" out passion; he is terrified of sexuality,
fleeing from the "poor innocent" at the seacoast (5) and studiously
resisting Nelly's suggestion that he court Cathy Linton Heathcliff.
He is consigned to the position of the observer, locked into the gaze
of the peeping tom, enviously "staring" at "smiting beauty" (233).
Confronted with powerful feeling, he will even *pay* to get out,
thrusting a coin into Nelly's hand and flinging a sovereign at Joseph's feet (256). His response to proffered passion is not mere fear,
it is a violent and sadistic rejection: when Catherine Earnshaw
grasps his hand in his dream, begging to come in, he brutally
"rubbed it to and fro till the blood ran down and soaked the bed-
clothes" (20). Divorced from authentic feeling, Lockwood's lan-

guage is false, affected, artificial; he self-deludingly refers to Cathy Linton Heathcliff as Heathcliff's "amiable lady," "presiding genius" and "beneficent fairy" (10–11), words which in this context can only mark the gap between the codes of courtesy and propriety and the realm of the actual. Trapped within the prison house of civilized language (good words and good books), Lockwood cannot speak of the thing-in-itself; hence he cannot literally narrate the story, but must defer to Nelly Dean, with the acknowledgement that "She is, on the whole, a very fair narrator and I don't think I could improve her style" (120).

The embodiment of civilized common sense, of "true benevolence and homely fidelity" as Charlotte Brontë put it (321), Nelly Dean serves to define the distance between rationality and passion.[96] Hardly the Titanic Eve of Shirley Keeldar's adoration, Nelly Dean is Milton's Eve or more precisely, Milton's cook. She is a woman who cannot comprehend passion because she has never felt it. A physically robust, healthy woman, she dislikes the sickly; worse, she cannot grasp the connection between mental and physical imbalance. She is both conventional, siding with Edgar and Cathy Linton against the willfulness and fierceness of Catherine and Heathcliff, and a compromiser, someone who wants to ignore or deny conflict. She tries to smooth over rough surfaces, softening the harshness of Edgar's refusal to see the abused and humbled Isabella, failing to report Linton Heathcliff's true character and physical condition to Edgar, attempting to bridge the gap between Thrushcross Grange and Wuthering Heights with the false language of etiquette (she continues to call the abused and sullen Cathy Linton Heathcliff an "angel" and a "queen"), and most importantly, refusing to hear what she does not understand. As a result, as John K. Mathison shrewdly observed, Nelly Dean does a great deal of damage: she does not listen to Catherine's dream in which Catherine wished to speak her secret knowledge that she should *not* marry Edgar (62); she does not tell Catherine until after his departure that Heathcliff overheard her statement that it would "degrade" her to marry him; she foments the battle between Edgar and Heathcliff; and she does not tell Edgar that Catherine is starving herself to death after Heathcliff's banishment from their house. As narrators, both Nelly Dean and Lockwood function to define the limits of rationality and common sense, to reveal by omission all that reason cannot apprehend, and to subtly shift our sympathies away from the values of civilization to the greater energy and passion of Catherine and Heathcliff, to nature itself.

The first half of *Wuthering Heights* explores and subtly affirms the masculine Romantic values of love or Eros, of revolutionary energy, of imagination, of that life-force in nature and the mind which Percy Shelley called "Power." At the same time it reveals the inability of both language and reason to grasp that power, a power which in Brontë's text shatters the fragile orders imposed by both narrators, erupting in dreams, nightmares, ghosts, premonitions, superstitions, and even a buried face ghoulishly unchanged in the grave after eighteen years (218). The novel situates itself in that time and space when the rationalist Lockwood "had no longer my imagination under control" (22), where the human mind, usually bound by the manacles of reason, can "turn" itself inside-"out to another" (245).

The second half of the novel registers the ways in which Emily Brontë complicated the masculine Romantic ideology she initially inhabited. Unlike the male Romantic poets she admired and emulated, Emily Brontë shared a female concern with biological generation, with the fate of women. The story of Catherine's daughter repeats her mother's story in reverse, and her marriage to Hareton Earnshaw fuses Wuthering Heights and Thrushcross Grange, nature and culture. Readers have responded differently to this culminating marriage, some arguing that it represents the dwindling of a primal female into a bourgeois wife, while others believe that it constitutes a triumphant reconciliation of nature and civilization, in which Cathy, combining her mother's energy with her father's education, unites with Hareton, who fuses Heathcliff's masculine vigor with a capacity for enduring affection or agape.[97]

In terms of the ideological investments I have been exploring, the novel continues to uphold a masculine Romanticism, as Lockwood's final statement ironically clarifies:

> I sought, and soon discovered, the three head-stones on the slope next the moor—the middle one, grey, and half buried in heath—Edgar Linton's only harmonized by the turf, and moss creeping up its foot—Heathcliff's still bare.
>
> I lingered round them, under that benign sky; watched the moths fluttering among the heath and hare-bells; listened to the soft wind breathing through the grass; and wondered how any one could ever imagine unquiet slumbers for the sleepers in that quiet earth. (256)

Immediately preceding Lockwood's reflections, the text has "imagined" Heathcliff and Catherine walking on the moors. Lockwood's statement, so patently false in its attempt at narrative closure, is a final textual irony which destabilizes not only his concept of death as "peace" but also his notion that nature is "benign." His sentimental tropes are further undercut by his description of the three graves, a description that provides a literal embodiment of the figural metaphors proposed earlier in the text by both Nelly and Catherine to represent Heathcliff and Edgar. As Nelly observed, "the contrast [between the two men] resembled what you see in exchanging a bleak, hilly, coal country, for a beautiful fertile valley" (54). Catherine changes Nelly's prejudice in favor of cultivated valleys back to an affirmation of enduring rocks: "My love for Linton is like the foliage in the woods. Time will change it, I'm well aware, as winter changes the trees. My love for Heathcliff resembles the eternal rocks beneath—a source of little visible pleasure, but necessary" (64). Catherine's grave, now blended into the moors she loved, and Heathcliff's grave, as bare as a rock, stand together against Edgar's cultivated, "harmonizing" moss and grass. By returning us to Catherine, Heathcliff and Edgar, by privileging the figures of death over life, Emily Brontë upholds her discursive commitment to masculine Romantic love as the entrance to transcendence.

By offering an alternative, however diminished, to such erotic passion, Brontë registers her femaleness, her obligation to her sex, her need to imagine *what is the best possible* for women who wish to survive, to bear children, to become mothers. Had a man committed to the triumph of Eros written this novel, the story of Cathy Linton and Hareton Earnshaw would not have been told—Shakespeare did not imagine a happy marriage for Octavius or Tybalt, nor did the medieval chronicler offer an alternative to the *liebestod* of Tristan and Isolde. Keats leaves his Knight-at-arms alone without his *belle dame,* his Lycius dead; while the narrator of Shelley's *Epipsychidion,* divided from his "Spouse! Sister! Angel!," collapses both psychologically and linguistically—"I pant, I sink, I tremble, I expire!"

Significantly, the growing love between Cathy Linton Heathcliff and Hareton Earnshaw is explicitly mediated by books, by reading, by literacy. Cathy and Hareton meet in nature, over a dogfight, but culture immediately intervenes to divide them: Cathy can read and write and speak a polite discourse, but Hareton can speak only "bad words" and thus, in the social class Cathy inhabits, not at all (167). Only after Cathy has discovered the limitations of an entirely literary love with Linton Heathcliff, a "little romance" (175) begun with notes and the exchange of books and carried out entirely in written words (love-letters and books), a love that for the narcissistic and finally tyrannical Linton is no love at all, can she turn her attention to the illiterate, "degraded" Hareton. Their larger "romance" is also mediated by books. Hareton lifts books off the shelf for Cathy Heathcliff when she can't reach them (224); deprived of books himself, he takes her favorites in order to teach himself to read (228); mortified by her mockery of his mispronunciations and stumbling speech, he proudly but self-destructively hurls these books into the fire (229); and finally, she initiates their friendship through the gift of a book, which is first flung away, but finally accepted. Significantly, this acceptance is preceded by the recognition that a gap between language and feeling can exist, that the signifier may not be motivated. As Cathy tells Hareton, "When I call you stupid, I don't mean anything—I don't mean that I despise you" (237).

Books, the desire to read, the desire to learn to read and to teach to read, can signify and even generate passionate love, as it did for Dante's Paolo and Francesca, but the love Cathy and Hareton feel, mediated by books, is not Eros. Rather it is agape, a love based on the recognition of otherness, on mutual esteem, affection, and self-respect. It is sexual passion tamed, domesticated. The first activity Cathy and Hareton engage in together is the cultivating of a garden. This is the love advocated by Mary Wollstonecraft in *A Vindication of the Rights of Woman*, in which the wife and husband are, in Wollstonecraft's favorite word, "companions." As Nelly tells Hareton, "You should be friends with your cousin. . . . It would do you a great deal of good—it would make you another man, to have her for a companion" (237).

But Nelly's exultation in the love between Cathy and Hareton— "the crown of all my wishes will be the union of those two; I shall envy no one on their wedding-day" (240)—ought to give us pause. Cathy and Hareton have perhaps found the best kind of love that one can have *within the bounds of culture*. Begun as a rebellion against the tyranny of Heathcliff, their union fuses nurture and nature, the blond and the dark (Lockwood observes them reading together, "her light shining ringlets blending, at intervals, with his brown locks" [233]. Both Nelly and Joseph approve: their marriage restores both "the ancient stock" and "the lawful master," the patriarch whose name is inscribed on the door, a door carved with "griffins and shameless little boys" (4). But as Sandra Gilbert and Susan Gubar have emphasized,[98] this means that Cathy Linton

Heathcliff Earnshaw has been entirely inscribed within the ancient patrilineal system of Western civilization: she has become the "wife." For in marrying Cathy, Hareton immediately takes legal possession both of her body and of all the property (both landed and personal) that she inherited upon Heathcliff's death.

Nor should we overlook the violence that sustains the relationship of Cathy and Hareton. When she cruelly mocks his efforts to improve himself by reading a ballad "in the drawling tone of a beginner," he gives "a manual check. . .to her saucy tongue" (229); when he fails to pronounce a word correctly, she gives him "a smart slap on the cheek" (233). Emily Brontë wants us to see that even the most civilized marriages are grounded on power, on physical violence. Cathy can defy Heathcliff verbally if the physical strength of Hareton supports her ("If you strike me, Hareton will strike you! . . .so you may as well sit down" [242]). But Hareton also has the power to *silence* Cathy's speech—"Catherine was waxing cross at this [Hareton's insistence that she not criticise Heathcliff]; but he found means to make her hold her tongue. . .indeed, I don't believe she has ever breathed a syllable, in the latter's hearing, against her oppressor, since" (243).

As Hareton's wife, Cathy's speech will finally be determined by Hareton's desire. In any physical struggle between them, the larger and stronger Hareton will easily subdue the "slender" form and "exquisite little face" of Cathy (9). Their marriage not only lacks the fierce passion and erotic consummation of Heathcliff's and Catherine's love; it also demonstrates that Western, "Christian" marriage is but another construction of male desire, of male power, at the expense of the female. For how can that "twisted tree" Hareton Earnshaw, degraded as Heathcliff was, attached to Heathcliff "by ties stronger than reason could break" (243), identified with Heathcliff ("I can sympathise with all his feelings, having felt them myself" [168]), as fond of hanging defenseless puppies as Heathcliff was (140, 117), not treat his wife as Heathcliff treated Isabella? To see Hareton as a devoted and loving husband is to read him through the same genre of sentimental romance that persuaded Isabella to elope with Heathcliff.[99] Yet Cathy is given no alternative but to depend on his continuing good will.

Thus Brontë acknowledges her female body, and the boundaries it imposes. A female can remain within culture, a dependant on male affection and pity. She can become a socially constructed woman, a mother. Significantly, in this novel mothers are not biological but socially assigned. The biological mothers either die

(Catherine Earnshaw, Francis Earnshaw) or disappear (Heathcliff's "mother," Isabella Linton); the only person who literally mothers children is Nelly Dean, who has no biological children. For Emily Brontë, a universal maternal *instinct* does not exist, as the cuckoo's story makes clear; mothering is a social construction.

Or a female can devote her body to sexual passion, to eros, to an integrated wholeness possible only outside of culture in nature, in death. For Emily Brontë herself, there was finally no choice but eros, the return to nature, the refusal of culture.[100] She published her novel and willed her death, refusing medical treatment till she knew it was too late. In her quest for "something far more deeply interfused," she followed the masculine Romantic ideology to its final consummation in the fusion of the self with a divine Power, a God of Visions. But she remained a female in her enduring consciousness that the *body* determines one's options: to die—and thus enable the ultimate triumph of the body, the reabsorption of the self into nature—or to live and be socially constructed as a woman—a daughter, sister, wife or mother—and hence a dependent on patriarchal power.

CONCLUSION
Why "Romanticism"?

As my last two chapters have tried to show, the binary oppositions of masculine and feminine Romanticism become far more complexly interwoven when we scrutinize individual authors and specific works. Yet the tension created by gender difference remains central to the structure, the content and the production of Romantic literary texts. In the future we can no longer continue to speak monolithically of "British Romanticism," of a "Romantic spirit of the age," of "*the* Romantic ideology." If we are to present ourselves as students and teachers of literary Romanticism, we can no longer confine our attention to the work of the six canonical male poets. In conversation and contestation with masculine Romanticism, we must learn to hear at the very least one other voice, what I have been calling feminine Romanticism.

To recapitulate, feminine Romanticism was based on a subjectivity constructed in relation to other subjectivities, hence a self that is fluid, absorptive, responsive, with permeable ego boundaries. This self typically located its identity within a larger human nexus, a family or social community. Taking the family as the grounding trope of social organization, feminine Romanticism opposed violent military revolutions, especially the French Revolution, in favor of gradual or evolutionary reform under the guidance of benevolent parental instruction, the model proposed by Mary Wollstonecraft. This involved a commitment to an ethic of care (as opposed to an ethic of individual justice), an ethic that takes as its highest value the insuring that, in any conflict, no one should be hurt. In this context, nature became not a source of divine creative power so much as a female friend or sister with needs and capacities, one who both provides support and requires cultivation, with whose life-giving powers one willingly cooperates. In this ideology, moral reform both of the individual and of the family-politic is achieved, not by utopian imaginative vision, but by the communal exercise of reason, moderation, tolerance and the domestic affections that can embrace even the alien Other. Contesting the hegemonic construction of gender, the cult of "true womanhood" and female beauty subscribed to by Felicia Hemans and Letitia Landon, feminine Romanticism insisted on the equal value and rational capacities of women. And finally, this ideology found its appropriate mode of linguistic expression in specific genres: in the novel which enables the author to represent in the vernacular a human community whose multiple relationships extend over time, and in those poetic genres which celebrate the value of the quotidian,[1] of daily domestic and social involvements.

Of course, other ideological positions existed in dialogue and contestation with what I have called masculine Romanticism, ideologies grounded on class and religion and ethnicity, as well as on gender. We need to pay attention to the voices of the aristocracy and gentry threatened by the bourgeoisie, and to the equally powerful voices of the working class, the religious dissenters, the foreign nationals, the emancipated slaves. These last subjectivities are multiply constructed: in the discourses of the movement to abolish the slave trade, in religious tracts, in political journalism, in the broadsides, poems and autobiographies of the working class, in the confessions of condemned criminals. Not until we can hear all these voices, these myriad subjectivities, in dialogue with each other, can we claim to understand British Romanticism as either a literary or a cultural or a historical phenomenon.

One final question I wish to pose. While writing this book, I frequently asked myself whether it any longer makes sense to use the term "Romanticism" to refer to the writings of British women during the period 1780 to 1830, given that the concepts and cultural practices we have traditionally identified with the British Romantic movement were produced primarily by men. Would it be simpler to assign the word Romanticism to what I have been calling *masculine* Romanticism and find another word altogether for what I have termed *feminine* Romanticism? Since the ideological investments of most of the women writing between 1780 and 1830 in England have more in common both with their eighteenth-century forebears, both male and female, and with their Victorian descendants, again both male and female, might we not want to call them "post-Enlightenment" or "pre-Victorian" writers? Certainly such terms would draw attention to the *continuity* in British literary culture from 1750 to 1900, a continuity which has been obscured both by our exclusive focus on the male poets of the Romantic period and by our post-modernist desire—stimulated by Foucault's concept of an epistemic cultural break in Europe between the eighteenth and the nineteenth century—to establish a definitive category of "the Romantic/Modern" distinct from earlier literary culture.

I argue for the preservation of the term Romanticism, with the necessary further specifications of masculine and feminine Romanticism, on grounds both pragmatic and theoretical. The academic curriculum in English literary studies is based on a historical chronology which locates Romanticism between Eighteenth-Century Literature and Victorian Literature. If those of us who wish to transform the canon and the curriculum cede the category of, and the courses in, Romanticism to the canonical male poets, then either there will continue to be no place in the existing curriculum for the numerous women writers of the Romantic period or they will be taught only in courses on women writers. Either way, the gendered dialogue between male- and female-authored texts in this historical era will go unheard.

On the other hand, we might wish to give up the term Romanticism altogether as a misnomer for the period 1780 to 1830, as scholars of the eighteenth-century have given up the terms Enlightenment and Neoclassicism to describe the period 1680 to 1780. If we seek a purely chronological term for the Romantic period, we will have to call it "Late Eighteenth- and Early Nineteenth-Century Literature" ("LEEN Lit" for short?), which many will find unbearably cumbersome. The possible political term, "Georgian" literature, would once again inscribe literary history within a political history dominated by the court and the aristocracy, the very social hierarchy under attack in much of the literature of the period.

More important than these pragmatic curricular considerations, however, are the theoretical issues at stake in the term "Romanticism." Philologically derived from *romaunt* ("romance," "roman," i.e. the novel), "Romanticism" has long connoted an association with the imagination, the fictive, the ideal, the utopian, the revolutionary, especially in matters of love and politics. I have argued that many of the women writers in England between 1780 and 1830 collectively produced an ideology that was both revolutionary and utopian. As opposed to their Enlightenment forebears, they insisted that women as well as men are rational creatures who must be educated in the same way to develop their rational faculties to the highest possible point. The concepts of the rational woman and of rational love as the basis of the ideal marriage are in large part direct responses to the political agenda and ramifications of the French Revolution and the work of such feminist theorists as Olympe de Gouges and Mary Wollstonecraft. Even more radical, the demand in the writings of many women of the Romantic era for genuinely *egalitarian* marriages goes beyond the lover-as-mentor marriages recommended by earlier British women novelists, especially insofar as this demand is grounded on a claim for the equal public and private legal and social rights of the common woman. And finally, as opposed to their Victorian heirs, these women writers insisted that the values of domesticity—of such private virtues as sympathy, tolerance, generosity and a commitment to the preservation of familial affections—should become the guiding program for all *public* action.

In contrast, most of the male and female writers of the Victorian period followed Hemans and Landon in promoting a doctrine of the separate spheres which relocated the domestic virtues, and the authority of women, exclusively within the private sphere. Indeed, from a late twentieth-century feminist perspective, we might see Victorian literature as a *regression* from the more liberated stance of feminine Romanticism, a backlash in which female intelligence, activity and power was once again *restricted* to the arena of the domestic household.

Feminine Romanticism was truly a "revolution," in Raymond Williams' terms, in the sense that it envisioned the making of a new social order which would overthrow an old order; it was what Wollstonecraft rightly called "a revolution in female manners." It envisioned the creation of this new order through peaceful and pedagogical means, through gradual social evolution and what we would now call "consciousness-raising." And in this sense, as Donna Landry and others have recently reminded us,[2] feminine Romanticism, like masculine Romanticism,[3] was a reformist bourgeois movement, one that served the interests of upper- and middle-class women at the expense of working-class women. Having aligned itself with the educated classes, feminine Romanticism too easily fell prey to a conservative Victorian backlash that reasserted a bourgeois patriarchal authority over both the public and the private sphere.

Notes

Introduction

1. For recent studies of the prose essay in the Romantic period, primarily of those written by men, see David Bromwich, *Hazlitt—The Mind of a Critic*; D. D. Devlin, *De Quincey, Wordsworth and the Art of Prose*; John C. Whale, *Thomas De Quincey's Reluctant Autobiography*; Thomas McFarland, *Romantic Cruxes: The English Essayists and The Spirit of the Age*; Annette Wheeler Cafarelli, *Prose in the Age of Poets: Romanticism and Biographical Narrative from Johnson to De Quincey*; and, for the only treatment of a female essayist, Jane Aaron, *A Double Singleness: Gender and the Writing of Charles and Mary Lamb*.

2. On the origin of the novel in feminine discourse, see Jane Spencer, *The Rise of the Woman Novelist — From Aphra Behn to Jane Austen*; Janet Todd, *Sensibility—An Introduction*; Ruth Perry, *Women, Letters and the Novel*; Patricia Meyer Spacks, *Gossip*, esp. pp. 34–46, 65–78, 147–170, 258–63; on the general theory of the novel as a feminine genre, see Mary Eagleton, ed. *Feminist Literary Theory: A Reader*, Part 3.

3. Michael McKeon, *The Origins of the English Novel 1600–1740*. Also see J. Paul Hunter, *Before Novels—The Cultural Contexts of Eighteenth-Century English Fiction*, chaps. 1–2.

4. William Beatty Warner, in a paper delivered to the American Association of Eighteenth-Century Studies annual convention in Minneapolis in 1990, and Deborah Nestor, in her forthcoming UCLA Ph.D. Thesis, "Women's Discourse in Eighteenth-Century England and The Rise of the Novel," have argued for the central importance of Eliza Haywood's fiction to the formation of the English novel.

5. Michael McKeon, *Origins of the English Novel*, pp. 20, 265–70.

6. Terry Eagleton, *The Rape of Clarissa—Writing, Sexuality and Class Struggle in Samuel Richardson*, p. 13, cf. pp. 1–17, 95–101.

7. Nancy Armstrong describes this transformation in her *Desire and Domestic Fiction—A Political History of the Novel*.

8. Irene Tayler and Gina Luria, "Gender and Genre: Women in British Ro-

mantic Literature," in *What Manner of Woman—Essays in English and American Life and Literature*, ed. Marlene Springer, pp. 98–123.

9. Gaye Tuchman, *Edging Women Out—Victorian Novelists, Publishers and Social Change.*

10. Ann H. Jones, in *Ideas and Innovations—Best Sellers of Jane Austen's Age*, lists the nine most popular novelists of the period 1800–1820 as Maria Edgeworth, Walter Scott, Elizabeth Hamilton, Amelia Opie, Mary Brunton, Jane Porter, Sydney Owenson, Thomas S. Surr and Anna Maria Porter (pp. 3–6), while the most popular novelists of the earlier period 1780–1800 were Charlotte Smith, Frances Burney and Ann Radcliffe (see J. M. S. Tompkins, *The Popular Novel in England 1770–1800*). Commenting on the circulating library novels in 1810, Anna Laetitia Barbauld declared that "notwithstanding the many paltry books of this kind published in the course of every year, it may be safely affirmed that we have more good writers in this walk living at the present time than at any period since the days of Richardson and Fielding. A very great proportion of these are ladies; and surely it will not be said that either taste or morals have been losers by their taking pen in hand. The names of D'Arblay, Edgeworth, Inchbald, Radcliffe, and a number more, will vindicate these assertions" ("On the Origin and Progress of Novel-Writing," Introductory Essay to her edition of *The British Novelists*, London: Bentley and Colburn, 1810, p. 59). See also Mitzi Myers, "Sensibility and the 'Walk of Reason'—Mary Wollstonecraft's Literary Reviews as Cultural Critique," in *Sensibility in Transformation—Creative Resistance to Sentiment from the Augustans to the Romantics*, ed. Syndy McMillen Conger, p. 122.

11. On the presence of women writers in the literary production of the Romantic period, see Stuart Curran, "The 'I' Altered," in *Romanticism and Feminism*, ed. Anne K. Mellor, pp. 185–207, and Judith Phillips Stanton, "Statistical Profile of Women Writing in English from 1660–1800," in *Eighteenth-Century Women and the Arts*, ed. Frederick M. Keener and Susan E. Lorsch, pp. 247–254. The major role of women in literary publication in the early nineteenth century in England is also supported by the data concerning Macmillan's Publishing House collected by Gaye Tuchman in *Edging Women Out—Victorian Novelists, Publishers and Social Change* (1989), and by Coral Ann Howells' comments on the circulating libraries and especially on Lane's Minerva Press in *Love, Mystery, and Misery—Feeling in Gothic Fiction*, pp. 80–82.

12. Stuart Curran, *A Textbase of Women's Writing in English, 1330–1830: Bibliography of British Women Poets, 1760–1830*, pp. 1–42, available from the Brown University Women Writers Project or from the author.

13. Richard D. Altick, in *The English Common Reader—A Social History of the Mass Reading Public 1800–1900*, argues for the growing literacy of English women in the eighteenth-century, and especially for the surge of popular interest in reading during the 1790s spurred by the Sunday School Movement and the availability of books through the circulating and itinerating libraries (pp. 45, 65–72, 213–239). Although Altick does not concern himself specifically with the gender of readers, the tabulation compiled by the London Statistical Society of the contents of the ten leading circulating

libraries in London in 1800 cited on pp. 217–8 suggests that the subscribers to these libraries were predominantly female: three-quarters of the two thousand books in circulation were either "Fashionable Novels, well known" (439 volumes) or "Novels of the lowest character, being chiefly imitations of Fashionable Novels" (1008 volumes). Two additional categories also appealed primarily to women readers: "Romances" (76 volumes) and "Novels by Miss Edgeworth, and Moral and Religious Novels" (49 volumes).

J. Paul Hunter, in *Before Novels—The Cultural Contexts of Eighteenth-Century English Fiction*, also argues for the increasing literacy of women in the eighteenth-century (pp. 69–75) and points out that at least half of the popular Guides for Youth or conduct-books were addressed to female readers (pp. 265–266).

14. On the supposed "anxiety of authorship" experienced by female writers in the Romantic era, see Sandra Gilbert and Susan Gubar, *The Madwoman in the Attic*, chaps. 2–8; Mary Poovey, *The Proper Lady and the Woman Writer*; and Margaret Homans, *Women Writers and Poetic Identity*.

15. The use of the term "bluestockings" to refer to the learned or literary ladies of the late eighteenth century originally derived from the bluestockings worn by Benjamin Stillingfleet when he attended Lady Mary Wortley Montagu's Wednesday literary evenings with the leading female intellectuals of her day. On the friendships and literary productions of eighteenth-century literary women, see Sylvia Harcstark Myers, *The Bluestocking Circle: Women, Friendship, and the Life of the Mind in Eighteenth-Century England*. Myers discusses the origin of the term "bluestocking" (pp. 6–11), as well as Byron's, Moore's and Scargill's use of the term (pp. 290–97).

16. See, for example, Terry Eagleton, *The Rape of Clarissa*, pp. 1–17.

17. I owe these observations on *The Old Manor House* to David Blackmore and Lisa Gordis.

18. On the emergence of the cult of domesticity in the Romantic period, see Leonore Davidoff and Catherine Hall, *Family Fortunes: Men and Women of the English Middle-Class, 1780–1850*. On the dangers for women inherent in the bourgeois domestic ideology and represented in the female-authored fiction of the Romantic period, see my *Mary Shelley: Her Life, Her Fiction, Her Monsters*, esp. pp. 177–218.

19. Kingsley Amis, *The Faber Popular Reciter*, p. 14.

20. Anne Renier, *Friendship's Offering*, p. 5. Sonia Hofkosh has perceptively discussed the ways in which these elaborately engraved and bound books functioned culturally as articles of conspicuous literary consumption that defined women as the object of the male gaze within the category of beauty ("Disfiguring Economies: Mary Shelley's Stories," in *The Other Mary Shelley: Beyond Frankenstein*, ed. Audrey Fisch, Anne Mellor and Esther Schor) but I wish, like Renier, to emphasize their psychological and cultural function as gifts exchanged between women to document the existence of friendship.

Part I

1. M. H. Abrams, *Natural Supernaturalism—Tradition and Revolution in Romantic Literature.*

2. Geoffrey H. Hartman, *Wordsworth's Poetry 1787–1814.* For readings of English Romanticism influenced by deconstructive and hermeneutic methods, see Paul de Man, "The Rhetoric of Temporality," in *Interpretation: Theory and Practice*, ed. Charles S. Singleton, pp. 173–209; Frances C. Ferguson, *Wordsworth: Language as Counter-Spirit*; David Simpson, *Irony and Authority in Romantic Poetry*; Tilottama Rajan, *Dark Interpreter: The Discourse of Romanticism*; Anne K. Mellor, *English Romantic Irony*; Heather Glen, *Vision and Disenchantment: Blake's "Songs" and Wordsworth's "Lyrical Ballads"*; Cynthia Chase, *Decomposing Figures—Rhetorical Readings in the Romantic Tradition*; and William H. Galperin, *Revision and Authority in Wordsworth—The Interpretation of a Career.*

3. David Perkins, "The Construction of 'The Romantic Movement' as a Literary Classification," *Nineteenth-Century Literature* 45 (1990) pp. 129–143.

4. Gaye Tuchman, with Nina E. Fortin, *Edging Women Out—Victorian Novelists, Publishers, and Social Change*; and Paula Feldman, in private conversation, June, 1991.

5. Arguing from a more sophisticated perspective, Jerome McGann nonetheless reasserted the definition of Jane Austen as "un-Romantic" in *The Romantic Ideology—A Critical Investigation*, p. 19.

Chapter 1

1. On the social construction of gender, see Simone de Beauvoir, *The Second Sex*, trans. H. M. Parshley; *Woman, Culture and Society*, ed. Michelle Rosaldo and Louise Lamphere; Nancy Chodorow, *The Reproduction of Mothering*; Carol Gilligan, *In a Different Voice*; and Ruth Bleier, *Science and Gender.*

   On the social construction of biological sexuality, see Michel Foucault, *The History of Sexuality*, trans. Robert Hurley; John D'Emilio and Estelle B. Freedman, *Intimate Matters: A History of Sexuality in America*; Suzanne Kessler and Wendy McKenna, *Gender—An Ethnomethodological Approach*; Judith Butler, *Gender Trouble*; and Thomas Laqueur, *Making Sex.*

2. Marlon B. Ross, "Romantic Quest and Conquest—Troping Masculine Power in the Crisis of Poetic Identity," in *Romanticism and Feminism*, edited by Anne K. Mellor, pp. 26–51.

3. See Meyer Abrams, *Natural Supernaturalism*, pp. 27–8, 143–44.

4. Margaret Homans, *Bearing the Word—Language and Female Experience in Nineteenth-Century Women's Writing*, chap. 1.

5. Recent criticism has problematized the authority of both the narrator and the Pedlar in *The Ruined Cottage*; see, for instance, William Galperin, *Revision and Authority in Wordsworth*, pp. 71–75. Yet Wordsworth's manuscript revisions show an intensifying effort to assert an ultimate harmony between man and nature, a One Life that offers "comfort," "happiness" and

the benefits of the civilized mind—despite Margaret's suffering, grief and death—to the Pedlar, the narrator and the implied (male) reader. See James Butler, ed., William Wordsworth, *The Ruined Cottage and The Pedlar*, pp. 17–21; Peter J. Manning, "Wordsworth, Margaret, and the Pedlar," *Studies in Romanticism* 15 (1976) pp. 195–220, repr. in his *Reading Romantics—Text and Context*, pp. 9–34; and Marlon B. Ross, "Naturalizing Gender: Woman's Place in Wordsworth's Ideological Landscape," *ELH* 53 (1986) pp. 391–410, 406–8.

6. Marlon B. Ross, *The Contours of Masculine Desire—Romanticism and the Rise of Women's Poetry*, pp. 15–55.

7. Cf. Geoffrey Hartman, *Wordsworth's Poetry 1787–1814*, Part II: "The Via Naturaliter Negativa," and *passim*.

8. *William Wordsworth and the Age of Romanticism*, ed. Jonathon Wordsworth, *et al.* Catalogue entry #156, p. 218.

9. *The Letters of John Keats 1814–1821*, ed. Hyder Edward Rollins, 2 Vols., II p. 167.

   Without confronting the problematic issue of gender in "To Autumn," Helen Vendler bases her reading of this ode on the dubious assumption that Autumn is necessarily female, "a female corn-goddess derived from pagan myth," rather than the masculine figure of Autumn in Spenser's Mutability Cantos from which Keats, according to Vendler, "centrally" derived his poem. See Vendler, *The Odes of John Keats*, pp. 232–288, p. 242.

10. See Michael Ferber, *The Social Vision of William Blake*, and Irene Tayler, "The Woman Scaly," *Bulletin of the Midwest Modern Language Association* 6 (1973) pp. 74–87, repr. in *Blake's Poetry and Designs*, ed. Mary Lynn Johnson and John E. Grant, pp. 539–553.

11. David Erdman endorses the traditional identification of this figure as the female Jerusalem/Britannia, but adds that the figure also represents "all youth" in *The Illuminated Blake*, pp. 378, 375; while David Bindman in *Blake as an Artist* initially reads the nude figure as the male Albion but then acknowledges that the naked figure "could be either male or female" (pp. 180, 183).

12. For more detailed discussions of Blake's gender politics, see my "Blake's Portrayal of Women," *Blake: An Illustrated Quarterly* 16 (1982–3), pp. 148–155; Susan Fox, "The Female as Metaphor in William Blake's Poetry," *Critical Inquiry* 3 (1977), pp. 507–519; Diana Hume George, "Is She Also the Divine Image? Feminine Form in the Art of William Blake," *Centennial Review* 23 (1979), pp. 129–40; David Aers, "Blake: Sex, Society, and Ideology," in *Romanticism and Ideology*, ed. David Aers, Jonathan Cook, and David Punter, pp. 27–43; Alicia Ostriker, "Desire Gratified: William Blake and Sexuality," *Blake: An Illustrated Quarterly* 16 (1982–3), pp. 156–65; David Punter, "Blake, Trauma, and the Female," *New Literary History* 15 (1984), pp. 475–90; Norma A. Greco, "Mother Figures in Blake's *Songs of Innocence* and the Female Will," *Romanticism Past and Present* 10 (1986), pp. 1–15; Brenda Webster, "Blake, Women and Sexuality," in *Critical Paths: Blake and the Argument of Method*, ed. Dan Miller, Mark Bracher, and Donald Ault, pp. 204–24; Elizabeth Langland, "Blake's Feminist Revision of Literary Tradition in 'The Sick Rose'", also in *Critical Paths*, pp. 225–243;

Anne K. Mellor, "Blake's *Songs of Innocence and of Experience*: A Feminist Perspective," *Nineteenth Century Studies* 2 (1988), pp. 1–18; Mary Lynn Johnson, "Feminist Approaches to Teaching *Songs*," in *Approaches to Teaching Blake's Songs of Innocence and of Experience*, ed. Robert F. Gleckner and Mark L. Greenberg, pp. 57–66 (includes bibliography); Diana Long Hoeveler, *Romantic Androgyny—The Woman Within*, pp. 125–39, 210–225; and Margaret Storch, *Sons and Adversaries; Women in William Blake and D. H. Lawrence*.

13. Alan Richardson, "Romanticism and the Colonization of the Feminine," in *Romanticism and Feminism*, ed. Anne K. Mellor, pp. 13–25. For an extended case study of the way Percy Shelley appropriated the ideology of maternity into the ideology of the aesthetic, see Barbara Charlesworth Gelpi, *Shelley's Goddess: Maternity, Language, Subjectivity*.

14. Percy Shelley, *A Defense of Poetry*, in *Shelley's Prose*, ed. David Lee Clark, pp. 294, 294, 295, 297.

15. *The Letters of Percy Bysshe Shelley*, ed. Frederick Jones, I p. 402.

16. Percy Shelley, *On Love*, in *Shelley's Prose*, ed. David Lee Clarke, p. 170.

17. Percy Shelley, *A Defense of Poetry*, in *Shelley's Prose*, ed. David Lee Clark, p. 294.

18. Nathaniel Brown writes in *Sexuality and Feminism in Shelley*: "Utopian feminism . . . is precisely what Shelley offers in his literary prophecies of the future. . . . Shelley prophesies nothing less than woman's total emancipation—sexual, social, intellectual, moral, and spiritual—from centuries of male tyranny" (p. 180).

19. Nathaniel Brown, *Sexuality and Feminism in Shelley*, p. 182.

20. For a fine discussion of the role of gender in the construction of the hermeneutic community within the writings of Schleiermacher, Coleridge and Fuller, see Julie Ellison, *Delicate Subjects—Romanticism, Gender, and the Ethics of Understanding*. For other explorations of the role of gender in the writings of the canonical romantic poets, see, in addition to works cited elsewhere in this volume, forthcoming studies by Gerda Norvig, Karen Swann, Sonia Hofkosh, Julie Carlsen, Marlon Ross and Susan Wolfson.

Chapter 2

1. Edmund Burke, *Reflections on the Revolution in France, and on the Proceedings in Certain Societies in London, relative to that Event* (November, 1790), ed. Thomas H. D. Mahoney, pp. 35, 67, 82.

2. Mary Wollstonecraft, *A Vindication of the Rights of Men* (London, 1790), facsimile edition with introduction by Eleanor Louise Nicholes, pp. 41, 52. On the relation of Wollstonecraft's *Rights of Men* to Burke's *Reflections* and the tradition of Commonwealth dissent that Burke opposed, see Elissa S. Guralnick, "Radical Politics in Mary Wollstonecraft's *A Vindication of the Rights of Woman*," *Studies in Burke & His Time* 18 (1977), pp. 155–158; and G. J. Barker-Benfield, "Mary Wollstonecraft: Eighteenth-

Century Commonwealthwoman," *Journal of the History of Ideas* 50 (1989) pp. 95–115.

3. Mary Wollstonecraft, *A Vindication of the Rights of Woman* (1792), ed. Carol H. Poston, Second Edition, p. 192. All further citations from this volume will appear in the text.

   As Raymond Williams reminds us, it was in the 1790s that "revolution" acquired its full modern sense, moving beyond its earlier meanings of "a circular movement of history" or a "rebellion" to take on the additional meaning of "an attempt to make a new social order" (*Keywords—A Vocabulary of Culture and Society*, pp. 226–30).

4. That Wollstonecraft's intended readership was primarily middle- and upper-class men, the men who had the authority and power to institute the educational and political reforms she demanded, has been stressed both by Anca Vlasopolos in "Mary Wollstonecraft's Mask of Reason in *A Vindication of the Rights of Woman*," *Dalhousie Review* 60 (1980) pp. 462–71; and by Laurie A. Finke, "'A Philosophic Wanton': Language and Authority in Wollstonecraft's *A Vindication of the Rights of Woman*," in Robert Ginsburg, ed., *The Philosopher as Writer*, pp. 155–176. Anna Wilson has explored, from a contemporary deconstructive perspective, the failure of Wollstonecraft's rhetorical attempt to construct a readership of either men or women, in "Mary Wollstonecraft and the Search for the Radical Woman," *Genders* 6 (1989) pp. 88–101.

5. Mitzi Myers, "Reform or Ruin: 'A Revolution in Female Manners'," *Studies in Eighteenth Century Culture* 11 (1982) pp. 199–216, 206. Jane Roland Martin reaches a similar conclusion in her chapter on "Wollstonecraft's Daughters," in her *Reclaiming a Conversation—The Ideal of the Educated Woman*, pp. 70–102.

6. Cora Kaplan, "Wild Nights: Pleasure/Sexuality/Feminism," in her *Sea Changes—Essays on Culture and Feminism*, pp. 31–56.

7. On Mary Wollstonecraft's passionate love affairs with Fanny Blood, Gilbert Imlay and William Godwin, see Claire Tomalin, *The Life and Death of Mary Wollstonecraft*, and Emily W. Sunstein, *A Different Face—The Life of Mary Wollstonecraft*. On the contradictions and tensions in the text of *A Vindication*, see Mary Poovey, *The Proper Lady and the Woman Writer*, chap. 2.

8. Jean Jacques Rousseau, *Emile*, trans. Barbara Foxley, p. 333.

9. On the tensions inherent in nineteenth-century conceptions of female modesty, including Wollstonecraft's, and the significance of the female blush in nineteenth-century fiction, see Ruth Bernard Yeazell, *Fictions of Modesty—Women and Courtship in the English Novel*.

   On the parodic dimensions of Wollstonecraft's invocation of modesty in chapter seven of *A Vindication of the Rights of Woman*, see Laurie A. Finke, "'A Philosophic Wanton'," pp. 164–5.

10. For an anthology of eighteenth-century feminist writing, see *First Feminists—British Women Writers*, ed. Moira Ferguson. Ferguson's introduction provides a brief history of eighteenth-century British feminism, pp. 1–50.

11. See Hannah More, *Strictures on the Modern System of Female Education*

(1799); Catherine Macaulay, *Letters on Education* (1790); Priscilla Wake-field, *Reflections on the Present Condition of the Female Sex* (1798); Anne Frances Randall (Mary Robinson), *Letter to the Women of England, on the Injustice of Mental Subordination* (1799); and Mary Hays, *Appeal to the Men of Great Britain in Behalf of Women* (1798).

12. Regina M. Janes, "On the Reception of Mary Wollstonecraft's *A Vindication of the Rights of Woman*," *Journal of the History of Ideas* 39 (1978) pp. 293–302. Only Hannah More's *Strictures on the Modern System of Female Education* (1799) approached the impact of *A Vindication*; More's tract on the surface seemed more conservative—she advocated restricting women to the domestic sphere—but as Mitzi Myers has taught us, More's thought was potentially as subversive as Wollstonecraft's, since More allowed women virtually unlimited control over the private sphere, and asserted the equal importance of the private to the public sphere (Myers, "Reform or Ruin," pp. 199–216).

Chapter 3

1. Jane Spencer, *The Rise of the Woman Novelist—From Aphra Behn to Jane Austen*, pp. 140–80.

2. Claudia L. Johnson, *Jane Austen—Women, Politics, and the Novel*, pp. 19–21. Johnson comments tellingly on the gender politics of the "new and short-lived character-type" of the "freakish feminist, or 'female philosopher,' as she was then called." The use of this figure enabled the authors to make substantial social criticisms of the patriarchy while simultaneously assuring their readers they themselves were not such "uppity and insubordinate" women, to argue Wollstonecraft's ideas when her work was under a ban of disrepute, and to play the extreme ends of sexism and female superiority against a middle of gender relations distinctly more egalitarian than the status quo.

3. Maria Edgeworth, *Letters for Literary Ladies* (London: John Johnson, Second Edition, 1799), p. 89. Cited hereafter in text.

4. Maria Edgeworth, *Belinda* (London: John Johnson, 1801: repr. London: Pandora Books, 1986), p. 106. Cited hereafter in text.

5. Beth Kowaleski-Wallace, "Home Economics: Domestic Ideology in Maria Edgeworth's *Belinda*," *The Eighteenth Century* 29 (1988), pp. 242–3. Kowaleski-Wallace, writing from a 1980s feminist perspective, eloquently condemns the strategies of guilt and obligation inherent in the construction of motherhood under Edgeworth's "new-style patriarchy," strategies which resist women's usurpation of male prerogatives and define maternal self-sacrifice as the "natural" function of women.

6. On the results of the Rousseauistic experiment in the education of a wife carried out by Thomas Day, the author of *Sanford and Merton*, see Marilyn Butler, *Maria Edgeworth—A Literary Biography*, pp. 39n2, 309.

7. Frances Ann Edgeworth, *A Memoir of Maria Edgeworth*, London, 1867, I pp. 229–30.

8. Elizabeth Harden argues that Edgeworth condemns Belinda in *Maria Edgeworth*, pp. 53–55.

9. Frances Ann Edgeworth discusses Maria Edgeworth's love for Edelcrantz in her *Memoir*, pp. 141–144.

10. Helen Maria Williams, *Julia, A Novel, interspersed with some Poetical Pieces* (Dublin, 1790), p. 75. Cited hereafter in text.

11. Mary Hays, *Memoirs of Emma Courtney* (London, 1796; repr. London: Pandora Books, 1987), pp. 171–2.

12. The claim that Susan Ferrier attended James Stalker's Academy is put forth both by Aline Grant, in *Susan Ferrier of Edinburgh—A Biography*, p. 13, and by Elspeth Yeo, in The Catalogue for the National Library of Scotland, Edinburgh, exhibition *Susan Ferrier 1782–1854* (1982), p. 32. Mary Cullinan, in *Susan Ferrier*, p. 11, denies this, asserting that Susan Ferrier "may have gone briefly to an infant school, but otherwise she received a basic education at home."

13. Susan Ferrier, *Marriage* (written in 1810, first published in 1818), with introduction by Rosemary Ashton (London: Penguin-Virago, 1986), p. 5. Cited hereafter in text.

14. Nancy L. Paxton, "Subversive Feminism: A Reassessment of Susan Ferrier's *Marriage*," *Women & Literature* IV (1976) p. 23. Paxton emphasizes Ferrier's indebtedness to Wollstonecraft and Rousseau throughout the novel (pp. 18–29).

15. Mary Cullinan, *Susan Ferrier*, p. 60.

16. Both Nancy Paxton and Mary Cullinan have drawn attention to the subversive feminism of Emily Lindore; Paxton believes that Ferrier's irony is conscious, while Cullinan insists that it is unconscious, even as she acknowledges that Emily Lindore speaks with the same conversational manner and comic wit that characterizes Susan Ferrier's private correspondence (Paxton, "Subversive Feminism," pp. 24–26; Cullinan, *Susan Ferrier*, pp. 61–65).

17. The debate concerning Jane Austen's political and ideological allegiances has raged for years. Among the most powerful critical voices to sustain the traditional definition of her politics as a conservative investment in the landed gentry are Ian Watt, Alistair Duckworth, Marilyn Butler, Warren Roberts, David Monaghan and Mary Poovey; arguments for Jane Austen's radical feminism can be found in Lloyd W. Brown, "Jane Austen and the Feminist Tradition," *Nineteenth-Century Fiction* 28 (1973) pp. 321–38; Margaret Kirkham, *Jane Austen—Feminism and Fiction*; see also her "Feminist Irony and the Priceless Heroine of *Mansfield Park*," in Janet Todd, ed., *Jane Austen—New Perspectives*, pp. 231–47; and Mary Evans' *Jane Austen and the State*.

18. Claudia L. Johnson, *Jane Austen—Women, Politics, and the Novel*, and Alison G. Sulloway, *Jane Austen and the Province of Womanhood*, read Jane Austen as a "moderate feminist" engaged in a satirical attack upon patriarchal privilege. See also Tony Tanner, *Jane Austen*, who represents Austen as both exposing and criticising "the ideological assumptions which ground her society and which may seem to constrain her fiction" (pp. 5–6); Leroy Smith, *Jane Austen and the Drama of Women*; and the essays on Jane Austen as articulating "the woman's point of view" collected in *Jane*

Austen in a Social Context, ed. David Monaghan, and in *Jane Austen: New Perspectives*, ed. Janet Todd.

19. Critics have only begun to acknowledge Austen's overwhelming intellectual and rhetorical debts to Wollstonecraft's *A Vindication of the Rights of Woman*. See Lloyd W. Brown, "Jane Austen and the Feminist Tradition," *Nineteenth-Century Fiction* 28 (1973) pp. 321–38 and Margaret Kirkham, "Feminist Theory and the Priceless Heroine of *Mansfield Park*," in Janet Todd, ed., *Jane Austen—New Perspectives*, pp. 231–47. See also the brief but shrewd remarks of Cora Kaplan on Austen's "conservative recuperation" of Wollstonecraft in "Wild Nights," pp. 174–5, and of Ruth Bernard Yeazell on Austen's use of Wollstonecraft's concept of modesty in *Mansfield Park* in *Fictions of Modesty*, p. 155.

20. Here I am endorsing Claudia Johnson's persuasive interpretation of *Emma* in her *Jane Austen—Women, Politics and the Novel*, chap. 6, and rejecting the more traditional view of Emma as, in Susan Morgan's overly extreme formulation, "the most flawed of Austen's heroines" (*In the Meantime—Character and Perception in Jane Austen's Fiction*, p. 77).

21. *Emma*, pp. 331, 340: These lines, quoted by Jane Austen, from Cowper's *The Task*, Book IV, are of course the inspiration for Coleridge's celebration of the freely associative and unifying romantic imagination in *Frost at Midnight*. Jane Austen, in contrast to Coleridge, explicitly identifies the liberated imagination with the errors of perception to which Emma and others (here, possibly Mr. Knightley) are prone. Susan Morgan has recently reformulated the relationship between imagination, perception and error in *Emma*, arguing that Emma is not so much a flawed character as a bad novelist, one whose stories are too reliant on "sentimental and sexist cliches" (*Sisters in Time—Imagining Genders in Nineteenth-Century British Fiction*, p. 54).

22. Mary Hamilton, *Munster Village* (1778; repr. London: Pandora Books, 1987); the references to Lady Dorothea Bingley, Lady Eliza, and Mr. Bennet all occur in one paragraph on p. 60.

23. John Gregory, *A Father's Legacy to his Daughters* (London: John Sharpe, 1822), p. 66.

24. Austen, *Pride and Prejudice*, ed. Donald Gray (New York: Norton Critical Edition, 1966), p. 131. Cited hereafter in the text.

25. *Jane Austen's Letters to her Sister Cassandra and Others*, ed. R. W. Chapman, 2nd ed., p. 141.

26. Joseph Allen Boone, *Tradition Counter Tradition—Love and the Form of Fiction*, p. 96. See also Nina Auerbach, *Communities of Women—An Idea in Fiction*, pp. 35–55; and for a harsher reading of the Darcy/ Elizabeth marriage with which I largely concur, Susan Fraiman, "The Humiliation of Elizabeth Bennet," in *Refiguring the Father—New Feminist Readings of Patriarchy*, ed. Patricia Yaeger and Beth Kowaleski-Wallace, pp. 168–187.

27. Since the 1950s, critics have emphasized the role of money in Austen's fiction. See Mark Schorer, "Fiction and the 'Matrix of Analogy'," *Kenyon Review* 11 (1949) pp. 539–60; Dorothy Van Ghent, *The English Novel— Form and Function*, pp. 99–112; and David Daiches, "Jane Austen, Karl Marx and the Aristocratic Dance," *American Scholar* 17 (1948) pp. 289–98.

The feminist implications of Jane Austen's concern with property, money and women's economic situation have been emphasized by Judith Lowder Newton in *Women, Power & Subversion: Social Strategies in British Fiction, 1778–1860*, chap. 2. Also see Alistair M. Duckworth, "Jane Austen's Accommodations," *Tennessee Studies in Literature* 29 (1985) pp. 225–267.

28. For readings of the ending of *Pride and Prejudice* as comic or optimistic, see the essays by Reuben A. Brower, Andrew H. Wright, Howard S. Babb and A. Walton Litz collected in the Norton Critical Edition of *Pride and Prejudice*, ed. Donald J. Grey (New York, 1966); and more recently Julia Prewitt Brown, *Jane Austen's Novels—Social Change and Literary Form*, chap. 3; and Susan Morgan, *In the Meantime*, p. 105. Robert M. Polhemus, reading *Pride and Prejudice* with more sophistication and insight, sustains the view of the novel's ending as a comic affirmation of "reasoned love" over "being in love," a reasoned love that leads to good marriages, in *Erotic Faith—Being in Love from Jane Austen to D. H. Lawrence*, pp. 28–54.

29. For a compelling reading of *Mansfield Park*, see Ruth Bernard Yeazell, *Fictions of Modesty*, chap. 9.

30. "Somerset v. Stewart," Lord Mansfield presiding, *The English Reports* 98 (King's Bench Division 27) Lofft I (London: Stevens and Sons, Ltd; Edinburgh: William Green and Sons, 1909), p. 500. The relevance of Lord Mansfield's Judgment to *Mansfield Park* was first noted by Margaret Kirkham, *Jane Austen—Feminism and Fiction*, pp. 116–119.

31. Jane Austen, *Mansfield Park* (London: Penguin, 1966; repr. 1980), p. 216: "She was less and less able to endure the restraint which her father imposed."

32. Jane Austen, *Emma* (London: Penguin, 1966; repr. 1983), p. 300.

33. Nina Auerbach, "Jane Austen and Romantic Imprisonment," in *Romantic Imprisonment—Women and Other Glorified Outcasts*, p. 20.

34. See Mary-Elisabeth Fowkes Tobin, "Aiding Impoverished Gentlewomen: Power and Class in *Emma*," *Criticism* 30 (1988), pp. 413–430.

35. Elissa Guralnick has persuasively traced the trope of the standing-army officer as female in *A Vindication of the Rights of Woman*, "Radical Politics in Mary Wollstonecraft's *A Vindication*," pp. 159–161.

36. Nina Auerbach has emphasized the ways in which *Northanger Abbey* repeats—as well as parodies—the conventions of the Gothic romance, even likening the final wedding bells to funeral bells, in *Romantic Imprisonment*, pp. 18–19, 294 n. 16.

Chapter 4

1. Mary Shelley, *Frankenstein, or the Modern Prometheus* (The 1818 Text), ed. James Rieger (Chicago: University of Chicago Press, 1982), p. 51.

2. On Wollstonecraft's *Rights of Man* and Burke's *Reflections*, see Elissa S. Guralnick, "Radical Politics in Mary Wollstonecraft's *A Vindication of the Rights of Woman*," pp. 155–159.

3. Mary Wollstonecraft, *A Vindication of the Rights of Men* (December, 1790),

facsimile edition with introduction by Eleanor Louise Nicholes, p. 22. Cited hereafter in text.

4. Edmund Burke, *Reflections on the Revolution in France, and on the Proceedings in Certain Societies in London, relative to that Event* (November, 1790), ed. Thomas H. D. Mahoney, p. 53. Cited hereafter in text.

5. Mary Wollstonecraft, *An Historical and Moral View of the Origin and Progress of the French Revolution and the Effect it has Produced in Europe* (1795)—A Facsimile Reproduction with an Introduction by Janet Todd, p. 19. Cited hereafter in the text.

6. Lee Sterrenburg, "*The Last Man:* Anatomy of Failed Revolutions," *Nineteenth Century Fiction* 33 (1978) pp. 324–47; cf. Anne K. Mellor, *Mary Shelley,* pp. 162–69.

7. Helen Maria Williams, *Poems on Various Subjects* (London, 1823), p. 262. Cited hereafter in the text.

8. Mona Ozouf, *Festivals and the French Revolution,* trans. Alan Sheridan, chap. 1 and passim.

9. Helen Maria Williams, *Letters written in France, in the Summer 1790, to a Friend in England, containing Various Anecdotes relative to the French Revolution; and Memoirs of Mons. and Madame Du F——* (London: T. Cadell, 1796)—republished as *Letters from France,* Eight Volumes in Two, Facsimile Reproductions with an Introduction by Janet M. Todd, Vol. I pp. 5–6. All further citations from these two volumes will be given in the text, by original volume and page.

10. On the complex significance of the representation of Liberty as female in the French Revolution, see the essays by Joan Landes, Mary Jacobus and Joan Wallace Scott in *Rebel Daughters: Women and the French Revolution,* ed. Sara Melzer and Leslie Rabine.

11. On Williams' account of her experience in prison, see Judith Scheffler, "Romantic Women Writing on Imprisonment and Prison Reform," *The Wordsworth Circle* 19 (1988), pp. 100–101.

12. Helen Maria Williams, *A Tour in Switzerland; or, a View of the Present State of the Governments and Manners of those Cantons, with Comparative Sketches of the Present State of Paris* (London: G. G. & J. Robinson, 1798), Vol. II, pp. 55–56.

13. Helen Maria Williams, *A Narrative of the Events which have taken place in FRANCE; with an account of the Present State of Society and Public Opinion* (London: John Murray, 1816; 2nd edition), p. 271. Cited hereafter in the text.

14. Here I disagree with the conclusion reached by Chris Jones in his study of Williams' radical sensibility and its relationship to that of Wordsworth and Coleridge, namely that the sceptical Williams could finally "only assert the inner ideals of the imagination" rather than a belief in the social reform achievable by humanitarian feelings, "Helen Maria Williams and Radical Sensibility," *Prose Studies* 12 (1989) pp. 3–24.

15. *The Journals of Mary Shelley, 1814–1844,* ed. Paula R. Feldman and Diana Scott-Kilvert, Vol. I, pp. 20–21. For a fuller discussion of Mary Shelley's politics, see my *Mary Shelley,* chap. 4.

16. Michael Hurst, *Maria Edgeworth and the Public Scene—Intellect, Fine Feeling and Landlordism in the Age of Reform*, p. 87.

17. Maria Edgeworth, *The Grateful Negro; and The Cherry Orchard* (London: Routledge, n.d.), included in *Tales and Novels by Maria Edgeworth* (London, 1832), Vol. 5. Cited hereafter in the text.

18. Michael Hurst, *Maria Edgeworth and the Public Scene*, p. 23.

19. Maria Edgeworth, *Essay on Irish Bulls*, in *Tales and Novels by Maria Edgeworth*, Vol. I, p. 277.

20. Maria Edgeworth, *The Absentee*, 1812, ed. W. J. McCormack and Kim Walker. Cited hereafter in the text.

21. McCormack and Walker argue that Edmund Burke is the model for Edgeworth's good agent, Mr. Burke, in their Introduction to *The Absentee*, pp. xxxi–xxxiii.

22. Barbara Charlesworth Gelpi, *Shelley's Goddess: Maternity, Language, Subjectivity* (New York: Oxford University Press, 1992), p. 39. On the changing construction of the family and the ideology of maternity in the eighteenth century, also see Lawrence J. Stone, *The Family, Sex, and Marriage in England 1500–1800*; Randolph Trumbach, *The Rise of the Egalitarian Family*; Alice Ryerson, "Medical Advice on Childrearing, 1550–1900," *Harvard Educational Review* 31 (1961), pp. 302–23; and Leonore Davidoff and Catherine Hall, *Family Fortunes: Men and Women of the English Middle Class, 1780–1850*.

23. Alan Richardson, "Romanticism and the Colonization of the Feminine," in *Romanticism and Feminism*, ed. Anne K. Mellor, pp. 13–25.

24. Mary Wollstonecraft, *Maria, or The Wrongs of Woman*, ed. Moira Ferguson, p. 23.

25. Barbara Charlesworth Gelpi, *Shelley's Goddess*, p. 62.

Chapter 5

1. Perhaps no subject in contemporary academic discourse concerning the character of Romanticism has received so much attention as the sublime. The major studies are Samuel H. Monk, *The Sublime: A Study of Critical Theories in XVIII-Century England* (1935; repr. 1960); Marjorie Hope Nicolson, *Mountain Gloom and Mountain Glory: the Development of the Aesthetics of the Infinite* (1959); Herbert Lindenberger, *On Wordsworth's Prelude* (1963); Geoffrey H. Hartman, *Wordsworth's Poetry 1787–1814* (1964; repr. 1971); Thomas Weiskel, *The Romantic Sublime* (1976); Morton D. Paley, *Apocalyptic Sublime* (1986); Theresa M. Kelley, *Wordsworth's Revisionary Aesthetics* (1988); and Peter de Bolla, *The Discourse of the Sublime—Readings in History, Aesthetics and the Subject* (1989).

2. Edmund Burke, *A Philosophical Inquiry into the Origin of Our Ideas of the Sublime and the Beautiful*, Fifth Edition (London: J. Dodsley, 1767), pp. 58–9. Cited hereafter in the text.

3. Isaac Kramnick, *The Rage of Edmund Burke—Portrait of an Ambivalent Conservative*, pp. 92–98.

4. Immanuel Kant, *Critique of Judgement* (1790), trans. Werner S. Pluhar, Section 28, p. 120. Cited hereafter in text.

5. For his distinction between the positive and negative sublime (both of which I am identifying with the masculine sublime), see Thomas Weiskel, *The Romantic Sublime—Studies in the Structure and Psychology of Transcendence*, pp. 22–62. On the way in which the "discursive network" of the sublime produces (and is produced by) the autonomous subject, see Peter de Bolla, *The Discourse of the Sublime*.

6. For further discussion of Coleridge's conception and representation of the sublime in this poem, see my "Coleridge's 'This Lime-tree Bower My Prison' and the Categories of English Landscape," *Studies in Romanticism* 18 (1979) pp. 253–70.

7. For a discussion of "This Lime-tree Bower My Prison" that emphasizes the poem's failure to overcome the hermeneutic problems of reading and interpretation it thematizes, see Tilottama Rajan, *The Supplement of Reading—Figures of Understanding in Romantic Theory and Practice*, pp. 108–115.

8. For the original version of "This Lime-tree Bower My Prison" sent to Robert Southey on 17 July 1797, see *Collected Letters of Samuel Taylor Coleridge*, ed. Earl Leslie Griggs, I pp. 334–336.

9. Ann Radcliffe, *The Mysteries of Udolpho* (1794; repr. Oxford: Oxford University Press, 1980), p. 30. Cited hereafter in the text.
    For a discussion of Radcliffe's use of the categories of the sublime, the beautiful and the picturesque in her diaries and *A Journey made in the summer of 1794, through Holland and the Western Frontiers of Germany, with a return down the Rhine, to which are added Observations during a tour to the Lakes of Lancashire, Westmoreland and Cumberland* (London: G. G. and J. Robinson, 1795), see E. B. Murray, *Ann Radcliffe*, pp. 20–28.

10. Ann Radcliffe, *The Italian* (1797: repr. Oxford: Oxford University Press, 1981), p. 63. Cited hereafter in text.

11. Radcliffe, *Mysteries of Udolpho*, pp. 40, 611–20; *The Italian*, p. 113.

12. Kate Ferguson Ellis, *The Contested Castle—Gothic Novels and the Subversion of Domestic Ideology*, p. 50. On the transgression of boundaries in Radcliffe's fiction, see also Eugenia C. DeLamotte, *Perils of the Night—A Feminist Study of Nineteenth-Century Gothic*, pp. 29–35, 43–52.

13. Kate Ferguson Ellis discusses the initiative-taking, assertive heroines in Radcliffe's fiction in *The Contested Castle*, pp. xiii, 99–128. Coral Ann Howells also makes this point, in "The Pleasure of the Woman's Text: Ann Radcliffe's Subtle Transgressions," in *Gothic Fictions—Prohibition/Transgression*, ed. Kenneth W. Graham, pp. 151–162.
    Harriet Blodgett has explored Radcliffe's debt to Wollstonecraft for her portrayal of Emily as a rational heroine who believes in the value and virtues of the female, in "Emily Vindicated: Ann Radcliffe and Mary Wollstonecraft," *Weber Studies* 7 (1990), pp. 48–61.

14. Kate Ferguson Ellis has explored the ways in which Radcliffe endorses an agrarian or non-capitalist economy in her fiction, *The Contested Castle*, pp. 100–102.

15. Sydney Owenson, Lady Morgan, *The Wild Irish Girl* (1806; repr. London: Pandora Books, 1986), pp. 6–7. Cited hereafter in text.

16. Lady Morgan, *The Life and Times of Salvator Rosa* (London: Henry Colburn, 1824), 2 Volumes, I p. 106.

17. Morgan, *Salvator Rosa*, II p. 297.

18. Morgan, *Salvator Rosa*, II pp. 298–300.

19. Vineta Colby, *Yesterday's Woman—Domestic Realism in the English Novel*, pp. 100–01.

20. Susan Ferrier, *Marriage* (Blackwood, 1818; repr. London: Virago Press, 1986), pp. 205–6.

21. Susan Ferrier, *Inheritance* (Blackwood, 1824; repr. Bampton, Oxfordshire: Three Rivers Press, 1984), p. 16.

22. Susan Ferrier, *Inheritance*, p. 227.

23. Ferrier, *Destiny; or, The Chief's Daughter* (Edinburgh: Robert Cadell, 1831), p. 894.

24. Helen Maria Williams, *Poems on Various Subjects* (London, 1823), p. 262.

Chapter 6

1. Ruth Bernard Yeazell, *Fictions of Modesty*, p. 26; see also pp. 22–32.

2. For detailed description of this hegemonic domestic ideology, see Davidoff and Hall, *Family Fortunes*.

3. Isobel Armstrong, "Scandal and Sudden Death: A Nineteenth-Century Mystery," Inaugural Lecture, Birkbeck College, University of London, 30 April 1991. Armstrong reads Landon and her poetry as working to *expand* Burke's category of the beautiful, while I see Landon's life and poetry as defining the *limits* (and eventual annihilation) of female beauty.

4. Bulwer-Lytton's review is reprinted in *Nineteenth-Century Literature Criticism*, Vol. 15, p. 156.

5. Maclise's individual and group portraits of Landon appear in *The MACLISE Portrait-Gallery of Illustrious Literary Characters with Memoirs*, by William Bates (London, 1883), 2 Vols., I pp. 200–201, II p. 335.

6. Anne Renier, *Friendship's Offering—An Essay on the Annuals and Gift-Books of the Nineteenth Century*, p. 17.

7. Sonia Hofkosh, "Disfiguring Economies: Mary Shelley's Stories."

8. L. E. L., *Traits and Trials of Early Life* (London: Henry Colburn, 1837), pp. 291, 294, 297, 312. In this story we can see Landon defining the initial outlines of what Germaine Greer has subsequently called the "Woman of Genius Syndrome":

   The elements in the pathology include an impecunious father, female relatives who sought to exploit the child's gift, an apparently happy and sunny child's conviction that she was rejected and unloved, and the usual haphazard education afforded the gifted female children of impoverished middle class families. To these elements must be added the tremendous vogue of the Byronic hero, the burgeoning of the romantic concept of genius, and the particular brand of covert eroticism cultivated in the permissive era of the Regency, which L. E. L. ill-advisedly tried to carry with her into the Victorian age.

Germain Greer, "The Tulsa Center for the Study of Women's Literature: What We Are Doing and Why We Are Doing It," *Tulsa Studies in Women's Literature* I (1982) pp. 5–26, 19.
   This interpretation of Landon's career as "The Fate of Genius" was first put forth by William Jerdan, in *The Autobiography of William Jerdan* (London, 1835), Vol. III, pp. 168–206.

9. Laman Blanchard, *Life and Literary Remains of L. E. L.* (London: Henry Colburn, 1841), Vol. I, pp. 22–4, cf. pp. 6–20.

10. William Jerdan, *The Autobiography of William Jerdan*, Vol. II, p. 256.

11. Laman Blanchard, *Life and Literary Remains of L. E. L.*, I p. 33.

12. Laman Blanchard, *Life and Literary Remains of L. E. L.*, I p. 42.

13. William Jerdan, *The Autobiography of William Jerdan*, Vol. III, p. 185.

14. L. E. L., *The Venetian Bracelet, The Lost Pleiad, A History of the Lyre, and Other Poems* (London: Longman, Rees, Orme, Brown and Green, 1829), p. v.

15. L. E. L., *The Venetian Bracelet*, p. vi.

16. Letitia Elizabeth Landon, *The Troubadour*, in *Poetical Works of Letitia Elizabeth Landon "L. E. L."*, A Facsimile Reproduction of the 1873 Edition with an Introduction and Additional Poems, ed. F. J. Sypher (Delmar, New York: Scholars' Facsimiles & Reprints, 1990), p. 64. Cited hereafter in the text, by page number.

17. Samuel Carpenter Hall, in *A Book of Memories of Great Men and Women of the Age, from Personal Acquaintance* (London: Virtue and Co., 1871), insisted that with Landon, "the melancholy was real, the mirth assumed" (p. 270), while her biographer Laman Blanchard insisted that "there was not the remotest connection or affinity, not indeed a colour of resemblance, between her every-day life or habitual feelings, and the shapes they were made to assume in her poetry" (*Life and Literary Remains of L. E. L.*, p. 34).

18. Quoted by Laman Blanchard, *Life and Literary Remains of L. E. L.*, p. 55.

19. Landon herself described these letters to her friend, Mrs. Samuel C. Hall, as "notes, as pretty and flattering as I could make them, to Dr. Maginn, upon different literary matters, and one or two on business" (Landon's letter is reprinted in full in S. C. Hall, *A Book of Memories*, p. 276). On the address and "tone of affectionate friendship" in which these letters were written, see Dr. Shelton Mackenzie, ed., *Miscellaneous Writings of the late Dr. [William] Maginn* (London, 1855), Vol. V, p. lxxxv.

20. Quoted in Laman Blanchard, *Life and Literary Remains of L. E. L.*, p. 130.

21. *The Diaries of William Charles Macready, 1833–1851*, ed. William Toynbee (London: Chapman and Hall, 1912), I p. 262.

22. Samuel Carpenter Hall, *A Book of Memories*, p. 278.

23. Brodie Cruickshank, *Eighteen Years on the The Gold Coast of Africa, including an Account of the Native Tribes, and their Intercourse with Europeans* (London: Hurst and Blackett, 1853), Vol. I, pp. 169–230, see esp. his original verdict, p. 227.

24. D. E. Enfield, after reviewing the available theories, opted for suicide, arguing that Landon realized she had come to the end of the road, unable to return to London and miserable with her husband with whom she "was not really in love" and whom she "had married like any heartless society lady, like any provincial spinster, simply for the sake of being married, because she was tired of being talked about, because she was afraid of being an old maid, and because she cared more for the image of herself reflected in the eyes of the world than for her own integrity" (*L. E. L.—A Mystery of the Thirties* (London: Hogarth Press, 1928), pp. 182, 180).

25. Quoted by Henry F. Chorley, *Memorials of Mrs. Hemans, with illustrations of Her Literary Character from her Private Correspondence*, I p. 182. Cited hereafter in the text.

26. Writing to John Murray from Ravenna on August 12, 1820, Byron asked him to send "no *more modern* poesy—I pray—neither Mrs. Hewoman's— nor any female or male Tadpole of Poet Turdsworth's." Byron specifically accused Felicia Hemans of writing a "false stilted trashy style which is a mixture of all the styles of the day—which are all *bombastic*" and concluded that "if [she] knit blue stockings instead of wearing them it would be better" (*Byron's Letters and Journals*, Vol. 7, pp. 158, 182).

    Felicia Hemans was equally disappointed by Byron when she read extracts from Moore's *Memoirs* and an article on Byron in the *Quarterly Review:* "his character, as there portrayed, reminded me of some of those old eastern cities, where travellers constantly find a squalid mud hovel built against the ruins of a gorgeous temple; for, alas! the best part of that fearfully mingled character is but ruin—the wreck of *what might have been*" (Chorley II p. 147, cf. I p. 18).

    William Wordsworth also resented Hemans' poetic success. Although he eulogized her in his "Extempore Effusion upon the death of James Hogg" (1835):

    > Mourn rather for that holy Spirit,
    > Sweet as the spring, as ocean deep;
    > For Her who, ere her summer faded,
    > Has sunk into a breathless sleep,

    he commented testily that "it is a great thing to have said of her that she has given so much innocent pleasure—and that her verses may be more useful to the Americans—with whom she is a favourite—in their present state of intellectual culture, than more powerful productions" (presumably by himself). (William Wordsworth, *Letters* VI p. 139n).

27. That women poets earned as much or more than their male rivals was irritably confirmed by John Gibson Lockhart in a long *Quarterly* article in 1840: "they can, and do, write, print and publish whatever they like. Is there any fear of the Press before their eyes? Do Reviews fright them out of their own way? . . . are publishers wanting? There is Mr. Henry Colburn.

Are they underpaid? They obtain thousands. Are they without readers? We wish Milton had as many" (quoted by Janet E. Courtney, *The Adventurous Thirties—A Chapter in the Woman's Movement*, p. 6).

Although Felicia Hemans died at the age of 41 in 1835, her popularity continued unabated through the 1860s; she led all other poets in her appearances in American gift-books and annuals and in British anthologies in this period, outdistancing even Tennyson (James D. Hart, *The Popular Book—A History of American Literary Taste*, p. 133).

28. All quotations are taken from *The Poetical Works of Felicia Hemans*, ed. William Michael Rossetti (London: Ward Lock and Co., 1878), p. 228. Cited hereafter in text by page number.

29. Mrs. Harriet Hughes, *The Works of Mrs. Hemans; with a Memoir of Her Life by Her Sister*, I p. 8. Cited hereafter in text.

30. Felicia Hemans claimed that *Records of Woman* was the volume "in which 'she had put her heart and individual feelings more than in anything else she had written' " (Hughes I p. 136; cf. Chorley I pp. 103–4).

31. That Hemans remained emotionally embroiled in this failed marriage is evidenced by her reaction to her husband's letters. As Mrs. Rose Lawrence records, "paroxysms of beating of the heart, in almost audible pulsations, . . . used to seize her (as one of the children said) 'after she got her letters'," an anxiety that also produced "her harassed, feverish, countenance" (*The Last Autumn at a Favorite Residence, with other Poems; and Recollections of Mrs. Hemans*, p. 298).

32. William Wordsworth commented in 1836, reflecting on his acquaintance with Felicia Hemans, whom he had hosted for two weeks at Rydal Mount in July, 1830: "Poor woman! She was sorely tried—and a beautiful trait in her character was, that she never uttered a complaint of her husband" (William Wordsworth, *Letters* VI p. 314).

33. Peter W. Trinder, *Mrs. Hemans*, pp. 20, 38–9.

34. Mrs. Rose Lawrence, *The Last Autumn*, p. 296.

35. The best modern account of what Hemans suffered from the disparity between her poetic espousal of "the cult of true womanhood" (which was the basis of her literary fame) and the failure of her marriage is by Norma Clarke, *Ambitious Heights—Writing, Friendship, Love—The Jewsbury Sisters, Felicia Hemans, and Jane Welsh Carlyle* (London and New York: Routledge, 1990), pp. 44–51, 98–102.

36. Wordsworth to Isabella Fenwick, *Poetical Works of William Wordsworth*, p. 737.

37. Numerous references in her letters and journals document Felicia Hemans' passionate love for her mother. After her mother's death on January 11, 1827, she lamented: "I have lost the faithful, watchful, patient love, which for years had been devoted to me and mine; and I feel that the void it has left behind, must cause me to bear 'a yearning heart within me to the grave'; but I have her example before me, and I must not allow myself to sink" (Hughes I p. 100). Her sister noted that their mother's death was an "irreparable loss" to Felicia: "From henceforth she was to be a stranger to any thing like an equal flow of quiet, steadfast happiness" for "the old

home feeling of shelter and security was gone for ever" (Hughes I p. 105). On her mother's "unremitting care" of Felicia, see Chorley I p. 25.

Felicia Hemans' intense bonding with her mother is evidenced by her decision, within a year of her wedding, after the birth of her first son Arthur, to return with her husband to Bronwylfa, in Wales, to live with her mother and sister. She remained in her mother's house, first at Bronwylfa and then across the Clyde at Rhyllon, until her mother's death. Left to provide alone for her sons' care and education, Felicia Hemans then moved to Wavertree, near Liverpool, for three years, and finally joined her brother in Dublin until her death on May 16, 1835.

38. Henry Chorley first identified *The Siege of Valencia* as Hemans' best work, marked "by more distinct evidences of originality" than her previous poetry: "None of her after poems contain finer bursts of strong, fervid, indignant poetry than 'The Siege of Valencia'" (Chorley I pp. 89–90).

39. Anticipating Rossetti's opinion, Lord Jeffrey, in his famous review of Hemans' *Collected Poems* for *Edinburgh Review* (XCIX), both described at length what women writers can and cannot do, and defined Hemans' work as "a fine exemplification of female poetry," "infinitely sweet, elegant, and tender," a poetry which achieves a "delicate blending" of the human emotions with the objects of the external world and brings "all that strikes the sense into unison with all that touches the heart" (Jeffrey's review is reprinted in Volume V of the 1839 Blackwood edition of *The Works of Mrs. Hemans*).

Chapter 7

1. Margaret Homans, *Women Writers and Poetic Identity,* chap. 1–2; James Holt McGavran, Jr., "Dorothy Wordsworth's Journals—Putting Herself Down," in *The Private Self—Theory and Practice of Women's Autobiographical Writings,* ed. Shari Benstock, p. 232; Susan Levin, *Dorothy Wordsworth and Romanticism,* pp. 26, 4. Meena Alexander offers a similar reading of Dorothy's subjectivity, in "Dorothy Wordsworth: the grounds of writing," *Women's Studies* 14 (1988), pp. 195–210; see also her *Women in Romanticism: Mary Wollstonecraft, Dorothy Wordsworth, and Mary Shelley* (1989).

2. For readings of Wordsworth which emphasize his hermeneutic and rhetorical doubts, see Paul de Man, "The Rhetoric of Temporality," in *Interpretation: Theory and Practice,* ed. Charles S. Singleton, pp. 173–209, *Blindness and Insight,* and *The Rhetoric of Romanticism;* Cynthia Chase, *Decomposing Figures;* Jonathan Arac, "Bounding Lines: *The Prelude* and Critical Revision," *Boundary* 7 (1979), pp. 31–48; Susan Wolfson, *The Questioning Presence—Wordsworth, Keats, and the Interrogative Mode in Romantic Poetry;* William Galperin, *Revision and Authority in Wordsworth—The Interpretation of a Career;* David Simpson, *Irony and Authority in Romantic Poetry;* Tilottama Rajan, *Dark Interpreter—The Discourse of Romanticism;* and Frances C. Ferguson, *Wordsworth: Language as Counter-Spirit.*

3. M. H. Abrams, *Natural Supernaturalism,* see esp. pp. 71–140.

4. Herbert Lindenberger, *On Wordsworth's Prelude.*

5. All references to Wordsworth's *Prelude* are to the 1805 edition, *The Prelude—1799, 1805, 1850*, ed. Jonathan Wordsworth, M. H. Abrams, and Stephen Gill (New York: W. W. Norton & Co., 1979). Cited hereafter in text.

6. Geoffrey Hartman, *Wordsworth's Poetry, 1787–1814.*

7. Marlon B. Ross, *The Contours of Masculine Desire—Romanticism and the Rise of Women's Poetry*, see esp. pp. 15–55; Alan Liu, *Wordsworth—The Sense of History.*

8. Richard J. Onorato, *The Character of the Poet—Wordsworth in The Prelude*, see esp. pp. 174–182. Here I accept the arguments of Nancy Chodorow (in *The Reproduction of Mothering*), Juliet Mitchell (in *Psychoanalysis and Feminism*) and other feminist psychologists that the Oedipal complex applies *only* to male children, and that females follow a very different model of psychic maturation than the one posited by Freud as the "Electra-complex," a model that discourages the development of strong ego boundaries.

9. Harold Bloom, *The Anxiety of Influence—A Theory of Poetry.*

10. Wordsworth's sexual liaison with Annette Vallon is of course never mentioned in *The Prelude*, and is rhetorically displaced into the love story of Vaudracour and Julia; even the "slight shocks of young love-liking" that he attributes to the festal company of maids and youths whom he joins during his summer vacation is rhetorically depersonalized: they "mounted up like joy into *the* head,/ And tingled through *the* veins" (not *my* head, *my* veins; IV:325–8, italics mine).

11. For discussion of the way Wordsworth precariously represses the Other, see Susan J. Wolfson, *The Questioning Presence: Wordsworth, Keats, and the Interrogative Mode in Romantic Poetry;* Cynthia Chase, *Decomposing Figures: Rhetorical Readings in the Romantic Tradition*, chaps. 2–3; Mary Jacobus, *Romanticism, Writing and Sexual Difference: Essays on the Prelude;* and E. Douka Kabitogou, "Problematics of Gender in the Nuptials of *The Prelude*," *The Wordsworth Circle* 19 (1988) pp. 128–135.

12. Kurt Heinzelman discusses this passage as a *locus amoenus* in which Wordsworth's male body becomes the landscape which Dorothy's feminine art of gardening refines and improves, in "The Cult of Domesticity—Dorothy and William Wordsworth at Grasmere," in *Romanticism and Feminism*, ed. Anne K. Mellor, p. 66.

13. Although they approach the issue from very different methodological perspectives, both the traditional historian of ideas Karl Joachim Weintraub in *The Value of the Individual—Self and Circumstance in Autobiography*, and Michel Foucault in his enquiry into "the archaeology of knowledge" initiated in *The Order of Things* (1966) concur in defining the late eighteenth century as a pivotal moment in the evolution of the idea of the self, the beginning of an episteme in which the individual has a new sense "of something taking place in himself, often at an unconscious level, in his subjectivity, in his values, that traverses the whole of his action in the world" (*Michel Foucault: The Will to Truth*, pp. 82–3). It is probably not accidental that this is also the historical moment when the very word "autobiography" is coined, by the poet Robert Southey in 1809.

This modern self is assumed as a given in the canonical Victorian autobiographies by John Stuart Mill, Cardinal John Henry Newman, John Ruskin and Edmund Gosse; for studies of the Victorian/modern self, see Linda H. Peterson, *Victorian Autobiography—The Tradition of Self-Interpretation;* Avrom Fleischman, *Figures of Autobiography—The Language of Self-Writing in Victorian and Modern England;* Susanna Egan, *Patterns of Experience in Autobiography;* Jerome Hamilton Buckley, *The Turning Key—Autobiography and the Subjective Impulse since 1800;* and Heather Henderson, *The Victorian Self—Autobiography and Biblical Narrative.* For other modes of Victorian subjectivity, see Regenia Gagnier's study of Victorian working-class autobiographies in her *Subjectivities: A History of Self-Representation in Britain, 1832–1920.*

14. Carole Pateman has demonstrated the way in which the individual assumed capable of entering into the social contract in both classical and modern social contract theory is exclusively male, in *The Sexual Contract;* John Locke's equation of the individual with the ownership of his own capacities, attributes and physical body occurs in his *Two Treatises of Government,* ed. P. Laslett, 2nd ed., II, p. 27.

15. "Metaphors ... are that by which the lonely subjective consciousness gives order not only to itself but to as much of objective reality as it is capable of formalizing and controlling," writes James Olney in *Metaphors of Self—the Meaning of Autobiography,* p. 30. Despite its rhetorical status, Olney argues that the self so constituted in metaphor is "a coherent and integral self, potential at first and destined, though no one can foredraw the exact shape of destiny, to be realized through many experiences until it shall become this one, and no other, self" (p. 326).

16. The most subtle studies of the relationship between the fictive and the referential self in autobiography are by Paul John Eakin, *Fictions in Autobiography—Studies in the Art of Self-Invention* and *Autobiography as a Referential Art;* Huntington Williams, *Rousseau and Romantic Autobiography;* William C. Spengemann, *The Forms of Autobiography—Episodes in the History of a Literary Genre;* and the essays collected in two volumes edited by James Olney, *Autobiography: Essays Theoretical and Critical* and *Studies in Autobiography.*

17. Georges Gusdorf, "Conditions and Limits of Autobiography," trans. James Olney, in James Olney, ed., *Autobiography: Essays Theoretical and Critical,* p. 38.

18. Gusdorf, pp. 35, 39, 29.

19. Philippe Lejeune, *On Autobiography,* foreword by Paul John Eakin, trans. Katherine Leary, p. 4. This definition first appeared in Lejeune's *Autobiographie en France* (Paris: A. Colin, 1971).

20. Elizabeth W. Bruss, "Eye for I: Making and Unmaking Autobiography in Film," in James Olney, ed., *Autobiography: Essays Theoretical and Critical,* p. 297. Bruss first proposed her generic rules for autobiography in her *Autobiographical Acts—The Changing Situation of a Literary Genre,* pp. 10–18.

21. Lejeune, "The Autobiographical Pact" and "The Autobiographical Pact (bis)," in *On Autobiography,* pp. 3–30, 119–137.

22. Bruss, "Eye for I," p. 298n.

23. Bruss, "Eye for I," p. 301.

24. Friedrich Nietzsche, *The Will to Power*, trans. Walter Kaufman and R. J. Hollingdale, ed. Walter Kaufmann, p. 267. This deconstructive reading of both the subject and the autobiographical compact was first undertaken by Paul de Man, "Autobiography as De-facement," *MLN* 94 (December 1979) pp. 919–930, and by Paul Jay, *Being in the Text: Self-Representation from Wordsworth to Roland Barthes* (1984). Mary Jacobus repeats this deconstructive reading of the self in *The Prelude*, in *Romanticism, Writing, and Sexual Difference* (1989), Chap. 1.

25. Julia Kristeva, *Desire in Language*, ed. Leon S. Roudiez, p. 125.

26. The influence of gender upon autobiography is a rich field that has only recently begun to be explored. The most useful texts to date are Estelle Jelinek, ed. *Women's Autobiography: Essays in Criticism* (1980); Sidonie Smith, *A Poetics of Women's Autobiography* (1987); *The Female Autograph*, ed. Domna C. Stanton (1984); *Life/Lines—Theorizing Women's Autobiography*, ed. Bella Brodzki and Celeste Schenck (1988); *The Private Self—Theory and Practice of Women's Autobiographical Writings*, ed. Shari Benstock (1988); and Felicity Nussbaum, *The Autobiographical Subject—Gender and Ideology in Eighteenth-Century England* (1989).

27. "The Collected Poems of Dorothy Wordsworth," in Susan Levin, *Dorothy Wordsworth and Romanticism*, Appendix One, pp. 207–9.

28. On Dorothy's resistance to her brother's psychic and poetic strategies, see Susan J. Wolfson, "Individual in Community: Dorothy Wordsworth in Conversation with William," in *Romanticism and Feminism*, ed. Anne K. Mellor, pp. 139–166.

29. Margaret Homans, *Women Writers and Poetic Identity*, pp. 83–85.

30. Susan J. Wolfson, "Individual in Community," p. 145.

31. Susan Levin's fine study of Dorothy Wordsworth stresses the similarity of Dorothy's concept of subjectivity to Chodorow's concept of feminine identity, *Dorothy Wordsworth and Romanticism*, p. 5; but Levin insists, wrongly I think, on Dorothy Wordsworth's *fear* of the self-annihilation implicit in an identity founded on relationship, on the other. The classic texts of the Self-in-Relation school of psychology are Nancy Chodorow's *The Reproduction of Mothering* (1974); Jean Baker Miller's *Toward a New Psychology of Women* (1976); and Carol Gilligan's *In a Different Voice* (1982).

32. Mary G. Mason has analyzed the "evolution and delineation of an identity by way of alterity" in the writings of Cavendish, Julian, Kempe and Bradstreet in "The Other Voice: Autobiographies of Women Writers," in *Life/Lines*, ed. Brodzki and Schenck, 19–44.

33. Shirley Neuman argues that all autobiography, whether written by men or by women, represses the body, seeing the representation of a feminine body in the texts by Kate Simon and Violette Leduc that she discusses in " 'An Appearance walking in a forest the sexes burn': Autobiography and the Construction of the Feminine Body," *Signature: A Journal of Theory and Canadian Literature* (1989) pp. 1–26, as "anomalous" (p. 2). I would argue instead that the body is prominent in several female-authored, working-class and African-American autobiographies (e.g. by Joanna Southcott,

Mary Prince, Maya Angelou, Sally Morgan, Olaudah Equiano, Malcolm X, and the Victorian laborers surveyed in Regenia Gagnier's study of British working-class subjectivity) as well as in the genre of the journal and diary, whether authored by men or women, that academic studies of autobiography have unjustifiably excluded. Moreover, despite Newman's claim, the body does appear in a few canonical male-authored autobiographies—I think especially of Rousseau's catheters and Thoreau's sweating labor at Walden—but this somatic dimension of the self has been overlooked in most critical interpretations of these texts.

In this context, we might consider Patricia Yaeger's telling comment that "if *somatophobia*, or fear of the body's fleshliness and mutability, characterizes our conflicts with women's bodies, then *asomia*, or bodilessness, characterizes our way of describing and thinking about the father," "The Father's Breasts," in *Refiguring the Father—New Feminist Readings of Patriarchy*, ed. Patricia Yaeger and Beth Kowaleski-Wallace, p. 9.

34. On the ways in which diaries represent a self that is not unified, rational or intentional and thus register an ideological contestation with a dominant ideology of a unitary self, see Felicity A. Nussbaum, "Toward Conceptualizing Diary," in James Olney, ed. *Studies in Autobiography*, pp. 128–140.

35. *Byron's Letters and Journals*, ed. Leslie A. Marchand, Vol. 3, pp. 109, 119. I discussed these passages as examples of Byron's romantic irony in my *English Romantic Irony*, pp. 31–32.

36. Roman Jakobson, "The Metaphoric and Metonymic Poles," in Roman Jakobson and Morris Halle, *Fundamentals of Language*, pp. 90–96.

37. On the use of metonymy to figure an individual woman's participation in a larger community from which she draws her sense of identity, see Doris Summer, " 'Not Just a Personal Story': Women's *Testimonios* and the Plural Self," in *Life/Lines*, ed. Brodzki and Schenck, pp. 107–130.

38. *Journals of Dorothy Wordsworth*, ed. Mary Moorman, p. 1. Cited hereafter in text, by page number.

39. Levin, *Dorothy Wordsworth and Romanticism*, p. 21.

40. *Letters of Dorothy Wordsworth*, ed. Alan Hill: to Mrs. Thomas Clarkson, dated 9 December 1810, p. 113. Margaret Homans' influential argument in *Women Writers and Poetic Identity* that Dorothy Wordsworth's poetic talent was silenced by her brother's identification of nonverbal nature with the female has little textual basis, since Dorothy never expressed a desire to write or publish, regarding her verses as occasional and her *Journals* as private, to be read only by her immediate family circle. Because she assumes the universal validity of a masculinist poetics and subjectivity, Homans fails to consider the possibility that Dorothy possessed both a subjectivity and an ideology different from her brother's, one grounded in the belief that making a home is as valuable a human activity as making a poem.

41. For the details of Dorothy's life, see the biography by Robert Gittings and Jo Manton, *Dorothy Wordsworth*.

42. Kurt Heinzelman also reads Dorothy Wordsworth's *Journals* as a successful resolution of a psychic trauma, one that he identifies as the "crisis of

the empty nest," in "The Cult of Domesticity," Anne K. Mellor, *Romanticism and Feminism*, pp. 68–78.

43. William Wordsworth, in his *Poems on the Naming of Places*, also domesticated the sublime in this feminine fashion. As I have indicated, the binary oppositions between masculine and feminine Romanticism are not grounded on biological sex. Moreover, they finally break down into a more fluid continuum of literary constructions produced by the male and female writers of the Romantic period.

44. Dorothy Wordsworth, *George and Sarah Green—A Narrative*, ed. E. de Selincourt. On the construction of community in the *Narrative*, see Susan J. Wolfson, "Individual in Community," pp. 154–163.

45. James Holt McGavran, Jr., "Dorothy Wordsworth's Journals—Putting Herself Down," pp. 237–8.

46. *The Love Letters of William and Mary Wordsworth*, ed. Beth Darlington, p. 82, cf. p. 229.

47. Kurt Heinzelman, "The Cult of Domesticity," pp. 75–76.

48. The model of identity as affiliation rather than achievement has been proposed for the lives of many nineteenth-century American women both by Nancy Cott, *The Bonds of Womanhood*, p. 165, and by Carol Holly, "Nineteenth-Century Autobiographies of Affiliation: The Case of Catherine Sedgwick and Lucy Larcom," in *American Autobiography: Retrospect and Prospect*, ed. Paul John Eakin, pp. 216–234.

    In an essay that came to my attention only after completing this chapter, Kay K. Cook reaches conclusions concerning Dorothy Wordsworth's construction of her subjectivity in her *Journals* that support the argument I am making here, "Self-Neglect in the Canon: Why Don't We Talk about Romantic Autobiography?," *Auto/biography Studies* 5 (1990) pp. 88–98.

49. For examples of this negative reading of Dorothy's self, see Richard Fadem, "Dorothy Wordsworth: A View from 'Tintern Abbey,'" *The Wordsworth Circle* 9 (1978) pp. 17–32; Homans, *Women Writers and Poetic Identity*, pp. 20–23; Donald Reiman, "Poetry of Familiarity: Wordsworth, Dorothy, and Mary Hutchinson," in *The Evidence of the Imagination*, ed. Donald Reiman, Michael C. Jaye, and Betty T. Bennett, pp. 142–77; and McGavran, Jr., "Dorothy Wordsworth's Journals—Putting Herself Down," pp. 230–33. Anita Hemphill McCormick also reads the Journals as a narrative of repressed anxieties and hostilities, in "'I shall be beloved—I want no more': Dorothy Wordsworth's Rhetoric and the Appeal to Feeling in *The Grasmere Journals*," *Philosophical Quarterly* (Fall 1990) pp. 471–493.

50. This is the conclusion of her biographers, Gittings and Manton, *Dorothy Wordsworth*, 233.

51. The phrase is Elizabeth Kincaid-Ehlers' (cited in Levin, *Dorothy Wordsworth and Romanticism*, p. 68n).

52. For the details of Dorothy's dementia, see Levin, *Dorothy Wordsworth and Romanticism*, pp. 68–9; Gittings and Manton, *Dorothy Wordsworth*, pp. 271–5.

53. The medical diagnosis of Dorothy Wordsworth's condition is given in Gittings and Manton, *Dorothy Wordsworth*, Appendix Two, pp. 282–3.

54. First published in Gittings and Manton, *Dorothy Wordsworth*, p. 278.

55. The gender politics in this sonnet are given a different twist in Wordsworth's letter to Lady Beaumont in which he explains that the

> Ship in this Sonnet may . . . be said to come upon a mission of the poetic
> Spirit, because in its own appearance and attributes it is barely suffi-
> ciently distinguished to rouse the creative faculty of the human mind;
> to exertions at all times welcome, but doubly so when they come upon
> us when in a state of remissness. The mind being once fixed and rouzed,
> all the rest comes from itself; it is merely a lordly Ship, nothing more:
>> This ship was nought to me, nor I to her,
>> Yet I pursued her with a lover's look.
> My mind wantons with grateful joy in the exercise of its own powers,
> and, loving its own creation,
>> This ship to all the rest I did prefer,
> making her a sovereign or a regent, and thus giving body and life to all
> the rest; mingling up this idea with fondness and praise—
>> where she comes the winds must stir;
> and concluding the whole with
>> On went She, and due north her journey took.
> Thus taking up again the Reader with whom I began, letting *him* know
> how long I must have watched this favorite Vessel, and inviting *him* to
> rest his mind as mine is resting. (my italics)
>   Letter to Lady Beaumont, 21 May 1807, in *Selected Letters of William
> Wordsworth* (London: Oxford University Press—The World's Classics,
> 1954), pp. 92–3.

Wordsworth's equation of the ship with the poetic imagination enables
him both to possess the female entirely ("My mind wantons . . . its own
creation") and to dismiss the Othered object, the ship, without regret, secure now in a community of exclusively male readers. For the interchange
of sympathy between two genders, Wordsworth here substitutes the (masculine) imagination's playing with itself, exhausting itself, coming to rest
among an accepting band of brothers.

Part III

1. William Hazlitt, in his essay "On Effeminacy of Character," cites the poetry of John Keats as his primary example of "an effeminacy of style, in
some degree corresponding to effeminacy of character," and concludes, "I
cannot help thinking that the fault of Mr. Keats's poems was deficiency in
masculine energy of style. He had beauty, tenderness, delicacy, in an un-
common degree, but there was a want of strength and substance." See
William Hazlitt, *Table Talk*, p. 254.

2. On Brontë's writing as "crude", "coarse" and hence implicitly masculine,
see G. W. Peck, Review of *Wuthering Heights*, *American Review* VII, June
1848, pp. 572–85; and other reviews cited below.

3. Susan J. Wolfson has persuasively studied Keats as a figure who complicates the definitions and rhetorical strategies of gender in poetry for both

nineteenth- and twentieth-century readers, in "Feminizing Keats," *Critical Essays on John Keats*, ed. Hermione de Almeida, pp. 317–56. In an essay that appeared only after I had completed this chapter, and which covers much of the same material, Margaret Homans reaches conclusions different from, and harsher than, my own, asserting that Keats finally invokes "an exclusively male readership," writes "only for men" and thus "makes of his poetry a masculine preserve, and in so doing he elects himself a member of the male club that poets in the classical tradition, and especially the high romantics, have always claimed literature to be, but which it is not," "Keats Reading Women, Women Reading Keats," in *Studies in Romanticism* 29 (Fall, 1990) pp. 341–370, p. 368. Mario L. D'Avanzo first noted Keats' engendering of poetry as female, in *Keats's Metaphors for the Poetic Imagination*, pp. 25–31.

4. The best biographies of Keats are by Walter Jackson Bate, *John Keats;* Aileen Ward, *John Keats—The Making of a Poet;* and Robert Gittings, *John Keats.*

5. Susan Wolfson, "Feminizing Keats," pp. 322–23; Byron, *Don Juan,* Canto 11:60.

6. John Gibson Lockhart, *Blackwood's Edinburgh Magazine* III (August, 1818) pp. 519–524; repr. in Donald H. Reiman, ed. *The Romantics Reviewed*, Vol. I pp. 90–95.

7. Marjorie Levinson most fully explored the class implications of Lockhart's attack in her *Keats's Life of Allegory—The Origins of a Style*, see esp. pp. 1–25. Susan Wolfson also notes the class implications of Lockhart's remarks on Keats, "Feminizing Keats," pp. 319–20. On the equation of Keats' Cockney poetics with Cockney—or liberal, anti-Establishment—politics, see David Bromwich, "Keats's Radicalism," and William Keach, "Cockney Couplets: Keats and the Politics of Style," both in *Studies in Romanticism* 25 (1986), pp. 197–219 and 182–196 respectively.

8. In his "Second Letter to John Murray, Esq., on the Rev. W. L. Bowles's Strictures on the Life and Writings of Pope" (25 March 1821), Byron described the poetry of the Cockneys (Keats and Leigh Hunt): "The grand distinction of the under forms of the new school of poets is their *vulgarity.* By this I do not mean that they are *coarse,* but 'shabby-genteel', as it is termed. A man may be *coarse* and yet not *vulgar,* and the reverse. . . . It is in their *finery* that the new under school are *most* vulgar, and they may be known by this at once; as what we called at Harrow 'a Sunday blood' might be easily distinguished from a gentleman, although his clothes might be the better cut, and his boots the best blackened, of the two:— probably because he made the one, or cleaned the other, with his own hands. In the present case, I speak of writing, not of persons." (*The Works of Lord Byron*, ed. Rowland E. Prothero, London, 1898–1904, *Letters and Journals*, Volume V p. 591). Marjorie Levinson analyses the class implications of Byron's remarks on Keats in detail, *Keats's Life of Allegory*, chap. 1.

Until Keats' death, with the exception of *Hyperion,* Byron repeatedly referred to Keats' poems as "the *Onanism* of Poetry": *Byron's Letters and Journals*, ed. Leslie Marchand, Vol. 7, pp. 200, 225, 217.

9. *Byron's Letters and Journals*, ed. Marchand, Vol. 7 p. 202.

10. I owe these observations to Claire Tomalin, *The Life and Death of Mary Wollstonecraft*, p. 18 and 18n; see also *Thraliana—the Diaries of Mrs. Piozzi*, ed. K. Balderstone; and *The Ladies' Dispensatory; or Every Woman her Own Physician* (London, 1740), which gives six detailed case histories of female masturbators; in one case, the girl had been "taught the sin" of masturbation "by her Mother's Chambermaid, with whom she continued to practice it seven years, they trying all Means to pleasure each other, and heighten the titillation" (p. 10). For evidence of lesbian sexual activity among upper- and middle-class women in eighteenth- and early nineteenth-century England, see *I Know My Own Heart: The Diaries of Anne Lister (1791–1840)*, ed. Helena Whitbread (London: Virago Press, 1988), pp. 104–5, 121, 158–9. For the practice of passionate but perhaps nonsexual "romantic friendship" among upper- and middle-class women, see Lillian Faderman, *Surpassing the Love of Men—Romantic Friendship and Love Between Women from the Renaissance to the Present*, pp. 74–144; and Elizabeth Mavor, *The Ladies of Llangollen: A Study of Romantic Friendship*.

11. On the nature and impact of Tissot's theories of masturbation, see Ludmilla Jordanova, "The Popularization of Medicine: Tissot on Onanism," *Textual Practice* 1 (1987) pp. 68–79.

12. Adrienne Rich and Barbara Charlesworth Gelpi, "Three Conversations," in *Adrienne Rich's Poetry*, ed. Barbara Charlesworth Gelpi and Albert Gelpi, pp. 114–115.

13. *The Letters of John Keats 1814–1821*, ed. Hyder Edward Rollins, 2 Vols., To Richard Woodhouse, 27 October 1818, I p. 387.

14. On the Self-in-Relation school of psychology, see Nancy Chodorow, *The Reproduction of Mothering;* Jean Baker Miller, *Toward a New Psychology of Women;* Carol Gilligan, *In A Different Voice;* and Sara Ruddick, *Maternal Thinking*. On Lacan and the French feminist psychoanalytic school, see the Introductions by Juliet Mitchell and Jacqueline Rose to Jacques Lacan, *Feminine Sexuality—Jacques Lacan and the Ecole Freudienne*.

15. *Letters of Keats*, I p. 387.

16. To George and Tom Keats, 21–27 December 1817, *Letters of Keats*, I p. 193.

17. On the ways in which the new "man of feeling" absorbed the female, see Janet Todd, *Sensibility—An Introduction;* and Alan Richardson, "Romanticism and the Colonization of the Feminine," in *Romanticism and Feminism*, ed. Anne K. Mellor, pp. 13–25.

18. To the George Keatses, 14 February–3 May 1819, *Letters of Keats*, II p. 66.

19. To James Rice, December 1819, *Letters of Keats*, II p. 236. I am grateful to Frederick Burwick for drawing this letter to my attention.

20. The best psychoanalytic study of the role of the female imago in Keats' personal and literary development is by Leon Waldoff, *Keats and the Silent Work of Imagination*.

    In a view with which I largely concur, Margaret Homans, Sonia Hofkosh, Marlon Ross and Alan Richardson have all seen the male romantic poet's imaging of himself as "impregnated" with a poem as an act of usurpation of female authority, even as a cannibalization of the female. However, in the case of Keats, I shall argue here, this metaphor functions as an act of dependence and submission rather than of colonization and exploitation. See Homans, "Keats Reading Women, Women Reading Keats," p. 343; Hofkosh, "The Writer's Ravishment: Women and the Romantic Author—The Example of Byron," pp. 105–109; Ross "Romantic Quest and Conquest—Troping Masculine Power in the Crisis of Poetic Identity," p. 48; Richardson, "Romanticism and the Colonization of the Feminine," pp. 15–21—the essays by Hofkosh, Ross and Richardson all appear in *Romanticism and Feminism*, ed. Anne K. Mellor.

21. To the George Keatses, 14 February–3 May 1819, *Letters of Keats*, II pp. 102–5.

22. To John Hamilton Reynolds, 19 February 1818, *Letters of Keats*, I pp. 231–2.

23. Patricia Klindienst Joplin has emphasized the origin of the identification of women's weaving with women's speech in the classical myth of Philomela, in "The Voice of the Shuttle is Ours," in *Rape and Representation*, edited by Lynn A. Higgins and Brenda R. Silver, pp. 35–63.

24. See Mary Field Belencky, *et al. Women's Ways of Knowing;* and Sara Ruddick, *Maternal Thinking* (1989). I should underline that the arguments of Belencky and Ruddick, like Nancy Chodorow's from which they are derived, posit not an essentialist but a socially constructed concept of gender.

25. Mary E. Hawkesworth, "Knowers, Knowing, Known: Feminist Theory and Claims of Truth," *Signs* 14 (Spring, 1989), p. 550. Major contributions to the field of feminist epistemology include Genevieve Lloyd, *The Man of Reason;* Sandra Harding and Merrill Hintikka, eds. *Discovering Reality;* Sandra Harding, *The Feminist Question in Science;* and Jean Grimshaw, *Philosophy and Feminist Thinking*.

26. To Benjamin Bailey, 13 March 1818, *Letters of Keats*, I pp. 242–3.

27. Stanley Cavell has developed the philosophical implications of this Romantic epistemology, of what he calls "mutual attunement," in his *The Claim of Reason*, Part IV. See also Michael Fischer's discussion of Cavell's Romanticism in his *Stanley Cavell and Literary Skepticism*, pp. 60–75.

28. Hawkesworth, p. 551. Hawkesworth specifies that such a concept of knowing embraces the following: perception, intuition, conceptualization, inference, representation, reflection, imagination, remembrance, conjecture, rationalization, argumentation, justification, contemplation, ratiocination, speculation, meditation, validation, deliberation—all of which are present in Keats' letters.

29. Margaret Homans, "Keats Reading Women, Women Reading Keats," pp. 344–45.

30. To John Hamilton Reynolds, 21 September 1817, *Letters of Keats*, I pp. 163–5.

31. Quoted by Margaret Drabble, ed., *The Oxford Companion to English Literature*, p. 662.

32. To the George Keatses, December 1818–4 January 1819, *Letters of Keats*, II pp. 18–9.

33. To Benjamin Bailey, 14 August 1819, *Letters of Keats*, II p. 139. For a discussion of Keats' anxiety in relation to women writers, and especially to the letter-writing Fanny Brawne, see Sonia Hofkosh, "The Writer's Ravishment: Women and the Romantic Author—The Example of Byron," in *Romanticism and Feminism*, ed. Anne K. Mellor, pp. 106–110.

34. Grant Scott, unpub. diss. UCLA 1989.

35. On the construction of the romance as a feminine genre in the eighteenth and nineteenth centuries, see Laurie Langbauer, *Women and Romance—The Consolations of Gender in the English Novel*.

36. To John Hamilton Reynolds, 21 September 1819, *Letters of Keats*, II p. 167.

37. Anne K. Mellor, *English Romantic Irony*, chap. 3.

38. To the George Keatses, 14 February–3 May 1819, *Letters of Keats*, II p. 62.

39. To John Hamilton Reynolds, 14 March 1818, *Letters of Keats*, I p. 245. On Ann Radcliffe's influence on Keats, also see Homans, "Keats Reading Women, Women Reading Keats," pp. 359–362.

40. To Richard Woodhouse, 21 September 1819, *Letters of Keats*, II p. 174.

41. Karen Swann, "Harassing the Muse," in *Romanticism and Feminism*, ed. Anne K. Mellor, pp. 81–92.

42. For a discussion of the connection of Moneta to Athena and a tragic consciousness, see Anne K. Mellor, "Keats' Face of Moneta: Source and Meaning," *Keats-Shelley Journal* 25 (1976), pp. 65–80.

43. For a study of the complexities of Keats' letters, see David Luke, "Keats's Letters: Fragments of an Aesthetic of Fragments," *Genre* II (1978), pp. 209–26; and Susan Wolfson, "Keats the Letter-Writer: Epistolary Poetics," *Romanticism Past and Present* 6 (1982), pp. 43–61.

44. Walter Pater, "Postscript" to *Appreciations* (1889); reprinted in *The Brontës—The Critical Heritage*, ed. Miriam Allott, p. 445. Pater, like so many critics of Romanticism influenced by his work, could conceive of "Romanticism" only in terms of what I have been calling the masculine Romantic ideology.

45. Ellen Nussey, "Reminiscences of Charlotte Brontë," *Scribner's Magazine*, May 1871, np.

46. Nussey, "Reminiscences."

47. C. Day Lewis, *Notable Images of Virtue*, pp. 1–25.

48. Winifred Gerin, *Emily Brontë—A Biography*, p. 34. For the above details of Emily Brontë's life, I am indebted to this still unsurpassed biography of Emily Brontë, as well as to the more recent effort of Edward Chitham, *A Life of Emily Brontë*.

49. Charlotte Brontë [Currer Bell], "Biographical Notice of Ellis and Acton Bell," Preface to Emily Brontë, *Wuthering Heights*, 2nd edition, September 19, 1850.

50. Elizabeth Gaskell, *The Life of Charlotte Brontë*, ed. Alan Shelston, p. 230.

51. Winifred Gerin, *Emily Brontë*, p. 259.

52. Elizabeth Gaskell, *The Life of Charlotte Brontë*, p. 358.

53. Margaret Homans, *Women Writers and Poetic Identity: Dorothy Wordsworth, Emily Brontë, and Emily Dickinson*, p. 109.

54. Emily's July 30, 1845, Diary entry is on display at the Brontë Parsonage in Haworth. It has been accurately transcribed in the Norton Critical Edition of *Wuthering Heights*, ed. William M. Sale, Jr., and Richard J. Dunn, third edition (New York, W. W. Norton & Company, 1990), p. 298. Teddi Lynn Chichester has discussed the significance of this letter in her "Evading 'Earth's Dungeon Tomb': Emily Brontë, A. G. A., and the Fatally Feminine," *Victorian Poetry* 29 (1991) pp. 1–15, 3.

55. Anonymous: Notice of *Wuthering Heights*. *Union Magazine of Literature and Art* 2 (June, 1848), p. 287.

56. Anonymous: Notice of *Wuthering Heights*. *Graham's Magazine* (July, 1848), p. 60.

57. Anonymous: Review of *Wuthering Heights*. *Examiner* (January, 1848), pp. 21–2. Anonymous Notice of *Wuthering Heights*. *Literary World* (April, 1848), p. 243.

58. George Washington Peck, Review of *Wuthering Heights*, *American Review* VII (June, 1848), pp. 572–85.

59. George Washington Peck, p. 575–6.

60. William Dearden, "Who Wrote *Wuthering Heights?*" *Halifax [England] Guardian* (June 15, 1867), np.

61. For definitive demonstrations of Emily Bronte's authorship, see Irene Cooper Willis, "The Authorship of *Wuthering Heights*," *The Trollopian* 2 (December 1947) pp. 157–68, and Winifred Gerin, *Branwell Brontë*, pp. 307–314.

62. Francis A. Leyland, *The Brontë Family with Special Reference to Patrick Branwell Brontë* (1886), 2 Vols. See esp. Vol. 2, Ch. 10, pp. 178–215, where Leyland argues that "there may have been some measure of collaboration between Branwell and his sister, that he originated the idea, moulded the characters, and wrote the earlier portion of the work, which she, taking, revised, amended, completed, and imbued with enough of the individual spirit to give unity to the whole."

63. T. W. Reid, *Charlotte Brontë, A Monograph* (London, 1877); cf. Winifred Gerin, *Emily Brontë*, pp. 197–201.

64. Nancy Armstrong, "Emily Brontë In and Out of Her Time," *Genre* XV (Fall 1982), pp. 243–264.

65. J. Hillis Miller, *Fiction and Repetition—Seven English Novels*, pp. 68, 50. For a recent statement of this argument from a French feminist perspective, see Patricia Yaeger, "Violence in the Sitting Room: *Wuthering Heights* and the Woman's Novel," *Genre* 21 (1988), pp. 203–229.

66. Judith Weissman, in her *Half Savage and Hardy and Free—Women and Rural Radicalism in the Nineteenth-Century Novel*, emphasized the commitment to an instinctual life and the "romantic radicalism" of *Wuthering Heights*, (pp. 85–99). Camille Paglia also reads Emily Brontë's nature as "primarily force, not nurturance," as "*a nature without a mother*," in her *Sexual Personae—Art and Decadence from Nefertiti to Emily Dickinson*, chap. 17, p. 449.

67. Emily Brontë, *Wuthering Heights*, ed. William M. Sale, Jr., and Richard

Dunn (New York: W. W. Norton, Critical Edition, 1990/1963), p. 250. Cited hereafter by page number in the text.

On Heathcliff as a "male muse" or the masculine dimension of a female writer's creative genius, here the masculine half of the divided Catherine Earnshaw, see Irene Tayler, *Holy Ghosts—The Male Muses of Emily and Charlotte Brontë*, p. 78 and chap. 2.

68. I am grateful to Lisa Gordis for drawing my attention to the image of child-birth in this passage. Mr. Earnshaw later refers to Heathcliff as a "poor *fatherless* child" (my italics, 30), reinforcing the suggestion that Earnshaw has functioned as mother rather than as father to Heathcliff. On Victor Frankenstein as a (failed) mother, see my *Mary Shelley*, chap. 2.

69. Many critics have emphasized the marginal social position of Heathcliff: either as a member of the lower classes (perhaps of the penniless, starving Gaelic Irish immigrants to Liverpool during the famines of the mid-eighteenth century); as a Romanian "gipsy brat" (28); or, in Nelly Dean's later fantasy, as the abandoned or kidnapped son of a lower-class East Indian Lascar or an upper-class Indian queen or even "the Emperor of China" (44). Both in appearance and in social class, Heathcliff is encoded as the racial Other, the foreign, the barbarian. On the class position of Heathcliff, see Terry Eagleton's fine discussion in *Myths of Power—A Marxist Study of the Brontes*, chap. 6.

70. Mary Douglas, *Purity and Danger—An Analysis of Concepts of Pollution and Taboo*, see esp. pp. 1–5, 113–121.

71. Emily Brontë's French essays, written for M. Heger in Brussels in 1842, are reprinted in French in Winifred Gerin, *Emily Brontë*, Appendix A.

72. Emily Brontë's drawing of "The North Wind" is reproduced in Winifred Gerin, *Emily Brontë*, Plate 1, facing p. 24.

73. Sandra Gilbert and Susan Gubar first noted the relevance of Levi-Strauss' distinction between the raw and the cooked to *Wuthering Heights*, in *The Madwoman in the Attic*, pp. 248–308, see esp. pp. 273–4.

74. For a persuasive Freudian reading of the sexual imagery in this scene, see Thomas J. Moser, "What is the Matter with Emily Jane? Conflicting Impulses in *Wuthering Heights*," *Nineteenth-Century Fiction* XVII (June, 1962) pp. 1–19.

75. Robert M. Polhemus, *Erotic Faith—Being in Love from Jane Austen to D. H. Lawrence*, pp. 79–107.

76. The classic analysis of Eros is Denis de Rougemont's *L'amour et l'occident* (1940), trans. as *Love in the Western World* by Montgomery Belgion (1956/ 1940). Jacques Blondel first emphasized the role of Eros in *Wuthering Heights* in his *Emily Brontë: expérience spirituelle et création poétique* (1955).

77. Barbara Ann Schapiro emphasized the narcissism of the English Romantic poets in *The Romantic Mother*, while Barbara Charlesworth Gelpi has explored the narcissistic and incestuous nature of Shelley's concept of love, in *Shelley's Goddess: Maternity, Language, Subjectivity*, chap. II. See also Atara Stein, who emphasizes the gender implications of Romantic narcissistic love, in *"I loved her and I killed her"—The Ambivalence of Love in Later English Romantic Poetry and Fiction*, unpub. diss., UCLA, 1990.

78. Eric Solomon, "The Incest Theme in *Wuthering Heights,*" *NCF* 14 (1959), pp. 80–83. Also see Ronald E. Fine, "Lockwood's Dreams and the Key of *Wuthering Heights,*" *Nineteenth-Century Fiction* 24 (1969) pp. 16–30.

79. Dorothy Van Ghent first explored the significance of the imagery of windows and boundaries in *Wuthering Heights,* in her *The English Novel— Form and Function* (1953), pp. 153–170. On the transgression of boundaries and the desire for the transcendental (masculine) Romantic self in *Wuthering Heights,* see Eugenia C. DeLamotte, *Perils of the Night—A Feminist Study of Nineteenth-Century Gothic,* chap. 4.

80. *The Complete Poems of Emily Jane Brontë,* ed. C. W. Hatfield, #A31, reduced and re-transcribed as #H489, p. 244.

81. Mark Schorer, "Fiction and the 'Analogical Matrix',," *Kenyon Review* XI (Autumn, 1949), reprinted in William M. Sale, Jr., ed., *Wuthering Heights,* pp. 356–361.

82. *Poems of Emily Brontë,* ed. Hatfield, #176, p. 208–9. For a fine study of the ways in which Emily Brontë's poetry was influenced by the male Romantic poets, see Irene Tayler, *Holy Ghosts—The Male Muses of Emily and Charlotte Brontë,* chap. 1.

83. Sandra Gilbert and Susan Gubar have emphasized the "crippling" of Catherine when she enters "cooked" Thrushcross Grange, *The Madwoman in the Attic,* pp. 271–278.

84. Margaret Homans has explored the relationship of the imaginary to the symbolic in Lacanian and Freudian terms in *Wuthering Heights,* in her fine essay, "Repression and Sublimation of Nature in *Wuthering Heights,*" *PMLA* 93 (1978) pp. 9–19.

85. Nancy Armstrong pointed out this gap in the narration of Heathcliff's history, in "Emily Brontë In and Out of Her Time," p. 375. For an early Marxist reading of Heathcliff's "rise," see Arnold Kettle, "Emily Brontë: *Wuthering Heights* (1847)," (1951), in Ian Watt, ed., *The Victorian Novel: Modern Essays in Criticism,* pp. 200–216. Also see Terry Eagleton, *Myths of Power: A Marxist Study of the Brontës.*

86. George Washington Peck, Review of *Wuthering Heights, American Review* VII (June, 1848), pp. 572–85.

87. On the image of Hercules as the self-representation of the revolutionary French republic, see Lynn Hunt, *Politics, Culture, and Class in the French Revolution,* chap. 5.

88. Without exploring its political ramifications, Nancy Armstrong applies the term "reign of terror" to Heathcliff, "Emily Brontë In and Out of Her Time," p. 373.

89. J. Hillis Miller, *Fiction and Repetition,* chap. 2; Margaret Homans, 'Repression and Sublimation of Nature in *Wuthering Heights,*" *PMLA* 93 (1978) pp. 9–19; Carol Jacobs, *Uncontainable Romanticism—Shelley, Brontë, Kleist,* chap. 3.

90. On the equation of the book with the values of civilization in *Wuthering Heights,* see Robert McKibben, "The Image of the Book in *Wuthering Heights,*" *Nineteenth-Century Fiction* 15 (1960) pp. 159–69.

91. Carol Jacobs, *Uncontainable Romanticism,* pp. 76–78.

92. Margaret Homans, "Repression and Sublimation in Nature," p. 15.

93. Carol Jacobs, *Uncontainable Romanticism*, p. 73.

94. Much has been written on the Romantic poets' recognition of the limitations of linguistic constructions. See for instance Geoffrey Hartman's *Wordsworth's Poetry, 1787–1814*; Paul de Man's *The Rhetoric of Romanticism*; and with a particular emphasis on Shelley and Byron, Jerrold E. Hogle's *Shelley's Process: Radical Transference and the Development of His Major Works*; William Keach's *Shelley's Style*; Jerome McGann's *Don Juan in Context*; my *English Romantic Irony*; and Peter Manning, *Reading Romantics—Texts and Contexts*; chap. 6, among many others.

    David Sonstroem argued that Emily Brontë was, in effect, a Romantic ironist, one who cancelled out all possible viewpoints as limited in understanding, in "*Wuthering Heights* and the Limits of Vision," *PMLA* 86 (1971) pp. 51–62. For this view, see also Inga-Stina Ewbank, *Their Proper Sphere: A Study of the Brontë Sisters as Early-Victorian Female Novelists*.

95. On Lockwood, see, in addition to Carol Jacob's *Uncontainable Romanticism*; Terence McCarthy, "The Incompetent Narrator of *Wuthering Heights*," *Modern Language Quarterly* 42 (1981) pp. 48–64; Edgar F. Shannon, "Lockwood's Dreams and the Exegesis of *Wuthering Heights*," *Nineteenth-Century Fiction* 14 (1959) pp. 95–109; and Carl Woodring, "The Narrators of *Wuthering Heights*," *Nineteenth-Century Fiction* 20 (1957) pp. 298–305.

96. On Nelly Dean see John K. Mathison, "Nelly Dean and the Power of *Wuthering Heights*," *Nineteenth-Century Fiction* XI (September 1956) pp. 106–29; and Carl Woodring, "The Narrators of *Wuthering Heights*," *Nineteenth-Century Fiction* 20 (1957) pp. 298–305.

97. Sandra Gilbert and Susan Gubar, *The Madwoman in the Attic*, chap. 8, have argued forcefully for the first view; while Arnold Kettle in his *An Introduction to the English Novel* (1951), Vol. I, Albert J. Guerard, in his Preface to *Wuthering Heights*, and William A. Madden, "*Wuthering Heights* and the Binding of Passion," *Nineteenth-Century Fiction* 27 (1972) pp. 127–54, have read the ending of the novel as a positive accommodation of nature to civilization. Carol A. Senf has further urged us to see the marriage of Hareton and Cathy as a feminist triumph, as the envisioning of a "more egalitarian, more feminine future," even though in the same sentence she defines their projected union as a "peaceful merger of capitalistic economic power with the traditional political power of the landed gentry," both systems of patriarchal privilege, in "Emily Brontë's Version of Feminist History: *Wuthering Heights*," *Essays in Literature* 12 (1985), pp. 201–214.

98. Sandra Gilbert and Susan Gubar, *The Madwoman in the Attic*, pp. 298–302.

99. Even Beth Newman, in her optimistic reading of the exchange of gazes between Cathy and Hareton as producing "a gaze that is strictly neither male nor female, thereby escaping the differential relations that express themselves in the hierarchical terms *active/passive, subject/object*" finally acknowledges that "a specular economy that fetishizes and appropriates women" controls the narration of *Wuthering Heights*, in her fine essay

" 'The Situation of the Looker-On': Gender, Narration, and Gaze in *Wuthering Heights*," *PMLA* 105 (1990), pp. 1029–1041.

100. Both Teddi Lynn Chichester, in "Evading 'Earth's Dungeon Tomb': Emily Brontë, A. G. A., and the Fatally Feminine," *Victorian Poetry* 29 (1991) pp. 1–15, and Irene Tayler, in *Holy Ghosts—The Male Muses of Emily and Charlotte Brontë*, chap. 1, have emphasized the alignment of the female with death in Bronte's poetry.

Conclusion

1. Stuart Curran has defined the concern of Romantic women poets with the representation of the "quotidian," in "The 'I' Altered," in *Romanticism and Feminism*, ed. Anne K. Mellor, pp. 184–207.

2. Whether or not Mary Wollstonecraft and her female peers were "revolutionary" has been the subject of some recent critical discussion. Janet Todd argues that the period of the 1790s was already a period of conservative backlash against the education of women and egalitarian marriages, in *The Sign of Angellica—Women, Writing and Fiction, 1660–1800*, chaps. 11–12; while Donna Landry more convincingly argues that from the perspective of the working-class female subaltern, the "revolution in female manners" proclaimed by Mary Wollstonecraft channeled potentially radical tendencies in British culture into a bourgeois reformism, in *The Muses of Resistance—Laboring-Class Women's Poetry in Britain, 1739–1796*, chap. 7.

3. Jon P. Klancher has explored the way in which the Romantic poets, especially Wordsworth and Coleridge, constructed an audience for themselves that would ensure their claim to authority within an educated, bourgeois public arena, in *The Making of English Reading Audiences 1790–1832*. For Marxist readings of the Romantic poets that highlight their class biases, see also David Simpson, *Wordsworth's Historical Imagination: The Poetry of Displacement;* John Barrell, *Poetry, Language and Politics;* and Marjorie Levinson, *Wordsworth's Great Period Poems: Four Essays*.

Works Cited

Aaron, Jane. *A Double Singleness: Gender and the Writing of Charles and Mary Lamb*. Oxford: Clarendon Press, 1991.

Abrams, Meyer H. *Natural Supernaturalism—Tradition and Revolution in Romantic Literature*. New York: W. W. Norton, 1971.

Aers, David. "Blake: Sex, Society, and Ideology," in *Romanticism and Ideology*. Eds. David Aers, Jonathan Cook, and David Punter. London: Routledge, 1981, pp. 27–43.

Alexander, Meena. "Dorothy Wordsworth: the grounds of writing." *Women's Studies* 14 (1988): 195–210.

———.*Women in Romanticism: Mary Wollstonecraft, Dorothy Wordsworth, and Mary Shelley*. Totowa, N.J.: Barnes & Noble, 1989.

Allott, Miriam, ed. *The Brontës—The Critical Heritage*. London and Boston: Routledge & Kegan Paul, 1974.

Altick, Richard D. *The English Common Reader—A Social History of the Mass Reading Public 1800–1900*. Chicago: University of Chicago Press, 1957.

Amis, Kingsley. *The Faber Popular Reciter*. London: Faber and Faber, 1978.

Arac, Jonathan. "Bounding Lines: *The Prelude* and Critical Revision." *Boundary* 7 (1979): 31–48.

Armstrong, Isobel. "Scandal and Sudden Death: A Nineteenth-Century Mystery," Inaugural Lecture, Birkbeck College, University of London, 30 April 1991.

Armstrong, Nancy. *Desire and Domestic Fiction—A Political History of the Novel*. New York: Oxford University Press, 1987.

———."Emily Brontë In and Out of Her Time." *Genre* XV (1982): 243–264.

Auerbach, Nina. *Communities of Women—An Idea in Fiction*. Cambridge, Mass.: Harvard University Press, 1987.

———. *Romantic Imprisonment—Women and Other Glorified Outcasts*. New York: Columbia University Press, 1985.

Austen, Jane. *Emma*. London: Penguin, 1966; repr. 1983.

———. *Jane Austen's Letters to her Sister Cassandra and Others*. Ed. R. W. Chapman. Second edition. London: Oxford University Press, 1952.

———. *Mansfield Park*. Ed. Tony Tanner. New York: Penguin Books, 1966.

————. *Persuasion*. Ed. D. W. Harding. New York: Penguin Books, 1965.

————. *Pride and Prejudice*. Ed. Donald Gray. New York: Norton Critical Edition, 1966.

Bakhtin, Mikhail. *The Dialogic Imagination: Four Essays by Mikhail Bakhtin*. Ed. Michael Holquist, trans. Caryl Emerson and Michael Holquist. Austin, Texas: University of Texas Press Slavic Series, no. 1, 1981.

Balderstone, K., ed. *Thraliana—the Diaries of Mrs. Piozzi*. Oxford, 1942.

Barbauld, Anna Laetitia. "On the Origin and Progress of Novel-Writing," Introductory Essay for *The British Novelists*, London: Bentley and Colburn, 1810.

Barker-Benfield, G. J. "Mary Wollstonecraft: Eighteenth-Century Commonwealthwoman." *Journal of the History of Ideas* 50 (1989): 95–115.

Barrell, John. *Poetry, Language and Politics*. Manchester: University of Manchester Press, 1988.

Bate, Walter Jackson. *John Keats*. Cambridge, Mass: Harvard University Press, 1963.

Belencky, Mary Field, *et al. Women's Ways of Knowing*. New York: Basic Books, 1986.

Benstock, Shari. *The Private Self—Theory and Practice of Women's Autobiographical Writings*. Chapel Hill: University of North Carolina Press, 1988.

Bindman, David. *Blake as an Artist*. Oxford: Phaidon, and New York: Dutton, 1977.

Blake, William. *The Poetry and Prose of William Blake*. Ed. David V. Erdman. Garden City, New York: Doubleday and Co., 1965.

Blanchard, Laman. *Life and Literary Remains of L. E. L.*. London: Henry Colburn, 1841. 2 Vols.

Bleier, Ruth. *Science and Gender*. New York: Pergamon Press, 1984.

Blodgett, Harriet. "Emily Vindicated: Ann Radcliffe and Mary Wollstonecraft." *Weber Studies* 7 (1990): 48–61.

Blondel, Jacques. *Emily Brontë: expérience spirituelle et création poétique*. Paris: Presses Universitaires de France, 1955.

Bloom, Harold. *The Anxiety of Influence—A Theory of Poetry*. London: Oxford University Press, 1973.

Boone, Joseph Allen. *Tradition Counter Tradition—Love and the Form of Fiction*. Chicago and London: University of Chicago Press, 1987.

Brodzki, Bella and Celeste Schenck. *Life/Lines—Theorizing Women's Autobiography*. Ithaca: Cornell University Press, 1988.

Bromwich, David. *Hazlitt—The Mind of a Critic*. New York and Oxford: Oxford University Press, 1983.

————. "Keat's Radicalism." *Studies in Romanticism* 25 (1986): 197–219.

Brontë, Charlotte [Currer Bell]. "Biographical Notice of Ellis and Acton Bell," Preface to Emily Brontë, *Wuthering Heights*, 2nd edition, September 19, 1850.

Brontë, Emily. *The Complete Poems of Emily Jane Brontë*. Ed. C. W. Hatfield. New York: Columbia University Press, 1941.

———. *Wuthering Heights*. Eds. William M. Sale, Jr., and Richard Dunn. New York: W. W. Norton, Critical Edition, 1990/1963.

Brown, Julia Prewitt. *Jane Austen's Novels—Social Change and Literary Form.* Cambridge, Mass.: Harvard University Press, 1979.

Brown, Lloyd W. "Jane Austen and the Feminist Tradition." *Nineteenth-Century Fiction* 28 (1973): 321–38.

Brown, Nathaniel. *Sexuality and Feminism in Shelley*. Cambridge, Mass: Harvard University Press, 1979.

Bruss, Elizabeth W. *Autobiographical Acts—The Changing Situation of a Literary Genre.* Baltimore: Johns Hopkins University Press, 1976.

———. "Eye for I: Making and Unmaking Autobiography in Film," in *Autobiography: Essays Theoretical and Critical*, edited by James Olney, pp. 296–320.

Buckley, Jerome Hamilton. *The Turning Key—Autobiography and the Subjective Impulse since 1800*. Cambridge: Harvard University Press, 1984.

Burke, Edmund. *A Philosophical Inquiry into the Origin of Our Ideas of the Sublime and the Beautiful*. Fifth Edition. London: J. Dodsley, 1767.

———. *Reflections on the Revolution in France, and on the Proceedings in Certain Societies in London, relative to that Event* (November, 1790). Ed. Thomas H. D. Mahoney. New York: Liberal Arts Press, 1955.

Butler, Judith. *Gender Trouble*. New York and London: Routledge and Chapman Hall, 1989.

Butler, Marilyn. *Jane Austen and the War of Ideas*. London: Oxford University Press, 1975.

———. *Maria Edgeworth—A Literary Biography*. Oxford: Clarendon Press, 1972.

Byron, George Gordon, Lord. *Byron's Letters and Journals*. Ed. Leslie A. Marchand. Cambridge, Mass.: Harvard University Press, 1974–1982. 10 Vols.

———. *Lord Byron: The Complete Poetical Works*. Ed. Jerome J. McGann. Oxford: Clarendon Press, 1980–90.

———. *The Works of Lord Byron*. Ed. Rowland E. Prothero, London, 1898–1904, *Letters and Journals*, Volume V.

Cafarelli, Annette Wheeler. *Prose in the Age of Poets: Romanticism and Biographical Narrative from Johnson to De Quincey*. Philadelphia: University of Pennsylvania Press, 1990.

Cavell, Stanley. *The Claim of Reason*. Oxford: Oxford University Press, 1979.

Chase, Cynthia. *Decomposing Figures—Rhetorical Readings in the Romantic Tradition*. Baltimore: Johns Hopkins University Press, 1986.

Chichester, Teddi Lynn. "Evading 'Earth's Dungeon Tomb': Emily Brontë, A. G. A., and the Fatally Feminine." *Victorian Poetry* 29 (1991) 1–15.

Chitham, Edward. *A Life of Emily Brontë*. Oxford: Basil Blackwell, 1987.

Chodorow, Nancy. *The Reproduction of Mothering*. Berkeley: University of California Press, 1978.

Chorley, Henry F., *Memorials of Mrs. Hemans, with illustrations of Her Literary Character from her Private Correspondence*. New York and London, 1836.

Clarke, Norma. *Ambitious Heights—Writing, Friendship, Love—The Jewsbury*

Sisters, Felicia Hemans, and Jane Welsh Carlyle. London and New York: Routledge, 1990.

Colby, Vineta. *Yesterday's Woman—Domestic Realism in the English Novel*. Princeton, N.J.: Princeton University Press, 1974.

Coleridge, Samuel Taylor. *Collected Letters of Samuel Taylor Coleridge*. Ed. Earl Leslie Griggs. Oxford: The Clarendon Press, 1956.

———. *The Poems of Samuel Taylor Coleridge*. Ed. Ernest Hartley Coleridge. London: Oxford University Press, 1912; repr. 1960.

Cook, Kay K. "Self-Neglect in the Canon: Why Don't We Talk about Romantic Autobiography?" *Auto/biography Studies* 5 (1990): 88–98.

Cott, Nancy. *The Bonds of Womanhood*. New Haven: Yale University Press, 1977.

Courtney, Janet E., *The Adventurous Thirties—A Chapter in the The Women's Movement*. London: Oxford University Press, 1933.

Cruickshank, Brodie. *Eighteen Years on the The Gold Coast of Africa, including an Account of the Native Tribes, and their Intercourse with Europeans*. London: Hurst and Blackett, 1853.

Cullinan, Mary. *Susan Ferrier*. Boston: Twayne Publishers, 1984.

Curran, Stuart. *A Textbase of Women's Writing in English, 1330–1830*: Bibliography of British Women Poets, 1760–1830. Available from the Brown University Women Writers Project or from the author.

———. "The 'I' Altered," in *Romanticism and Feminism*, ed. Anne K. Mellor, pp. 185–207.

Daiches, David. "Jane Austen, Karl Marx and the Aristocratic Dance." *American Scholar* 17 (1948): 289–98.

D'Avanzo, Mario L. *Keats's Metapors for the Poetic Imagination*. Durham, N.C.: Duke University Press, 1967.

Davidoff, Leonore and Catherine Hall. *Family Fortunes: Men and Women of the English Middle Class, 1780–1850*. London: Hutchinson; Chicago: Chicago University Press, 1987.

Deardon, William. "Who Wrote *Wuthering Heights*?" *Halifax* [England] *Guardian* (June 15, 1867), np.

De Beauvoir, Simone. *The Second Sex*. Trans. H. M. Parshley. New York: Alfred Knopf, 1953.

De Bolla, Peter. *The Discourse of the Sublime—Readings in History, Aesthetics and the Subject*. Oxford: Basil Blackwell, 1989.

DeLamotte, Eugenia C. *Perils of the Night—A Feminist Study of Nineteenth-Century Gothic*. New York and Oxford: Oxford University Press, 1990.

De Man, Paul. "Autobiography as De-facement." *MLN* 94 (1979): 919–930.

———. *Blindness and Insight*. New York: Oxford University Press, 1971.

———. *The Rhetoric of Romanticism*. New York: Columbia University Press, 1984.

———. "The Rhetoric of Temporality," in *Interpretation: Theory and Practice*, ed. Charles S. Singleton. Baltimore: Johns Hopkins Press, 1969, pp. 173–209.

D'Emilio, John and Estelle B. Freedman. *Intimate Matters: A History of Sexuality in America*. New York: Harper and Row, 1988.

De Rougemont, Denis. *L'amour et l'occident* (1940). Trans. as *Love in the Western World* by Montgomery Belgion. Greenwich, Conn.: Fawcett Publications, 1956/1940.

Devlin, D. D. *De Quincey, Wordsworth and the Art of Prose*. New York: St. Martin's Press, 1983.

Douglas, Mary. *Purity and Danger—An Analysis of Concepts of Pollution and Taboo*. London: Routledge & Kegan Paul, 1966.

Drabble, Margaret, ed., *The Oxford Companion to English Literature*. Oxford: Oxford University Press, 1985.

Duckworth, Alistair M. *The Improvement of the Estate—A Study of Jane Austen's Novels*. Baltimore: Johns Hopkins University Press, 1971.

———. "Jane Austen's Accommodations," *Tennessee Studies in Literature* 29 (1985): 225–267.

Eakin, Paul John. *Autobiography as a Referential Art*. Princeton: Princeton University Press, 1991.

———. *Fictions in Autobiography—Studies in the Art of Self-Invention*. Princeton: Princeton University Press, 1985.

Eagleton, Mary, ed. *Feminist Literary Theory: A Reader*. Oxford: Basil Blackwell, 1986.

Eagleton, Terry. *Myths of Power—A Marxist Study of the Brontës*. London: Macmillan, 1975.

———. *The Rape of Clarissa—Writing, Sexuality and Class Struggle in Samuel Richardson*. Oxford: Basil Blackwell, 1982.

Edgeworth, Frances Ann. *A Memoir of Maria Edgeworth*. London, 1867.

Edgeworth, Maria. *The Absentee* (1812). Eds. W. J. McCormack and Kim Walker. Oxford: Oxford University Press, 1988.

———. *Belinda*. London: John Johnson, 1801; repr. London: Pandora Books, 1986.

———. *Letters for Literary Ladies*. London: John Johnson, Second Edition, 1799.

———. *Tales and Novels by Maria Edgeworth*. London, 1832.

Egan, Susanna. *Patterns of Experience in Autobiography*. Chapel Hill: University of North Carolina Press, 1984.

Ellis, Kate Ferguson. *The Contested Castle—Gothic Novels and the Subversion of Domestic Ideology*. Urbana: University of Illinois Press, 1989.

Ellison, Julie. *Delicate Subjects—Romanticism, Gender, and the Ethics of Understanding*. Ithaca and London: Cornell University Press, 1990.

Enfield, D. E. *L. E. L.—A Mystery of the Thirties*. London: Hogarth Press, 1928.

Erdman, David. *The Illuminated Blake*. Garden City: Doubleday Anchor, 1974.

Evans, Mary. *Jane Austen and the State*. London: Tavistock, 1987.

Ewbank, Inga-Stina. *Their Proper Sphere: A Study of the Brontë Sisters as Early-Victorian Female Novelists*. Cambridge, Mass.: Harvard University Press, 1966.

Fadem, Richard. "Dorothy Wordsworth: A View from 'Tintern Abbey." *The Wordsworth Circle* 9 (1978) 17–32.

Faderman, Lillian. *Surpassing the Love of Men—Romantic Friendship and Love Between Women from the Renaissance to the Present*. New York: William Morow, 1981.

Felski, Rita. *Beyond Feminist Aesthetics—Feminist Literature and Social Change*. Cambridge, Mass.: Harvard University Press, 1989.

Ferber, Michael. *The Social Vision of William Blake*. Princeton: Princeton University Press, 1985.

Ferguson, Frances C. *Wordsworth: Language as Counter-Spirit*. New Haven: Yale University Press, 1977.

Ferguson, Moira, ed. *First Feminists—British Women Writers*. Bloomington: Indiana University Press, 1985.

Ferrier, Susan. *Destiny; or, The Chief's Daughter*. Edinburgh: Robert Cadell, 1831.

———. *Inheritance*. Edinburgh: Blackwood, 1824; repr. Bampton, Oxfordshire: Three Rivers Press, 1984.

———. *Marriage*. Introduction by Rosemary Ashton. London: Penguin-Virago, 1986.

Fine, Ronald E. "Lockwood's Dreams and the Key of *Wuthering Heights*." *Nineteenth-Century Fiction* 24 (1969): 16–30.

Finke, Laurie A. "'A Philosophic Wanton': Language and Authority in Wollstonecraft's *A Vindication of the Rights of Woman*," in *The Philosopher as Writer*. Ed. Robert Ginsburg. London and Toronto: Associated University Press, 1987, pp. 155–176.

Fischer, Michael. *Stanley Cavell and Literary Skepticism*. Chicago and London: Chicago University Press, 1989.

Fleischman, Avrom. *Figures of Autobiography—The Language of Self-Writing in Victorian and Modern England*. Berkeley: University of California Press, 1983.

Foucault, Michel. *The History of Sexuality*. Trans. Robert Hurley. New York: Pantheon Books, Vol. I, 1978; Vol. 2, 1985; Vol. 3, 1987.

———. *Michel Foucault: The Will to Truth*. New York: Methuen, 1980.

Fox, Susan J. "The Female as Metaphor in William Blake's Poetry." *Critical Inquiry* 3 (1977): 507–519.

Fraiman, Susan. "The Humiliation of Elizabeth Bennet," in *Refiguring the Father—New Feminist Readings of Patriarchy*, edited by Patricia Yaeger and Beth Kowaleski-Wallace. Carbondale: Southern Illinois University Press, 1989, pp. 168–187.

Gagnier, Regenia. *Subjectivities: A History of Self-Representation in Britain, 1832–1920*. New York: Oxford University Press, 1991.

Galperin, William H. *Revision and Authority in Wordsworth—The Interpretation of a Career*. Philadelphia: University of Pennsylvania Press, 1989.

Gaskell, Elizabeth. *The Life of Charlotte Brontë*. Ed. Alan Shelston. London: Penguin, 1975; repr. 1980.

Gelpi, Barbara Charlesworth. *Shelley's Goddess: Maternity, Language, Subjectivity*. New York: Oxford University Press, 1992.

George, Diana Hume. "Is She Also the Divine Image? Feminine Form in the Art of William Blake." *Centennial Review* 23 (1979): 129–40.

Gerin, Winifred. *Branwell Brontë*. London: Hutchinson, 1961; 1972.

———. *Emily Brontë—A Biography*. Oxford: Clarendon Press, 1971.

Gilbert, Sandra and Susan Gubar. *The Madwoman in the Attic—The Woman Writer and the Nineteenth-Century Literary Imagination*. New Haven: Yale University Press, 1979.

Gilligan, Carol. *In a Different Voice*. Cambridge, Mass: Harvard University Press, 1982.

Gittings, Robert. *John Keats*. London: Heinemann, 1968.

Gittings, Robert and Jo Manton. *Dorothy Wordsworth*. Oxford: Clarendon Press, 1985.

Glen, Heather. *Vision and Disenchantment: Blake's "Songs" and Wordsworth's "Lyrical Ballads"*. Cambridge: Cambridge University Press, 1983.

Grant, Aline. *Susan Ferrier of Edinburgh—A Biography*. Denver: Alan Swallow Press, 1957.

Greco, Norma A. "Mother Figures in Blake's *Songs of Innocence* and the Female Will." *Romanticism Past and Present* 10 (1986): 1–15.

Greer, Germain. "The Tulsa Center for the Study of Women's Literature: What We Are Doing and Why We Are Doing It." *Tulsa Studies in Women's Literature* I (1982): 5–26.

Gregory, John. *A Father's Legacy to his Daughters*. London: 1822.

Grimshaw, Jean. *Philosophy and Feminist Thinking*. Minneapolis: University of Minnesota Press, 1986.

Guerard, Albert J. Preface to *Wuthering Heights*. New York; Washington Square Press, 1960.

Guralnick, Elissa S. "Radical Politics in Mary Wollstonecraft's *A Vindication of the Rights of Woman*." *Studies in Burke & His Time* 18 (1977): 155–158.

Gusdorf, Georges. "Conditions and Limits of Autobiography." Trans. James Olney, in *Autobiography: Essays Theoretical and Critical*, ed. James Olney, pp. 28–38.

Hall, Samuel Carpenter. *A Book of Memories of Great Men and Women of the Age, from Personal Acquaintance*. London: Virtue and Co., 1871.

Hamilton, Mary. *Munster Village* 1778; repr. London: Pandora Books, 1987.

Harden, Elizabeth. *Maria Edgeworth*. Boston: Twayne, 1984.

Harding, Sandra. *The Feminist Question in Science*. Ithaca: Cornell University Press, 1986.

Harding, Sandra and Merrill Hintikka, eds. *Discovering Reality*. Dordrecht: D. Reidel, 1983.

Hart, James D., *The Popular Book—A History of America's Literary Taste*. Berkeley and Los Angeles: University of California Press, 1963.

Hartman, Geoffrey H. *Wordsworth's Poetry 1787–1814*. New Haven: Yale University Press, 1964.

Hawkesworth, Mary E. "Knowers, Knowing, Known: Feminist Theory and Claims of Truth." *Signs* 14 (1989): 533–557.

Hays, Mary. *Memoirs of Emma Courtney*. London, 1796; repr. London: Pandora Books, 1987.

Hazlitt, William. *Table Talk*. London and New York: J. M. Dent, Everyman Library, 1959.

Heinzelman, Kurt. "The Cult of Domesticity—Dorothy and William Wordsworth at Grasmere," in *Romanticism and Feminism*, ed. Anne K. Mellor, pp. 52–78.

Hemans, Felicia Browne. *The Poetical Works of Felicia Hemans*. ed. William Michael Rossetti. London: Ward Lock and Co., 1878.

Henderson, Heather. *The Victorian Self—Autobiography and Biblical Narrative*. Ithaca: Cornell University Press, 1989.

Hoeveler, Diana Long. *Romantic Androgyny—The Woman Within*. University Park and London: Pennsylvania State University Press, 1990.

Hofkosh, Sonia. "Disfiguring Economies: Mary Shelley's Stories," in *The Other Mary Shelley: Beyond Frankenstein*, eds. Audrey Fisch, Anne Mellor and Esther Schor. Oxford: Oxford University Press, 1992.

———. "The Writer's Ravishment: Women and the Romantic Author—The Example of Byron," in *Romanticism and Feminism*, edited by Anne K. Mellor, pp. 93–114.

Holly, Carol. "Nineteenth-Century Autobiographies of Affiliation: The Case of Catherine Sedgwick and Lucy Larcom," in *American Autobiography: Retrospect and Prospect*, ed. Paul John Eakin. Madison: University of Wisconsin Press, 1991, pp. 216–234.

Homans, Margaret. *Bearing the Word—Language and Female Experience in Nineteenth-Century Women's Writing*. Chicago: Chicago University Press, 1986.

———. "Keats Reading Women, Women Reading Keats." *Studies in Romanticism* 29 (1990): 341–370.

———. "Repression and Sublimation of Nature in *Wuthering Heights*." *PMLA* 93 (1978) 9–19.

———. *Women Writers and Poetic Identity*. Princeton: Princeton University Press, 1980.

Howells, Coral Ann. *Love, Mystery, and Misery—Feeling in Gothic Fiction*. London: Athlone Press, 1978.

———. "The Pleasure of the Woman's Text: Ann Radcliffe's Subtle Transgressions," in *Gothic Fictions—Prohibition/Transgression*, ed. Kenneth W. Graham, New York: AMS Press, 1989, pp. 151–162.

Hogle, Jerrold E. *Shelley's Process: Radical Transference and the Development of His Major Works*. New York: Oxford University Press, 1988.

Hughes, Harriet, *The Works of Mrs. Hemans; with a Memoir of Her Life by Her Sister*. Edinburgh: Blackwood, 1839. 7 Vols.

Hunt, Lynn. *Politics, Culture, and Class in the French Revolution*. Berkeley: University of California Press, 1984.

Hunter, J. Paul. *Before Novels—The Cultural Contexts of Eighteenth-Century English Fiction*. New York and London: W. W. Norton and Co., 1990.

Hurst, Michael. *Maria Edgeworth and the Public Scene—Intellect, Fine Feeling and Landlordism in the Age of Reform.* London: Macmillan, 1969.

Jacobs, Carol. *Uncontainable Romanticism—Shelley, Brontë, Kleist.* Baltimore: Johns Hopkins University Press, 1989.

Jacobus, Mary. *Romanticism, Writing and Sexual Difference: Essays on the Prelude.* New York: Oxford University Press, 1990.

Jakobson, Roman. "The Metaphoric and Metonymic Poles," in Roman Jakobson and Morris Halle, *Fundamentals of Language.* Janua Linguarum, Series Minor, I, The Hague: Mouton, 1971/1956, pp. 90–96.

Janes, Regina M. "On the Reception of Mary Wollstonecraft's *A Vindication of the Rights of Woman.*" *Journal of the History of Ideas* 39 (1978): 293–302.

Jay, Paul. *Being in the Text: Self-Representation from Wordsworth to Roland Barthes.* Ithaca and London: Cornell University Press, 1984.

Jelinek, Estelle, ed. *Women's Autobiography: Essays in Criticism.* Bloomington: Indiana University Press, 1980.

Jerdan, William. *The Autobiography of William Jerdan.* London, 1835. 4 Vols.

Johnson, Claudia L. *Jane Austen—Women, Politics, and the Novel.* Chicago and London: University of Chicago Press, 1988.

Johnson, Mary Lynn. "Feminist Approaches to Teaching *Songs,*" in *Approaches to Teaching Blake's Songs of Innocence and of Experience,* eds. Robert F. Gleckner and Mark L. Greenberg. New York: Modern Language Association, 1989, pp. 57–66.

Jones, Ann H. *Ideas and Innovations—Best Sellers of Jane Austen's Age.* New York: AMS Press, 1986.

Jones, Chris. "Helen Maria Williams and Radical Sensibility." *Prose Studies* 12 (1989): 3–24.

Joplin, Patricia Klindienst. "The Voice of the Shuttle is Ours," in *Rape and Representation,* eds. Lynn A. Higgins and Brenda R. Silver, New York: Columbia University Press, 1991, pp. 35–63.

Jordanova, Ludmilla. "The Popularization of Medicine: Tissot on Onanism." *Textual Practice* 1 (1987) 68–79.

Kabitogou, E. Douka. "Problematics of Gender in the Nuptials of *The Prelude.*" *The Wordsworth Circle* 19 (1988): 128–135.

Kaplan, Cora. "Wild Nights: Pleasure/Sexuality/Feminism," in Kaplan, Cora. *Sea Changes—Essays on Culture and Feminism.* London: Verso, 1986, pp. 31–56.

Kant, Immanuel. *Critique of Judgment* (1790). trans. Werner S. Pluhar. Indianapolis, Indiana: Hackett Publishing Co., 1987.

Keach, William. "Cockney Couplets: Keats and the Politics of Style." *Studies in Romanticism* 25 (1986): 182–196.

———. *Shelley's Style.* New York and London: Methuen, 1984.

Keats, John. *The Letters of John Keats 1814–1821.* ed. Hyder Edward Rollins. Cambridge: Harvard University Press, 1958, 2 Vols.

———. *The Poems of John Keats.* ed. Jack Stillinger. Cambridge: Harvard University Press, 1978.

Kelley, Theresa M. *Wordsworth's Revisionary Aesthetics*. Cambridge: Cambridge University Press, 1988.

Kessler, Suzanne and Wendy McKenna. *Gender—An Ethnomethodological Approach*. Chicago: University of Chicago Press, 1978.

Kettle, Arnold. "Emily Brontë: *Wuthering Heights* (1847)" (1951), in *The Victorian Novel: Modern Essays in Criticism*, ed. Ian Watt, London: Oxford University Press, 1971, pp. 200–216.

Kirkham, Margaret. *Jane Austen—Feminism and Fiction*. Sussex: Harvester Press, and New Jersey: Barnes and Noble, 1983.

———. "Feminist Irony and the Priceless Heroine of *Mansfield Park*," in *Jane Austen—New Perspectives*, ed. Janet Todd, New York and London: Holmes & Meier Publishers, Inc., 1983, pp. 231–47.

Klancher, Jon P. *The Making of English Reading Audiences 1790–1832*. Madison: University of Wisconsin Press, 1987.

Kowaleski-Wallace, Beth. "Home Economics: Domestic Ideology in Maria Edgeworth's *Belinda*." *The Eighteenth Century* 29 (1988): 242–262.

Kramnick, Isaac. *The Rage of Edmund Burke—Portrait of an Ambivalent Conservative*. New York: Basic Books, 1977.

Kristeva, Julia. *Desire in Language*. ed. Leon S. Roudiez. New York: Columbia University Press, 1980.

Lacan, Jacques. *Feminine Sexuality—Jacques Lacan and the école freudienne*. Introductions by Juliet Mitchell and Jacqueline Rose. New York: Norton, 1982; 1985.

Landon, Letitia Elizabeth. *Poetical Works of Letitia Elizabeth Landon "L. E. L."*, A Facsimile Reproduction of the 1873 Edition with an Introduction and Additional Poems, ed. F. J. Sypher. Delmar, New York: Scholars' Facsimiles & Reprints, 1990.

———. *Traits and Trials of Early Life*. London: Henry Colburn, 1837.

———. *The Venetian Bracelet, The Lost Pleiad, A History of the Lyre, and Other Poems*. London: Longman, Rees, Orme, Brown and Green, 1829.

Landry, Donna. *The Muses of Resistance—Laboring-Class Women's Poetry in Britain, 1739–1796*. Cambridge: Cambridge University Press, 1990.

Langbauer, Laurie. *Women and Romance—The Consolations of Gender in the English Novel*. Ithaca: Cornell University Press, 1990.

Langland, Elizabeth. "Blake's Feminist Revision of Literary Tradition in "The SICK ROSE." In *Critical Paths: Blake and the Argument of Method*. eds. Dan Miller, Mark Bracher, and Donald Ault. Durham, N. C.: Duke University Press, 1987, pp. 225–243.

Laqueur, Thomas. *Making Sex: Body and Gender from the Greeks to Freud*. Cambridge, Mass.: Harvard University Press, 1992.

Lawrence, Mrs. Rose, *The Last Autumn at a Favorite Residence, with other Poems; and Recollections of Mrs. Hemans*. Liverpool and London, 1836.

Lejeune, Philippe. *On Autobiography*. Foreword by Paul John Eakin, trans. Katherine Leary. Minneapolis: University of Minnesota Press, 1989.

Levin, Susan. *Dorothy Wordsworth and Romanticism*. New Brunswick: Rutgers University Press, 1987.

Levinson. Marjorie. *Keats's Life of Allegory—The Origins of a Style*. Oxford: Basil Blackwell, 1988.

———. *Wordsworth's Great Period Poems: Four Essays*. Cambridge: Cambridge University Press, 1986.

Lewis, C. Day. *Notable Images of Virtue*. Toronto, Canada: The Ryerson Press, 1960.

Leyland, Francis A. *The Brontë Family with Special Reference to Patrick Branwell Brontë*. London: Hurst & Blackett, 1886, 2 Vols.

Lindenberger, Herbert. *On Wordsworth's Prelude*. Princeton: Princeton University Press, 1963.

Lister, Anne. *I Know My Own Heart: The Diaries of Anne Lister (1791–1840)*. ed. Helena Whitbread. London: Virago Press, 1988.

Liu, Alan. *Wordsworth—The Sense of History*. Stanford: Stanford University Press, 1989.

Lloyd, Genevieve. *The Man of Reason*. Minneapolis: University of Minnesota Press, 1984.

Locke, John. *Two Treatises of Government*. ed. P. Laslett. Cambridge: Cambridge University Press, 1967. Second edition.

Lockhart, John Gibson. Review of Keats in *Blackwood's Edinburgh Magazine* III (August, 1818): 519–524; reprinted in Donald H. Reiman, ed. *The Romantics Reviewed*. New York and London, 1972, Vol. I: 90–95.

Luke, David. "Keats's Letters: Fragments of an Aesthetic of Fragments." *Genre* II (1978): 209–26.

McCarthy, Terence. "The Incompetent Narrator of *Wuthering Heights*." *Modern Language Quarterly* 42 (1981): 48–64.

McCormick, Anita Hemphill. " 'I shall be beloved—I want no more': Dorothy Wordsworth's Rhetoric and the Appeal to Feeling in *The Grasmere Journals*." *Philological Quarterly* (1990) 471–493.

McFarland, Thomas. *Romantic Cruxes: The English Essayists and The Spirit of the Age*. Oxford: Clarendon Press and New York: Oxford University Press, 1987.

McGann, Jerome J. *Don Juan in Context*. Chicago: University of Chicago Press, 1976.

———. *The Romantic Ideology—A Critical Investigation*. Chicago: Chicago University Press, 1983.

McGavran, James Holt, Jr. "Dorothy Wordsworth's Journals—Putting Herself Down," in *The Private Self—Theory and Practice of Women's Autobiographical Writings*, ed. Shari Benstock. Chapel Hill: University of North Carolina Press, 1988, pp. 230–253.

McKeon, Michael. *The Origins of the English Novel 1600–1740*. Baltimore: Johns Hopkins University Press, 1987.

McKibben, Robert. "The Image of the Book in *Wuthering Heights*." *Nineteenth-Century Fiction* 15 (1960): 159–69.

Maclise, Daniel. *The MACLISE Portrait-Gallery of Illustrious Literary Characters with Memoirs*, by William Bates. London, 1883. 2 Vols.

Macready, William Charles. *The Diaries of William Charles Macready, 1833–1851,* ed. William Toynbee. London: Chapman and Hall, 1912.

Madden, William A. "*Wuthering Heights* and the Binding of Passion." *Nineteenth Century Fiction* 27 (1972): 127–54.

Maginn, William. *Miscellaneous Writings of the late Dr. [William] Maginn,* ed. Dr. Shelton Mackenzie. London, 1855.

Manning, Peter. *Reading Romantics—Texts and Contexts.* New York: Oxford University Press, 1990.

———. "Wordsworth, Margaret, and the Pedlar." *Studies in Romanticism* 15 (1976): 195–220. Reprinted in Manning, Peter J. *Reading Romantics—Text and Context,* pp. 9–34.

Mansfield, Lord. "Somerset v. Stewart," Lord Mansfield presiding, *The English Reports* 98 (King's Bench Division 27) Lofft I. London: Stevens and Sons, Ltd; Edinburgh: William Green and Sons, 1909.

Martin, Jane Roland. *Reclaiming a Conversation—The Ideal of the Educated Woman.* New Haven: Yale University Press, 1985.

Mason, Mary G. "The Other Voice: Autobiographies of Women Writers," in *Life/Lines,* eds. Bella Brodzki and Celeste Schenck, pp. 19–44.

Mathison, John K. "Nelly Dean and the Power of *Wuthering Heights.*" *Nineteenth-Century Fiction* XI (1956): 106–29.

Mavor, Elizabeth. *The Ladies of Llangollen: A Study of Romantic Friendship* (1971). Reprinted New York: Penguin Books, 1973.

Mellor, Anne K. "Blake's Portrayal of Women." *Blake: An Illustrated Quarterly* 16 (1982–3): 148–155.

———. "Blake's *Songs of Innocence and of Experience:* A Feminist Perspective." *Nineteenth-Century Studies* 2 (1988): 1–18.

———. "Coleridge's 'This Lime-tree Bower My Prison' and the Categories of English Landscape." *Studies in Romanticism* 18 (1979): 253–70.

———. *English Romantic Irony.* Cambridge, Mass.: Harvard University Press, 1980.

———. "Keats' Face of Moneta: Source and Meaning." *Keats-Shelley Journal* 25 (1976): 65–80.

———. *Mary Shelley: Her Life, Her Fiction, Her Monsters.* New York and London: Methuen and Routledge, 1988.

———, ed. *Romanticism and Feminism.* Bloomington: Indiana University Press, 1988.

Melzer, Sara and Leslie Rabine, eds. *Rebel Daughters: Women and the French Revolution.* New York: Oxford University Press, 1992.

Miller, Jean Baker. *Toward a New Psychology of Women.* Boston: Beacon Press, 1976.

Miller, J. Hillis. *Fiction and Repetition—Seven English Novels.* Cambridge, Mass.: Harvard University Press, 1982.

Mitchell, Juliet. *Psychoanalysis and Feminism—Freud, Reich, Laing and Women.* New York: Pantheon Books/ Vintage, 1974/1975.

Monaghan, David, ed. *Jane Austen in a Social Context.* Totowa, N.J.: Barnes & Noble, 1981.

Monk, Samuel H. *The Sublime: A Study of Critical Theories in XVIII-Century England.* Ann Arbor, Mich.: University of Michigan Press, 1935; repr. 1960.

Morgan, Lady. See Owenson, Sydney.

Morgan, Susan. *In the Meantime—Character and Perception in Jane Austen's Fiction.* Chicago and London: University of Chicago Press, 1980.

―――. *Sisters in Time—Imagining Genders in Nineteenth-Century British Fiction.* New York: Oxford University Press, 1989.

Moser, Thomas J. "What is the Matter with Emily Jane? Conflicting Impulses in *Wuthering Heights.*" *Nineteenth-Century Fiction* XVII (1962) 1–19.

Murray, E. B. *Ann Radcliffe.* New York: Twayne, 1972.

Myers, Mitzi. "Reform or Ruin: 'A Revolution in Female Manners'." *Studies in Eighteenth Century Culture* 11 (1982): 199–216.

―――. "Sensibility and the 'Walk of Reason'—Mary Wollstonecraft's Literary Reviews as Cultural Critique" in *Sensibility in Transformation—Creative Resistance to Sentiment from the Augustans to the Romantics,* ed. Syndy McMillen Conger. Rutherford, N.J.: Fairleigh Dickinson University Press, 1989, pp. 120–144.

Myers, Sylvia Harcstark. *The Bluestocking Circle: Women, Friendship, and the Life of the Mind in Eighteenth-Century England.* Oxford: Clarendon Press, and New York: Oxford University Press, 1990.

Neuman, Shirley. " 'An Appearance walking in a forest the sexes burn': Autobiography and the Construction of the Feminine Body." *Signature: A Journal of Theory and Canadian Literature* (1989) 1–26.

Newman, Beth. " 'The Situation of the Looker-On': Gender, Narration, and Gaze in *Wuthering Heights.*" *PMLA* 105 (1990) 1029–1041.

Newton, Judith Lowder. *Women, Power & Subversion: Social Strategies in British Fiction, 1778–1860* (1981), repr. New York: Methuen, 1985.

Nicolson, Marjorie Hope. *Mountain Gloom and Mountain Glory: the Development of the Aesthetics of the Infinite.* Ithaca, N.Y.: Cornell University Press, 1959.

Nietzsche, Friedrich. *The Will to Power.* Trans. Walter Kaufman and R. J. Hollingdale, ed. Walter Kaufman. New York: Vintage Books, 1968.

Nineteenth-Century Literature Criticism. Ed. Laurie Lanzen Harris. Detroit, Michigan: Gale Research Co., 1981–91. Vol. 15.

Nussbaum, Felicity A. *The Autobiographical Subject—Gender and Ideology in Eighteenth-Century England.* Baltimore: Johns Hopkins University Press, 1989.

―――. "Toward Conceptualizing Diary." In *Studies in Autobiography,* edited by James Olney, pp. 128–140.

Nussey, Ellen. "Reminiscences of Charlotte Brontë," *Scribner's Magazine,* May 1871, n.p.

Olney, James. *Autobiography: Essays Theoretical and Critical.* Princeton: Princeton University Press, 1980.

―――. *Metaphors of Self—the Meaning of Autobiography.* Princeton: Princeton University Press, 1972.

————. *Studies in Autobiography.* New York: Oxford University Press, 1988.

Onorato, Richard J. *The Character of the Poet—Wordsworth in The Prelude.* Princeton: Princeton University Press, 1971.

Ostriker, Alicia. "Desire Gratified—William Blake and Sexuality." *Blake: An Illustrated Quarterly* 16 (1982–3): 156–65.

Owenson, Sydney (Lady Morgan). *The Life and Times of Salvator Rosa.* London: Henry Colburn, 1824, 2 Volumes.

————. *The Wild Irish Girl* (1806). London: Pandora Books, 1986.

Ozouf, Mona. *Festivals and the French Revolution.* Trans. Alan Sheridan. Cambridge: Harvard University Press, 1988.

Paglia, Camille. *Sexual Personae—Art and Decadence from Nefertiti to Emily Dickinson.* New Haven: Yale University Press, 1990.

Paley, Morton D. *Apocalyptic Sublime.* New Haven: Yale University Press, 1986.

Pateman, Carol. *The Sexual Contract.* Cambridge: Polity Press, 1988.

Paxton, Nancy L. "Subversive Feminism: A Reassessment of Susan Ferrier's *Marriage.*" *Women & Literature* IV (1976): 18–29.

Peck, G. W. Review of *Wuthering Heights. American Review* VII, June 1848, pp. 572–85.

Perkins, David. "The Construction of 'The Romantic Movement' as a Literary Classification." *Nineteenth-Century Literature* 45 (1990): 129–143.

Perry, Ruth. *Women, Letters and the Novel.* New York: AMS Press, 1980.

Peterson, Linda H. *Victorian Autobiography—The Tradition of Self-Interpretation.* New Haven: Yale University Press, 1986.

Polhemus, Robert M. *Erotic Faith—Being in Love from Jane Austen to D. H. Lawrence.* Chicago and London: University of Chicago Press, 1990.

Poovey, Mary. *The Proper Lady and the Woman Writer.* Chicago and London: University of Chicago Press, 1984.

Punter, David. "Blake, Trauma, and the Female." *New Literary History* 15 (1984): 475–90.

Radcliffe, Ann. *The Italian* (1797). Oxford: Oxford University Press, 1981.

————. *A Journey made in the summer of 1794, through Holland and the Western Frontiers of Germany, with a return down the Rhine, to which are added Observations during a tour to the Lakes of Lancashire, Westmoreland and Cumberland.* London: G. G. and J. Robinson, 1795.

————. *The Mysteries of Udolpho* (1794). Oxford: Oxford University Press, 1980.

Rajan, Tilottama. *Dark Interpreter: The Discourse of Romanticism.* Ithaca: Cornell University Press, 1980.

————. *The Supplement of Reading—Figures of Understanding in Romantic Theory and Practice.* Ithaca and London: Cornell University Press, 1990.

Reid, T. W. *Charlotte Brontë, A Monograph.* London, 1877.

Reiman, Donald. "Poetry of Familiarity: Wordsworth, Dorothy, and Mary Hutchinson." In *The Evidence of the Imagination,* eds. Donald Reiman, Michael C. Jaye, and Betty T. Bennett, New York: New York University Press, 1978, pp. 142–77.

Renier, Anne. *Friendship's Offering—An Essay on the Annuals and Gift Books of the Nineteenth Century.* London: Private Libraries Association, 1964.

Rich, Adrienne, and Barbara Charlesworth Gelpi. "Three Conversations," in *Adrienne Rich's Poetry,* ed. Barbara Charlesworth Gelpi and Albert Gelpi, New York: W. W. Norton and Co., 1975, pp. 114–115.

Richardson, Alan. "Romanticism and the Colonization of the Feminine," in *Romanticism and Feminism,* ed. Anne K. Mellor, pp. 13–25.

Roberts, Warren. *Jane Austen and the French Revolution.* London: Macmillan, 1979.

Rosaldo, Michelle and Louise Lamphere, eds. *Woman, Culture and Society.* Stanford: Stanford University Press, 1974.

Ross, Marlon B. *The Contours of Masculine Desire—Romanticism and the Rise of Women's Poetry.* New York: Oxford University Press, 1989.

——. "Naturalizing Gender: Woman's Place in Wordsworth's Ideological Landscape." *ELH* 53 (1986): 391–410.

——. "Romantic Quest and Conquest—Troping Masculine Power in the Crisis of Poetic Identity," in *Romanticism and Feminism,* ed. Anne K. Mellor, pp. 26–51.

Rossetti, William Michael, ed. *The Poetical Works of Felicia Hemans* (London: Ward Lock and Co., 1878).

Rousseau, Jean Jacques. *Emile.* trans. Barbara Foxley. New York: Everyman's, 1911; repr. 1963.

Ruddick, Sara. *Maternal Thinking.* Boston: Beacon Press, 1989.

Ryerson, Alice. "Medical Advice on Childrearing, 1550–1900." *Harvard Educational Review* 31 (1961): 302–23.

Schapiro, Barbara Ann. *The Romantic Mother.* Baltimore: Johns Hopkins University Press, 1983.

Scheffler, Judith. "Romantic Women Writing on Imprisonment and Prison Reform." *The Wordsworth Circle* 19 (1988): 99–103.

Schorer, Mark. "Fiction and the 'Matrix of Analogy'." *Kenyon Review* 11 (1949): 539–60.

Senf, Carol A. "Emily Brontë's Version of Feminist History: *Wuthering Heights.*" *Essays in Literature* 12 (1985): 201–214.

Shannon, Edgar F. "Lockwood's Dreams and the Exegesis of *Wuthering Heights.*" *Nineteenth-Century Fiction* 14 (1959): 95–109.

Shelley, Mary. *Frankenstein, or the Modern Prometheus* (The 1818 Text). ed. James Rieger. Chicago: University of Chicago Press, 1982.

——. *The Journals of Mary Shelley, 1814–1844.* Eds. Paula R. Feldman and Diana Scott-Kilvert. Oxford: The Clarendon Press, 1987, 2 Vols.

Shelley, Percy Bysshe. *The Letters of Percy Bysshe Shelley.* ed. Frederick Jones. Oxford: Clarendon Press, 1964, 2 Vols.

——. *Shelley's Poetry and Prose.* ed. Donald H. Reiman and Sharon B. Powers. New York: Norton, 1977.

——. *Shelley's Prose.* ed. David Lee Clark. Albuquerque: University of New Mexico Press, 1954.

Simpson, David. *Irony and Authority in Romantic Poetry.* Totowa, N.J.: Rowman and Littlefield, 1979.

———. *Wordsworth's Historical Imagination: The Poetry of Displacement.* London and New York: Methuen, 1987.

Smith, Leroy. *Jane Austen and the Drama of Women.* New York: St. Martin's Press, 1983.

Smith, Sidonie. *A Poetics of Women's Autobiography.* Bloomington: Indiana University Press, 1987.

Solomon, Eric. "The Incest Theme in *Wuthering Heights.*" *Nineteenth-Century Fiction* 14 (1959): 70–83.

Sonstroem, David. "*Wuthering Heights* and the Limits of Vision." *PMLA* 86 (1971): 51–62.

Spacks, Patricia Meyer. *Gossip.* Chicago: University of Chicago Press, 1986.

Spencer, Jane. *The Rise of the Woman Novelist—From Aphra Behn to Jane Austen.* Oxford: Blackwell, 1986.

Spengemann, William C. *The Forms of Autobiography—Episodes in the History of a Literary Genre.* New Haven: Yale University Press, 1980.

Stanton, Domna C., ed. *The Female Autograph.* Chicago: University of Chicago Press, 1984.

Stanton, Judith Phillips. "Statistical Profile of Women Writing in English from 1660–1800," in *Eighteenth-Century Women and the Arts,* eds. Frederick M. Keener and Susan E. Lorsch. New York: Greenwood Press, 1988, pp. 247–254.

Sterrenburg, Lee. "*The Last Man:* Anatomy of Failed Revolutions," *Nineteenth-Century Fiction* 33 (1978): 324–47.

Stone, Lawrence J. *The Family, Sex, and Marriage in England 1500–1800.* New York: Harper and Row, 1977.

Storch, Margaret. *Sons and Adversaries: Women in William Blake and D. H. Lawrence.* Knoxville: University of Tennessee Press, 1990.

Sulloway, Alison G. *Jane Austen and the Province of Womanhood.* Philadelphia: University of Pennsylvania Press, 1989.

Summer, Doris. " 'Not Just a Personal Story': Women's *Testimonios* and the Plural Self," in *Life/Lines,* eds. Bella Brodzki and Celeste Schenck, pp. 107–130.

Sunstein, Emily W. *A Different Face—The Life of Mary Wollstonecraft.* Boston: Little, Brown and Co., 1975.

Swann, Karen. "Harassing the Muse," in *Romanticism and Feminism,* ed. Anne K. Mellor, pp. 81–92.

Tanner, Tony. *Jane Austen.* London: Macmillan, 1986.

Tayler, Irene. *Holy Ghosts—The Male Muses of Emily and Charlotte Brontë.* New York: Columbia University Press, 1990.

———. "The Woman Scaly." *Bulletin of the Midwest Modern Language Association* 6 (1973) 74–87.

Tayler, Irene and Gina Luria, "Gender and Genre: Women in British Romantic Literature," in *What Manner of Woman—Essays in English and American Life and Literature,* ed. Marlene Springer. New York: New York University Press, 1977, pp. 98–123.

Tobin, Mary-Elisabeth Fowkes. "Aiding Impoverished Gentlewomen: Power and Class in *Emma.*" *Criticism* 30 (1988): 413–430.

Todd, Janet, ed. *Jane Austen: New Perspectives.* London: Holmes & Meier, 1983.

——. *Sensibility—An Introduction.* London: Methuen, 1986.

——. *The Sign of Angellica—Women, Writing and Fiction, 1660–1800.* New York: Columbia University Press, 1989.

Tomalin, Claire. *The Life and Death of Mary Wollstonecraft.* New York and London: Harcourt Brace Jovanovich, 1974.

Tompkins, J. M. S. *The Popular Novel in England 1770–1800.* London: Constable, 1932; Methuen, 1969.

Trinder, Peter W., *Mrs Hemans* Cardiff: University of Wales Press, 1984.

Trumbach, Randolph. *The Rise of the Egalitarian Family.* New York: Academic Press, 1978.

Tuchman, Gaye, with Nina Fortin. *Edging Women Out—Victorian Novelists, Publishers and Social Change.* New Haven: Yale University Press, 1989.

Van Ghent, Dorothy. *The English Novel—Form and Function.* New York: Rinehart & Co., Inc., 1953.

Vendler, Helen. *The Odes of John Keats.* Cambridge, Mass: The Belknap Press of Harvard University Press, 1983.

Vlasopolos, Anca. "Mary Wollstonecraft's Mask of Reason in *A Vindication of the Rights of Woman.*" *Dalhousie Review* 60 (1980): 462–71.

Waldoff, Leon. *Keats and the Silent Work of Imagination.* Urbana: University of Illinois Press, 1985.

Ward, Aileen. *John Keats—The Making of a Poet.* New York: Viking Press, 1963.

Watt, Ian. *The Rise of the Novel—Studies in Defoe, Richardson and Fielding.* Berkeley and Los Angeles: University of California Press, 1967.

Webster, Brenda. "Blake, Women and Sexuality," in *Critical Paths: Blake and the Argument of Method.* eds. Dan Miller, Mark Bracher, and Donald Ault. Durham, NC: Duke University Press, 1987, pp. 204–24.

Weintraub, Karl Joachim. *The Value of the Individual—Self and Circumstance in Autobiography.* Chicago: University of Chicago Press, 1978.

Wieskel, Thomas. *The Romantic Sublime—Studies in the Structure and Psychology of Transcendence.* Baltimore: Johns Hopkins University Press, 1976/1986.

Weissman, Judith. *Half Savage and Hardy and Free—Women and Rural Radicalism in the Nineteenth-Century Novel.* Middletown, Conn.: Wesleyan University Press, 1987.

Whale, John C. *Thomas De Quincey's Reluctant Autobiography.* London: Croom Helm and Totowa, N.J.: Barnes & Noble, 1984.

Williams, Helen Maria. *Julia, A Novel, interspersed with some Poetical Pieces.* Dublin, 1790.

——. *Letters written in France, in the Summer 1790, to a Friend in England, containing Various Anecdotes relative to the French Revolution; and Memoirs of Mons. and Madame Du F*————. London: T. Cadell, 1796. Republished as *Letters from France*, Eight Volumes in Two, Facsimile Reproductions with an Introduction by Janet M. Todd. Delmar, New York: Scholars' Facsimiles & Reprints, 1975.

————. *A Narrative of the Events which have taken place in FRANCE; with an account of the Present State of Society and Public Opinion.* London: John Murray, 1816. Second edition.

————. *Poems on Various Subjects.* London, 1823.

————. *A Tour in Switzerland; or, a View of the Present State of the Governments and Manners of those Cantons, with Comparative Sketches of the Present State of Paris.* London: G. G. & J. Robinson, 1798.

Williams, Huntington. *Rousseau and Romantic Autobiography.* Oxford: Oxford University Press, 1983.

Williams, Raymond. *Keywords—A Vocabulary of Culture and Society.* New York: Oxford University Press, 1976.

Willis, Irene Cooper. "The Authorship of *Wuthering Heights.*" *The Trollopian* 2 (December 1947) 157–68.

Wilson, Anna. "Mary Wollstonecraft and the Search for the Radical Woman," *Genders* 6 (1989): 88–101.

Wolfson, Susan J. "Feminizing Keats." In *Critical Essays on John Keats*, ed. Hermione de Almeida. Boston: G. K. Hall, 1990, pp. 317–56.

————. "Individual in Community: Dorothy Wordsworth in Conversation with William," in *Romanticism and Feminism*, ed. Anne K. Mellor, pp. 139–166.

————. "Keats the Letter-Writer: Epistolary Poetics." *Romanticism Past and Present* 6 (1982): 43–61.

————. *The Questioning Presence—Wordsworth, Keats, and the Interrogative Mode in Romantic Poetry.* Ithaca and London: Cornell University Press, 1986.

Wollstonecraft, Mary. *An Historical and Moral View of the Origin and Progress of the French Revolution and the Effect it has Produced in Europe* (1795). A Facsimile Reproduction with an Introduction by Janet Todd. Delmar, New York: Scholars' Facsimiles & Reprints, 1975.

————. *Maria, or The Wrongs of Woman.* ed. Moira Ferguson. New York: Norton, 1975.

————. *A Vindication of the Rights of Men.* London, 1790: facsimile edition with introduction by Eleanor Louise Nicholes. Gainesville, Florida: Scholar's Facsimiles & Reprints, 1960.

————. *A Vindication of the Rights of Woman* (1792). Ed. Carol H. Poston. Second Edition. New York: Norton Critical Editions, 1988/1975.

Woodring, Carl. "The Narrators of *Wuthering Heights.*" *Nineteenth-Century Fiction* 20 (1957) 298–305.

Wordsworth, Dorothy. "The Collected Poems of Dorothy Wordsworth," in Susan Levin, *Dorothy Wordsworth and Romanticism*, Appendix One.

————. *George and Sarah Green—A Narrative.* ed. E. de Selincourt. London: The Folcroft Press, 1936; repr. 1969.

————. *Journals of Dorothy Wordsworth.* ed. Mary Moorman. London: Oxford University Press, 1958, 1971; repr. 1981.

———. *Letters of Dorothy Wordsworth.* ed. Alan Hill. Oxford: Oxford University Press, 1981.

Wordsworth, Jonathan, Michael C. Jaye, and Robert Woof, ed. *William Wordsworth and the Age of English Romanticism.* New Brunswick: Rutgers University Press, 1987.

Wordsworth, William. *The Complete Poetical Works of Wordsworth*, Cambridge Edition, ed. Alice N. George. Boston: Houghton Mifflin, 1932.

Wordsworth, William. *The Letters of William and Dorothy Wordsworth*, ed. Alan G. Hill, Vol. VI. Oxford: Clarendon Press, 1982.

Wordsworth, William. *The Prelude—1799, 1805, 1850.* eds. Jonathan Wordsworth, M. H. Abrams, and Stephen Gill. New York: W. W. Norton & Co. 1979.

———. *The Ruined Cottage and The Pedlar.* ed. James Butler. Ithaca: Cornell University Press, 1979.

Wordsworth, William and Mary Wordsworth. *The Love Letters of William and Mary Wordsworth.* ed. Beth Darlington. Oxford: Clarendon Press, 1982.

Yaeger, Patricia. "The Father's Breasts." In *Refiguring the Father—New Feminist Readings of Patriarchy,* eds. Patricia Yaeger and Beth Kowaleski-Wallace. Carbondale: Southern Illinois University Press, 1989, pp. 6–28.

———. "Violence in the Sitting Room: *Wuthering Heights* and the Woman's Novel." *Genre* 21 (1988): 203–229.

Yeazell, Ruth Bernard. *Fictions of Modesty—Women and Courtship in the English Novel.* Chicago and London: University of Chicago Press, 1991.

Yeo, Elspeth. The Catalogue for the National Library of Scotland, Edinburgh, Exhibition: *Susan Ferrier 1782–1854* (1982).

INDEX

Coroner